A PENGUIN IN A SPARROW'S NEST

The Story of a Freelance Motorcycling Journalist

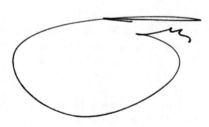

FRANK MELLING

Llanfest 2015

A Collie Press Book

First published in Great Britain in 2015 by:
The Collie Press
Manley Lane Manley Cheshire WA6 0PB

Text and Design © Frank Melling

Layout by Geoff Fisher

Whilst every effort has been made to ensure the accuracy of this book, the author
and publisher cannot be held responsible for any errors, omissions or inaccuracies.
Unless otherwise indicated, opinions expressed herein are those of the author of the
book and do not necessarily represent the views of persons or companies
represented.

A CIP catalogue record for this book is available in the British Library
ISBN 978-0-9527987-1-2

Printed and bound by CPI Books UK, Croydon CR0 4YY

Praise for "A Penguin in a Sparrow's Nest"

"Autobiographies are usually clouded by false humility, massive egos, and the natural inability to see ourselves as others do. What results is rarely more trustworthy than a ghost-writer's fantasy.

"A Penguin in a Sparrow's Nest is different. Frank suffers from none of these conditions and this inspirational meander through the life of an ordinary man proves that he is anything but ordinary.

"Adversity, sackings, hard work, determination, love, success, and the ability to cheat death all play their part – all under the umbrella of Fate – and leave you convinced of two things above all else: Penguins are categorically superior to sparrows and that life is very much what you choose to make it."

Richard Newland – *Deputy Editor Motorcycle News*

"A Penguin in a Sparrow's Nest " is the fascinating story of Frank's early life. It is warm funny and informative - and told by a master story teller. I could not put it down."

Jim Redman MBE – *Six Times World Champion*

"I've known Frank for a very long time and learnt long ago never to be surprised by what he took on, but he caught me on the back foot with this book. It's brilliant!"

Malc Wheeler – *Editor Classic Racer*

"A funny and observant personal account of what a man can learn, and do, in his life in such an easy and enjoyable read. Every page is packed with fascinating stories."

Sammy Miller MBE – *European Champion*

"With Frank Melling's love for motorcycles spread like butter through the pages, this utterly absorbing autobiography proves beyond doubt that self-belief, and single-mindedness, is far more important than where you come from in establishing where you get to in life."

Pete Kelly – *Editor Old Bike Mart*

"Frank's enthusiasm for motorcycles is unshakeable. Reading "A Penguin in a Sparrow's Nest" I see why he is like he is... read it yourself."

Tim Britton – *Editor Classic Bike Dirt*

"Once you have picked up "A Penguin in a Sparrow's Nest" you will not want to put it down.

Frank has interviewed, worked with, written about, and raced with many of the world's top motorcycling stars both on and off road, as well as having ridden and written about some of the world's most exotic machines.

The ups and downs of growing up, motorcycling, and freelance journalism, are all well documented here in Frank's own inimitable, amusing, and informative style.

A thoroughly enjoyable read."

Les Trotter – *North-West Evening Mail*

"A captivating, and quite often hilarious, journey through the life of a guy who simply loves all things motorcycles.

There are parts of this book that I shall visit again and again…"

David England – *Mortons Media Group*

"At its core, 'A Penguin in a Sparrow's Nest' tells an entertaining tale of an unconventional young man's motorcycling life.

"Melling's memories in this book span the period from the 1960s through the 70s, so they encapsulate the end of the British bike industry. The behind-the-scenes anecdotes from the dying days at BSA-Triumph are fascinating.

"The book is pure nostalgia for those who rode in the 1960s and 70s – and an eye-opening revelation for anyone who's taken to two wheels in more recent years."

Rowena Hoseason – *RealClassic magazine*

Acknowledgements

I hope that you will read this short section because I want, and need, to express my thanks to all those people who have helped me progress from being a sixteen year old shelf painter to my present, very happy, position.

On the way I have been privileged to work with some very lovely, and clever, people who taught me a lot and whose skills have been invaluable to the success I have achieved. I have also received a lot of kindness and support during the journey - and I am very grateful for this.

To those who have tried, and failed, to make life difficult for me – always remember folks, I'm writing this book and you aren't!

"A Penguin in a Sparrow's Nest" came about first because my wonderful daughter, Elizabeth, asked me to write down the stories I used to tell her on the way to race meetings. They had become family folklore and she wanted to have them in some form of permanent record – probably, being Ibby, to check that I wasn't telling fibs from one version to the next! Elizabeth keeps a close eye on me at all times…

The next important person in the gestation of the book was Harry Moffatt, the hardest of hard core motorcycle fans, who must have asked me five hundred times to write down the bits and pieces of paddock gossip we have shared over many years. Together, Elizabeth and Harry persuaded me to actually sit down and start typing.

The early drafts of the book – and there have been five versions – were sent to Elizabeth and Harry for their comments and as a result, major revisions took place. My thanks to them both.

David Clarke, the kindest person in motorcycle racing, also read an early version of the book and his comments were most welcome too.

The third incarnation of the work was sent to Peter Wilson, a life-long friend from my College days. Peter is not only highly intelligent but philosophically a very deep thinker. Peter made many thoughtful, sagacious comments as well as doing the hard graft of toiling through the book letter by letter correcting my typing errors.

However, the greatest thanks of all must go to Carol – my wife, best friend, soulmate, business partner - and much more.

She has worked as hard at editing the book as I have in writing it. If you enjoy reading the work, thank Carol for smoothing out all the rough edges.

Carol has many talents but near to the top must be her skill as an editor.

Carol and I decided to publish this book ourselves because we weren't happy with what mainstream publishers wanted to do with it. Good or bad, we wanted "A Penguin in a Sparrow's Nest" to be exactly what it is and not emasculated so that it became "more commercial" – whatever that expression means!

Philosophically, self-publishing is a wonderful thing and by far the best way for an author to see a book in a print. However, the metamorphosis through which a manuscript becomes a book is hard work and I owe a huge debt of thanks to Mark Jarvis, who designed the front and back covers, and to Geoff Fisher who typeset the text. I harassed them both endlessly, and in a way which must have driven them mad, but we are all - Mark, Geoff, Carol and me – happy that the finished product is that the best we can do as a team."

Finally my thanks to you, the readers, who have done me the great honour of reading what I have had to say since 1971. No-one could be more blessed and privileged.

Thanks to everyone for everything.

Frank Melling

Contents

For Ibby

Who wanted to be mentioned in a book

1

A Penguin in a Sparrow's Nest

THIS is the story of how I have ricocheted through life, starting out as a sixteen year old shelf painter and progressing to become quite a good scrap metal burner, a fairly competent teacher and then owning, and organising, The Thundersprint - one of the biggest motorcycling festivals in the world.

On the way I sold 5,400 motorcycle helmets in four months, using a two bedroomed bungalow as a warehouse, mentored and taught some of Britain's most prolific young drugs dealers and violent criminals, published and directed the largest children's magazine ever produced, owned my own race teams and have come to know many World Champions as personal friends.

However, throughout these many different career paths there has always been one constant - and that has been writing. Now, I have written well over 1000 articles as well as short stories, film scripts and eleven books.

All my life, I have been a freelancer – someone who writes anything for anyone - provided that there is a fee at the end and the work is interesting.

The fact that I have been paid to write about motorcycles has always been a source of particular amazement to me. Making any money from being involved with bikes, which are my passion and love, seems to be a bigger slice of good fortune than anyone can justifiably deserve.

So what is a freelancer?

"A freelancer, freelance worker, or freelance is a person who is self-employed and is not committed to a particular employer long-term."

Clearly, as a professional freelancer and, therefore always conscious of the time versus profit equation, I took the easy way out and ripped this definition off from Wikipedia - but it's not a bad one.

The only problem is that it doesn't really do justice to the hard core freelancer serving the self-imposed life sentence of never having a steady income – or a steady boss!

This group, to which I proudly belong, is not so much self-employed but rather utterly unemployable. We don't see freelancing as a means to a real job, with a pension scheme and paid holidays, but instead as a way of avoiding a real job.

We don't hope to be noticed, and so head hunted by some prestigious company, but rather ache to remain in the uncertain, fragile - and very happy - state of self-employment where we belong to no-one and have no master.

For us, the "free" part of "freelancer" is the golden key. We're not "self-employed" or on "zero hours contracts" or any of the other descriptions which are currently in vogue to describe those not in regular employment. We are free to write for whomsoever we please – or not – because we can, not because we have to.

For better, and sometimes very much for the worse, this mind set has dominated every aspect of my life.

Here's how I became a professional freelance writer almost five decades ago.

★★★

I was first paid to write when I was 19 years old but the genesis of being a freelancer started much earlier than this.

I had a very sad and unhappy childhood, but so did a lot of other kids at the time so I was nothing special.

I learned two essential lessons for a future freelancer. First, cry in private. Second, if I wanted anything doing then the best, and usually the only, way was to do it myself.

The problem was that I wasn't so much a cuckoo in the family nest but a giant, half ton penguin who clearly looked and sounded completely out of place.

Let me give you an example. When I was ten years old I had an enormous, hands-on-hips argument with the Children's Librarian at Warrington Library. I was fed up, and bored, with the children's section in the library and wanted, in fact demanded, adult library tickets.

I had a working class Warrington accent as dense as the pink scum floating down the River Mersey, and a total lack of social skills, so it was an odds-on bet that I wasn't presenting my case very well. Also, in 1957, ten year olds didn't raise their voices to grown-ups and were taught to speak only when they were spoken to.

As the spectators gathered around this verbal punch up a rather severe looking woman, wearing a pleated grey skirt and a starched white blouse, came into the Children's Section and asked me to explain what I felt was the problem. This lady, it transpired, was a Senior Librarian. Certainly, she brought the Children's Librarian instantly to heel.

She listened patiently, and without intervention, whilst I explained that I was bored with children's books and wanted access to the main library. The boss of the kids' section chipped in and said that this was against Warrington Library's policy and I couldn't have Adult Tickets until I was eleven. She was quietly hushed and I was not so much encouraged to continue but rather allowed to proceed uninterrupted.

At the end of my sales pitch, the Head Book Lady said that she would personally grant me two adult tickets and she would personally take responsibility for my use of this privilege.

I didn't look upon this support as patronage or kindness but just as simple justice. That naivety was another, nascent, freelance skill.

When I arrived home with two grown up books – I can't remember what they were – my Mum was horrified: utterly bereft. How could I have argued with a lady as important as a Librarian? How could I have brought so much shame on the family? Did anyone we knew hear me?

I think that she was only a blink away from going down to the library and offering to polish the steps with "Cardinal Red" by way of penance for her son's wayward behaviour.

Me? Well, I had my library tickets, and my books, and so that was that. Tomorrow was going to be another day. Never look back because the next job is always around the corner. Tick that box on the Freelancer's list of essential skills too.

In fact, I was soon upgraded to four adult tickets and I read and read and read. I read Science Fiction. I read poetry. I read Borstal Boy by Brendan Behan. I read Viper by Raymond Thorp – a very early book on drug addiction. I read without control or monitoring or plan or purpose or pattern. I read everything, from HG Wells to Dickens to Asimov, for no reason and every reason. I read crisp packets and toothpaste tubes. Whereever there were words I read them. Without knowing it, I was already in training and on the road to becoming a professional writer.

***

Another important event in my life occurred when I was eleven years old: I fell in love. What I felt mustn't be confused with puppy love, or admiration for Mrs. Yates who was my history teacher, or even something as all consuming as Romeo's passion for Juliet. No, my love was far greater. I rode my first motorcycle.

In fact, calling a Cycle Master a motorcycle is a bit like saying that the bloke who won last Friday's pub Karaoke competition sings just like Paul McCartney because he knows the words to 'Yesterday'. Admittedly, they both sing and yes, they both know the song but their performance, and the end result, is ever so slightly different.

The Cycle Master was a tiny, 32cc engine which fitted in place of the normal rear wheel in a conventional pedal cycle. The rider pedalled like crazy, engaged the engine, and the little two stroke pulled both rider and bike along at a furious pace – anything up to 20mph was possible.

It was an incredibly successful design, with over 250,000 of these lovely little power plants being produced. This made it, by far, the most successful ever, British engined two-wheeler.

My Dad had a Cyclemaster and, mainly because he was inebriated most of the time, had a rather laissez faire attitude towards me using the bike.

Very near to our Council house were the remains of RAF Padgate. This base was where many thousands of RAF recruits had their first taste of military life. When I was a child it had been abandoned by the military but the road systems were still largely intact.

I took the Cyclemaster round to Padgate Camp and then pushed and pushed and pushed trying to make the little bike start. It didn't - until a kindly adult walking his dog turned the fuel on for me. A lack of mechanical awareness has remained with me to this day!

With fuel going to the engine, I ran alongside the full sized bicycle and then dropped the clutch. The motor fired and, somehow, I clambered on to the saddle and perched high in the air with no chance of ever getting my feet to the ground if there was a problem.

But why should there, or could there, ever be a problem? I opened the throttle lever and the Cyclemaster surged forward on what felt like a magic carpet wave of fire and power.

As I am writing these words, I can still remember the dark brown wooden huts flashing by on the right hand side of the road whilst I was transformed into some new creature - no longer boy but now a mechanical hybrid of motorcycle and man.

From now on, there would be no more walking to the shops. No more buses with the smell of sweat, stale beer and old ladies' dirt. No more pedalling up the ramp to the Cantilever Bridge at Grappenhall, with aching legs and panting lungs. Simply the God like power of pulling the lever towards me and feeling the power of the engine take me to new worlds.

There was no drug more addictive – nothing in the world I wanted to do more. I was hooked. An addict. It was a life sentence. From now on, bikes and books were to be inextricably wound into every day of my life.

***

When I was sixteen years old I left school and learned another valuable lesson for a freelancer: it was where to place an ad in the paper for best effect. My Mum told me to get a job – any job. It wasn't a case of being fulfilled or using my talents to their best advantage but simply that the family needed the money.

Again, it's important to see this in context. My Mum wasn't being cruel or selfish but was reflecting the realities of having an alcoholic husband and living on a Council Estate. My feelings, ambitions and desires were not so much ignored as irrelevant, in the same way that you might look at sheep with mild interest - but not empathy.

Sheep eat grass, get wet and are eaten. Working class kids from sink housing estates got a job, chipped in for their keep and made what they could of the leftovers.

I found that the best place for an ad is always the top right hand side of an odd numbered page. This is where the reader's eye scans most naturally. In my case, in this highly desirable placement in the Warrington Guardian, there appeared an advertisement for an assistant storeman, at an engineering business.

My Mum pointed this out to me and off I went for an interview. That was it. My total careers' counselling amounted to being told to apply for a well placed ad.

In truth, it was a marriage doomed to failure. I was highly literate, articulate, smiling and bursting with energy. The Chief Storeman was an ex-Navy gunner who was deaf after a mis-fire in the turret of a Cruiser.

He was deeply suspicious of young people, rock and roll, showers and especially reading and writing – skills which he felt were for Officers and posh people - not "Other Ranks", the like of whom who applied for jobs in stores.

To avoid a conflict of interest, I was sent deep into the bowels of the stores to paint shelves. There were a lot of them and so I spent many weeks down there, in the company of the occasional 60 watt light bulb, many gallon tins of Jellipex paint and a single brush – whilst wondering if the sky was blue outside, or if the rain was caressing the rooftops, or perhaps whether the trees were rustling in the summer breeze.

As a treat, I used to allow myself to stir the last quarter of the one gallon tin of Jellipex paint so that it was no longer non-drip but was liquid. Liquefied jelly paint – a blow for freedom!

At tea break I sat in the crude canteen, in a corner away from everyone else. My workmates studied the Sporting Pink for likely horses, and masturbated to the pictures in Health and Efficiency magazine - whilst I read a copy of Chaucer's Canterbury Tales. We didn't have a lot in common.

At lunch-time, I jogged around Warrington to forget about being hungry. My Mum was generous in terms of my wages. I was allowed to keep half and she retained the other half for my "keep." In fact, even this is not fair to her because she often bought clothes for me so I really was well treated.

However, funding lunches came out of my money and I needed every penny to feed my addiction because I had passed my motorcycle test the moment I could. This was hardly surprising in view of the amount of time I had spent on bikes by the time I was sixteen years old.

In fact, except for being rather talented on a bike I should never have passed my test at all - but would have been facing a manslaughter charge.

In those happy pre-computer days, you could apply for a cancellation and take any driving test slot which became available in the area. Doing this avoided waiting for your turn in the queue at your local test centre. In my case, I got an almost instant cancellation in Bolton, which is about 35 miles from Warrington, and so I took the test as near to my sixteenth birthday as I could.

My bike was a 250cc BSA C.15 – and what a real dog of a thing it was too! In Wigan, the nipple pulled out of the front brake cable so I had no brake at all. Worse still, I was going to lose my test fee if I didn't turn up – and this was unthinkable.

The answer was to bend the end of the cable round the clevis pin on the brake drum arm and keep it out of sight.

I turned up for my test - and rode like the paragon of virtue that I wasn't. The examiner was quietly impressed and made thorough notes on his clipboard. Then he explained that he was going to step off the pavement and hold up his clipboard. I should then bring the bike to a stop in front of him, as quickly as possible, and completely under control.

I did the lap of the houses where I was being tested and saw the examiner nice and early. He stepped out and raised his board and I did briefly wonder if he knew how big a bet he was putting on the fact that I had about a zillion hours' riding experience - before I had ever even been near a motorcycle legally.

The key factor in the emergency stop was to use the front brake. If you went near the rear brake, the rear wheel could lock and skid and, even by the very modest test standards of the day, this would mean an instant fail.

Out comes the examiner with his clipboard and I lunge for the front brake in a comic sweep which sees my hand describe a huge arc, as I clearly reach for the front brake lever – which is connected to nothing.

Now things get tricky. Anything other than the gentlest pressure on the front brake lever will pull out the cable. At the same time, I have got to stop the bike quickly and, preferably at least, without killing the examiner.

So I just caress the front brake lever, and feel the rear brake right up to the point of locking, then bring the bike to a gentle stop. The examiner nods. I smile and, after a couple perfunctory Highway Code questions, we're heading home to Warrington with no "L" Plates - and a licence to ride any bike of any kind and size.

St. Peter in his leather jacket had just thrown open the doors of Heaven.

***

The bike licence came at the right time because things were not going well at work – not well at all.

I was considered to have an "attitude problem" and a lack of respect for the Senior Storeman. I was guilty on both charges - but not in the conventional sense of the accusations.

I wasn't so much bad mannered, or difficult, but severely under, and mis, employed. Worse still, the jobs which I was given – fit and proper ones for a trainee assistant storeman – I found difficult and confusing. I didn't know the names of the parts in their dull, grey, galvanised boxes or which bearings were used for what - and the company's Byzantine system of parts' bin numbering left me utterly confused.

The "paperwork" which the Senior Storeman hated so much seemed to me to be an utter breeze, as was drafting notes for the secretary to type. In every way, it was another case of the half ton penguin chick in the sparrow's nest but, this time, not nearly as welcome as I was at home.

Matters came to a head with the Motorcycle Show which was held in the Royal Horticultural Halls in London. I was determined to go the Show and my employers were determined that I would remain in Warrington.

There wasn't a lot of drama in what followed. I took Saturday off, without permission, went to London and enjoyed the bike show. On Monday morning I was called into the Manager's Office, sacked on the spot and given a week's wages. By half past nine, I was walking home. Then the trouble really started.

There were two problems and, ironically, they were of about equal importance. My Mum was traumatised because I had been sacked. Me, a decent, well brought up lad - sacked. What would the neighbours say? And say they did, because the curtains were rustling at the sight of Flo Melling's lad home from work so early. In a few hours, I was the scandal of the street.

The second problem was that my Mum needed the £6 a week I was chipping into the family pot.

As for me, I had a rather ambivalent attitude towards the whole exercise. I was concerned that my Mum was upset but completely distant from the tirade I had faced in the Manager's Office. The dire warnings heaped on me regarding my attitude, work ethic, lack of responsibility and thought for others didn't so much bounce off me as skim by as if I was sitting in a bubble.

This was strange because I was a sensitive young man, and very easily hurt on an emotional level, but when it came to being abused by adults somehow it had no effect. I simply sat quietly until he ran out of verbal ammunition, picked up my gas mask bag containing my copy of "The Motorcycle" - and left.

The real trouble was about to come. When I arrived home my Mum cried. I had seen her cry a lot over the years and her tears penetrated deep inside me to private, vulnerable places which should only be entered with extreme caution.

I had given her all my wages after being sacked and so had only a few pennies left in the world. Mum ordered me to go to the Unemployment Exchange and sign on – and do it immediately.

The Dole Office was about three miles from home but there was no thought of using my bike, and its precious remaining petrol, or a bus. It was a case of jogging and walking down to Bank Park, home to Warrington's famous, and quite stunning, Victorian Golden Gates and sitting on the wall there whilst I picked up the courage to go through the door of the Dole Office.

By 11 o'clock, I was ready to cross Sankey Street - and another Rubicon in the process of growing up.

I watched with morbid interest as the unemployed filed in through the door. They looked broken men – I never saw a woman – and they exuded sadness and world weariness. They were on the Dole – out of work and scroungers. This, in a town which exemplified the Protestant work ethic.

Eventually, I took a deep breath, crossed the street and opened the door. I felt that ten thousand eyes were looking at me. A fit young man signing on for benefit – wanting money for not working: what could be more shameful?

In fact, I never actually crossed the threshold but, instead, turned and fled back to Bank Park where I sat on the grass and cried and cried until there was not a single tear left.

My Mum was neither condemnatory nor sympathetic. Yes, she understood how I felt and if that was my choice not to sign on then I had better find some work – any work – and fast too.

So began a maelstrom of employment, as I bounced from one job to another. Second-hand car salesman, bulldozer route planner (don't even ask), photographer's assistant, fitter's mate, farm labourer, administrator, trainee manager and scrap metal burner.

These days, Health and Safety Legislation has become manic and oppressive but if you had been in Warrington in the 1960s you would have seen that, at the start, there was a legitimate reason for trying to make things safer for workers.

Let me give you an example. As things transpired, I had something of a natural talent with an oxy-acetylene burning torch. These are the things you sometimes see on bank robbery films. A blue flame comes out of the end of the torch and, ten seconds later, the bank vault door falls conveniently open. In real life, it's not quite that easy – or fast.

The scrapman I was working for got a job to clear out one of Warrington's wire works. Part of the contract was to remove two, huge zinc plating tanks – each one half the size of a small shipping container.

The problem was that they were too big to move intact and so had to be cut up into manageable pieces. The money I was offered was incredible. The scrapman was prepared to pay me £6.00 a day if I would climb into the tanks and cut through the dividing walls from the inside. This would mean near triple the amount of money I was earning so I was inside the tank like a ferret up a drain.

I fired up the torch and began cutting. No breathing apparatus, or protective gear – just a pair of leather gloves, green tinted goggles and overalls. The zinc fumes were horrendous and breathing was difficult but £6.00 was a lot of money, so I carried on cutting even though my eyes were streaming and I was coughing like a 60 a day man.

At lunch-break, I felt really ill and coughed up all sorts of filth but with £6.00 dangling in front of my eyes, I didn't need any motivation to get back in the tank and fire up the oxy torch again.

Things got worse and by late afternoon I was beginning to feel really fuzzy so I shut off the torch with its normal satisfying pop, climbed out of the tank – and collapsed in a very undignified heap.

The next thing that I remember was one of the foremen from the wire works proffering an enamelled mug of tea and rubbing my shoulders.

It's wrong to think of those days as mindless, Victorian cruelty. The foreman rounded on my employer and told him that he was going to kill me and that I was not to go back in the tank under any circumstances – and neither was anyone else. The tank was to be shifted intact – or not at all.

I was kept on until the end of the week and then told that there was no more work for me. I wasn't particularly surprised or upset because this was the norm at the time. You did a hard job and got paid well, or didn't do it and got sacked. The equation was simple.

I became quite inured to getting sacked - and I was just as quick to leave the moment things didn't suit me. However, there was one job which I left with the utmost reluctance and only then because I was genuinely terrified.

The problem was a young lady who lived on our street. She had an archetypally English strawberries and cream complexion, a lovely smile and a bottom worthy of being painted by Botticelli.

The snag, as always, was money. I now had a car and a motorcycle and the bike addiction was growing by the minute. Wooing the lovely "S" would be pushing the fiscal envelope to breaking point.

My saviour was the Warrington Guardian once more. It was a less well placed ad. than the top right hand side of the page where I had found my first job, but it still jumped out at me. "Demolition workers wanted. Top rates of pay."

The job was down at the Sankey St. Helen's Canal where a factory was being demolished. I rocked up, showed that I could use an oxy torch and was welcomed with open arms by the Irish gang running the job. Better still, and without any haggling, I was offered £15 a week plus a £5.00 bonus if I performed as well with the torch as I said I could.

And this was all cash in hand – tax free. I could see chicken in a basket, and a romantic night by Pickmere Lake, coming very soon.

I started work burning the big steel beams – they're called RSJs – which were the skeleton of the factory. We started from the top floor and worked down. First, the outside wall was knocked out and then we began cutting up the steel beams. It was dirty work, and the fumes from years of industrial use were unpleasant, but I was winning the approval of the Irish lads and things were going really well.

I sat astride the beam, burnt the steel largely through, hooked a thick wire round it and then the crane driver gave a quick tug and a length of RSJ hit the floor. As the expression so aptly went, "T' job's a good 'un!"

I went home that night with a spring in my step and a very special smile when I passed "S's" house.

The Irish lads had a brew on when I came back the following morning and were fulsome in their praise. Then the Charge Hand had an idea. Would I mind working a bit further out along the beams? This meant sitting with my legs either side of the beam with nothing between me and a long, long drop down to the yard beneath. I wasn't keen but the Charge Hand reminded me of the £5 bonus so out I went.

I cut, the crane driver snatched and RSJs piled up in the yard below. Yes, things were going well. Then I sensed something was not quite right.

The "not quite right" was that, behind me, one of the Irish lads was cutting through the same beam on which I was perched whilst dangling over the yard. I hated heights to begin with and nearly fell off the RSJ with terror. I couldn't believe that someone was behind me, cutting through the beam I was sitting on and the argument that this helped, because the beam was sliced halfway through by the time I reached it, was not impressive. Yes, technically the beam could have held my weight but that was me on the dangling end and I was terrified!

This time, I had no hesitation in leaving. The Charge Hand was very kind and paid me for the whole day which was more than fair but, thwarted love life or not, I was fast going off the demolition business and beginning to think that perhaps my skills with an oxy torch needed retiring.

But then Sammy Green's wash house, and Warrington Tech College, intervened to change my life forever.

2

Through Sammy's
Wash House Door

ONE of the best known sayings is that the older you get, the quicker time passes.

In my case, the situation was reversed. First, the rocket was ignited when I left school. Then there was the initial period, during my time at the engineering merchants, where it sat on the launch pad with its engines running flat out but no apparent movement.

Lift off followed and then so many things happened, so quickly, that my life was changing not so much month by month, or even in weekly increments, but almost by the hour!

Following the "Great Pre-burnt RSJ Incident", retirement from the oxy-acetylene torch business didn't come a moment too soon because, even with the strong feeling of immortality I had at the time, the sense that something was going to go badly wrong was beginning to worry me.

Not that I had much time to ponder the prospects of dying because major events were happening all around me - and at a bewildering rate. They should all be listed as #1 in importance because each, in its own way, was vital but there has to be a start so let me begin by expressing my thanks to Sam Green - and his Dad's wash house.

I have been privileged to know Sam all my adult life and the reason I still give such heartfelt thanks to him is that he helped me when I had nothing – and no apparent prospects either. Such generosity to someone occupying the sludge in life's dung heap is not to be forgotten – ever. I was literally at the bottom, the very bottom, of the ecological ladder and yet Sam showed great kindness, and without ever asking for anything in return.

Sam lived in a Council House at the other side of Warrington but in a somewhat posher area than us. He was older than me and had the unimaginable luxury of a brand new 250cc Honda. Not metaphorically, but quite literally, I couldn't even dream of how anyone could be rich enough to afford a £300 motorcycle but, regardless of being a huge distance further down the motorcycling tree than Sam, our joint love of two wheels formed the basis of a strong friendship.

The great joy of Sam's house was that it had a large wash house attached to the rear of the property. Now, a wash house is a thing of wonder - not for the original intention of being somewhere the wife could wash clothes for the family but as a small, neat and dry premises. It was from Sam's wash house that I launched my first business.

Lusting after girlfriends apart, I was free of the normal teenage vices. I didn't like even the idea of smoking, knew absolutely nothing about drugs and had seen enough of alcohol to put me off for life.

I also had the bare minimum of clothes and didn't like parties. This frugality meant that I could scrape together enough capital to buy a batch of second-hand engine spares for the then ubiquitous Villiers engines, which were used by many of the smaller British motorcycle manufacturers.

The spares cost me £15 and left me destitute – absolutely penniless. It was back to jogging at lunch-time as a substitute for eating. But the situation was short lived. Dealing from Sam's wash house, I had my £15 back in a few days and, in another week, a profit of £10. I was in business!

The next step was unusual: I went to see the Manager at the Midland Bank. I put on my tweed sports jacket and a tie, brushed my Hush Puppy suede shoes and then made my pitch directly to the Branch Manager himself. What a difference from today where a computer scores every overdraft! In those happy days, a keen young person could appeal straight to someone who could make a reasoned decision and then help, or not, based on merit.

I asked for a £15 loan, to go with my £25, to enable me to buy a BSA Gold Star scrambler - and still live whilst it was being sold. At the time, £15 was an awful lot of money to lend to a young person with no credit rating, no business experience and, for that matter, no business either! Regardless, something must have touched a chord and so I was given my loan.

Just as important, I was also provided with an invaluable lesson in fiscal and business responsibility. The Manager explained that the £15 was his money, not mine, and that I was to spend it only on financing this one deal and nothing else. I did not have his permission to do anything else with it – only to buy the Gold Star and then return his money to him in his bank.

To make the loan so personal was such a wonderful lesson to a baby businessman like me. I had been taught, right from the outset, to borrow responsibly, spend responsibly and pay back responsibly too. What a shame the same help isn't available today.

In fact, I bought the "Goldie" for £35. I sold its racing gearbox for £25 and the engine for another £25. Within a week, all the other bits had gone too and for a further £20. I had re-paid the bank and, by still watching every penny, I now had £50 capital – and an overdraft facility.

The problem was that I had financial needs far in excess of my income because there were two big drains on my very limited resources.

***

First – I was love struck again. Clearly, I don't mean love in the sense of: "May I touch your left breast in the second-half of the film if we sit in the medium priced seats of the Ritz and I pay for the tickets?"

No, this was not so much love as more of a biological necessity – the sort of love which drives men to swim crocodile infested rivers and climb fiery volcanoes in order to show their unbridled commitment. Such real, true, passionate, all consuming, dream generating, eating distracting, limb aching lust only meant one thing: motorcycles.

Worse still, it was not just motorcycles – but motorcycle racing.

At the time, Warrington was a real hotbed of bike racing. Just up the road from us was Oulton Park – an international quality road racing circuit.

World Championship motocross was held at both Hatherton Hall, near Nantwich, and the iconic Hawkstone Park – both less than an hour away from our Council House. As well as superb motocross, the Cheshire Centre was home to some of the best grass track riders in the world.

Then there was high speed beach racing at New Brighton and Ainsdale, speedway at Belle Vue's legendary Hyde Road Stadium and many observed trials too. In short, Warrington was at the epicentre of motorcycle sport and lots of my peer group competed in something.

The truth was that I really wanted to road race. My heroes were the Grand Prix superstars of the day - Mike Hailwood, Jim Redman and Luigi Taveri but I could never afford to buy even a basic track racing machine. As a second best choice, I decided to enter motocross.

This sport was affordable – if it was done on a micro budget and with no knowledge. Both elements were important.

I met a lovely lad called Ken Bromley and we both wanted to ride motocross – or more accurately, "scrambles" as it was called at the time. Ken held two aces. First, he had a van and second, he was a tyre fitter.

My contribution was that I could find races in which to ride and also complete the entry forms.

The first job was to find a motocross bike. At the time, a half decent bike was £50 or £60 which was impossibly beyond my budget. However, I did find a wreck of an ancient 500 BSA and bought this for £15. With the addition of a pair of alloy mudguards and ball ended control levers, the bike was almost race ready – in the sense that an ice-cream looks forward to a long and happy retirement whilst sat in the middle of the Sahara Desert in August.

The one thing missing was a pair of knobbly tyres. Inevitably, these were too expensive to buy - but Ken did have a fix. His company supplied tyres to Warrington Council and one of their jobs was to replace the 21" Goodyear Grasshopper rubber on the big, commercial lawnmowers. With my need in mind, Ken became particularly zealous in terms of swapping the lawnmower tyres and I soon became the proud owner of only partly used rubber before it hit the scrap bin.

Our first race was in the hills outside Oswestry. The rain poured down in grey, irregular sheets and a thick, cold mist rolled across the track. Conditions were as bad as I have ever seen them in a lifetime of racing.

My BSA was wholly and totally unsuitable for off-road use, and the lawn-mower tyre clogged up in a few yards, so I was effectively riding a two wheeled toboggan. In practice, I managed about 150 yards of the mile and a half lap. Racing was slightly better and I got a few yards up the first hill before collapsing in a heap.

At the end of the day, I was classified last – but I was ecstatic. More than anything else, I loved the purity of racing – its absolute honesty.

Much later, I learned an American expression which summed up motorcycle racing and it has been very much at the centre of my life since that first event at Oswestry. It's this: "When the flag drops, the bullshit stops."

Rich or poor, well connected or utter nonentity, motorcycle racing is a naked place to be. You have no team mates to pass the ball or cover your mistakes - no referee to decide whether you have been fairly treated or not. It's you, your bike and the other competitors - whether it is a Grand Prix or an amateur race in a field where you are cheered on only by your girlfriend and pet dog.

Currently, it is the vogue for top racers to refer to "our efforts" and "our results." Depending on how you look at the situation this is either meticulously good manners, and an acknowledgement of the huge cost and team effort it takes to get a World Championship rider on to the grid, or it is cynical Political Correctness.

Either way, it is hypocritical. When you see the start of a MotoGP race, and twenty riders are tipping their bikes into the first corner at 120mph, believe me there is no "us" or "our" – but only "me."

It's me that is going to decide to go that fraction harder and either make up five places or end up in hospital.

It's my body which will break, not our body, and it's me who has to make those fine decisions which mean either success or failure. This utter purity and honesty is the joy of motorcycle racing.

Prior to racing I had been judged by things outside of my control, and which impacted my life in a way I didn't understand, and were impossible for me to influence.

By contrast, racing cared nothing for who you were or where you came from. If you were the fastest rider you won and if you weren't, you didn't. It was a hard core meritocracy – and still is. I loved it.

Ken not only had a van but he was also liquid nitrogen cool in terms of his driving skills. I used to watch him in utter admiration as he controlled the

Thames van with his elbows through the steering wheel. This was so incredible, so utterly stylish that I was surprised snow didn't form on the steering wheel.

Forget rock 'n' roll, Mods and Rockers and flower ties, nothing in the world was so mind blowingly impressive as being able to steer a van with your elbows whilst lolling back against the van's bench seat. It was the apogee of high fashion.

A few weeks after my seventeenth birthday, I was driving a car. This wasn't the rite of passage that it seems to be today. I could already drive because I had been in numerous cars and vans wherever there was a non-public road. We had a lot of ex-military bases in the area and so there were miles of viable practice tracks. All of my peer group could drive before they ever went near a public road.

Despite hundreds of hours of experience, I was advised that I had to take driving lessons in order to pass my test and so I did. They weren't a great success. After eleven, one hour lessons I was sacked for doing racing gear changes as I came through the lower gears. How else are you supposed to come down through the gearbox smoothly? I couldn't understand my instructor's problem.

Despite being shown the door by my Driving Instructor, I was relaxed about taking my test.

The key reason for my confidence was that I had been driving all over north-western England and Wales with my Mum as my supervising passenger. In the early days of driving licences there were no tests and anyone who said they could drive was given a licence. My Mum had a licence but to say that she wasn't very highly experienced is putting the matter kindly.

Regardless, she sat in the passenger seat of my Morris Oxford van and off we went racing.

My first test went brilliantly – at least in my eyes. I drove with all the flair and verve of a motorcycle racer and we did the course in record time. My examiner was not so pleased and failed me.

The rejection shocked me. I needed some thought before my second try. I asked everyone who had taken the test recently how they had passed and it became clear that the Highway Code had to be rigidly followed. Actual vehicle control wasn't the problem – delivering these skills in a way which was going to get my pass was.

The second time, my Mum came with me and as I was walking out of the test centre with the examiner she caught his arm and pleaded: "He really does need his licence for his job, love…" Things were very different then…

I sat bolt upright in the van, stretched my neck like a giraffe to show that I was looking in my rear view mirror and didn't take the racing line to straighten out any bend. Even my three point turn was a model of good behaviour.

I liked three point turns a lot. Smack the brakes on, into reverse, just a touch on the hand brake and then engage first gear and spin the wheels as you accelerate away with just a hint of opposite lock to correct the slide. Standard paddock practice for turning a van round!

The Department of Transport saw things differently and so I looked in the mirrors, indicated, braked, stopped gently, applied the handbrake, looked in the mirrors, released the handbrake, reversed, stopped, applied the handbrake, looked in the mirrors, released the handbrake and …

By the time I was half way through the exercise I had almost fallen asleep with boredom.

But the best was yet to come. The Morris was an excellent van, and very good value at £40, but it did have a fault. There was a notch in the steering box and so at the far end of the right-hand arc it would stick, quite firmly, until I gave it a sharp tug. Normally, driving along on a straight-ish road this wasn't a problem but it was an issue on a tight steering lock. For this reason, I was not welcoming the reversing element of the test. If I was given the wrong radius of corner this would be a real challenge.

The examiner stopped us and asked me to reverse round a lovely, near ninety degree corner. He was kinder than he needed to be because the Morris was a bit of an awkward thing to reverse, the rear of the van being a lot wider than the front. This being the case, the examiner re-assured me that I could open the driver's door and peer round the bulge behind me.

I had a good look, released the handbrake like the good boy that I was, and off we went. As I applied right-hand lock, the steering wheel twitched as the notch in the steering box engaged. Then it dawned on me – this was the perfect radius for the corner. I simply relaxed my hands and let the van do the work. We reversed round the bend magnificently. I stopped, applied the handbrake and beamed happily at the examiner. Mirror, indicator, release handbrake, mirror and off we go. Hey, I can do this test driving.

We arrived back at the centre and my Mum, rather than me, was actually given my pass paper so perhaps there was bit of kindness involved but, no matter, I was on the road.

★★★

Matters were also progressing on the writing front – well, after a fashion. I was an inveterate contributor to motorcycle club magazines and wrote voluble and highly opinionated letters on every subject with a vague relevance to the marque – and often no relevance at all.

Usually they weren't published because even when the magazine was desperate for anything to fill its pages, it wasn't so desperate that it would take long, rambling polemics from teenagers who should have known their place in society.

Another problem was that I had truly appalling hand writing which wandered over the page not so much like a spider but more like a centipede which had dipped its feet in ink and then ingested some very interesting narcotic substance.

So too long, irrelevant, too personal and illegible: overall, not a lot going for the work. Not that this stopped me writing something almost every night.

The highlight of my rejections came from Warrington Motorcycle Club. This club, still very much in existence today as it happens, met in a wooden hut in Appleton village, on the outskirts of Warrington. To be honest, I wasn't really a club person but I was thrashing around trying to find the real me in the maelstrom of teenage angst and I thought that a part of the "me" might be a club member.

The club had a large notice board on which members were allowed to place adverts for bike parts they had for sale. The spares business was progressing very nicely from Sammy's Dad's wash house and so I always had bits and pieces available.

From my perspective, the ads were mind numbingly dull – and then some. "For sale. BSA primary chaincase. Will fit BSAs. £5. Ask Steve."

What about a bit of pizzazz? Bring on the humour and social comment. My ads told little stories about the Villiers cylinder barrel which was all on its own and wanted a new Daddy to live with, or the cylinder head which was really so beautiful that it used to share a cushion in the Tower of London with the Queen's jewels.

They weren't great writing but they were excellent practice in terms of playing with words and ideas.

The committee, I really have come to love committees over the years, banned the ads on the grounds that they weren't real advertisements and therefore the holy notice board was being mis-used. Worse still, the ads appeared too often and constituted, roll of drums and wait for it, a business.

I briefly, and unsuccessfully, argued my case but the weight of club bureaucracy and opinion was against me so it was genocide for the ads.

★★★

Meanwhile, I had a strange experience at Warrington Technical College. The incident, short though it was, changed my life – although not immediately.

I had managed to get a job with an engineering company as a sort of office gofer – not so much employed as being a floating fixer. It soon became apparent that I was a rather good problem solver so I spent all day doing little bits and pieces of admin., answering the phone when someone wasn't there and generally being helpful.

As far as I was concerned, it was great. I had hours of spare time to read the bike papers, got to wear a shirt and tie and trousers and, with the demolition job still very much on my mind, I didn't have to sit on the end of an RSJ with an oxy torch!

Unfortunately, my abilities came to the attention of the little company's owner. He called me into his office, expressed his pleasure at how well I had settled in but also noted his sadness that someone with my academic achievement – I had a bag full of good "O" levels – and my generally positive attitude should be wasting my time effectively in a non-job. In fact, he was so impressed by me that he was going to put me on to an engineering course.

This offer needs to be seen in context, in view of society's current view of engineering. I despair at the sneering, mock bemused attitude, which is shown today by anyone when the subject of engineering related topics is raised. See a report about a plane crash on TV and the anchor-man, or woman, doesn't quite refer to the power plants as: "The engine thingies which go brumm, brumm, brumm under the wings and seem to have broken…" Not quite – but very nearly!

Bring on a film star, and talk about the pressures of keeping your make up fresh on set, and the reporter will be an authority on the subject. Mention metal fatigue, or CAD/CAM design, and you might as well be discussing the problems of erecting a Mongolian Yurt in the middle of a Gobi Desert blizzard

By contrast, the whole of Warrington was effectively one enormous, world class, multi-product, engineering works.

At one end were the huge companies like Greenings and Rylands making an immense range of wire products from hair fine, medical and scientific strands of precious metals to ships' anchor chains – and everything in between. These renowned firms were not only major manufacturers but also cutting edge leaders, with highly qualified staff in well-equipped technical and research centres.

Supporting these behemoths were hundreds of small firms, from instrument repairers to pump specialists and expert welders.

I still become really angry when I hear commentators describe these industries as "tin bashing" when nothing could be further from the truth. Currently, television – and particularly the BBC – seems to be dominated entirely by left of centre reporters, with degrees in arts related subjects, and no empathy with, or understanding of, what we have lost as a nation as our industrial base has been destroyed.

If you take a Lloyds Coded welder, capable of perfectly joining two sections of thin wall, stainless steel tube carrying nuclear waste, this isn't "tin bashing" – it's an awe inspiring combination of technology, art and physical skills equal to those of any sculptor. That weld can't be merely very good, or even excellent, it has to be perfect - otherwise a lot of decent people will die through poisoning. Tin bashing? Not for a moment.

Consider the tool maker who can look at a two dimensional drawing, see in his mind's eye what the engineer wants the finished tool to achieve, and then choose the materials and machinery to execute that drawing. No poet writing a sonnet in iambic pentameter has a greater grasp of the abstract or a deeper insight into the unseen.

These tradesmen, and there was no higher accolade in Warrington than to "have a trade", were the aristocracy of the industrial age and to refer to them in pejorative tones is both a gross insult to them – and also a telling window on the intelligence and perception of the commentator.

So, I was sent off to become an Engineer and so join Warrington's elite. I was expected to achieve competent trade skills, produce first class engineering drawings and then go on, as part of the Officer class in this industrial army, to lead my tradesmen into battle.

This was a good idea in theory and I was very excited at the prospect. The only, ever so tiny, problem was that I was a hopeless engineer.

Whilst my classmates saw moments of force as having a real, practical, tangible effect on the breaking point of a beam, to me they were an abstract, unseeable entity - first cousins of the storms which Poseidon hurled at irreligious seafarers.

Yes, they were clearly there. Yes, in the right circumstances they would smash your ship and drown you. Yes, obviously someone, or something, made them. As for what they were, or from whence they came, I had no idea or understanding. My fix for an excess of moments of force would be to walk out to the front of the class with some votive offerings and a prayer.

By contrast, my classmates not only understood these moments of force in an abstract, theoretical manner, and had a bewildering skill in executing the mathematics to calculate what was happening, but they felt them too. They could look at a piece of metal and say: "If you apply that amount of force to this point, then a piece of steel of this grade will break." And it would.

As I have said, if this was tin bashing then Michelangelo did "Painting by Numbers" for the Sistine Chapel!

If I struggled with Maths and Physics in the classroom, and goodness me I really did sweat blood in these subjects, it was nothing compared with my incompetence in the workshop. Just as Royal Marines' Officers have to undertake the same 32 week training course as the men they command, engineers were expected to have a decent level of trade skills so that they knew what they could ask of the tradesmen working for them.

My incompetence was first a matter of bemusement to my colleagues and tutors, then mockery and, finally, despair.

On one occasion, we were given a spec. sheet to turn a tapered brass bush, with an internal thread, on a basic Boxford lathe. Almost before the Ozalid drawing had hit the bench, my colleagues had a length of brass in the chuck and were well on their way to creating a piece of metal working art.

By contrast, I couldn't read the drawing (this means interpret it before you even start work); or cut the piece of brass square because I was so cack handed (what a wonderfully succinct and onomatopoeic expression) with the hacksaw; then I left the key in the lathe chuck (which was a true Court Martial offence because it could have flown out and killed someone) and, finally, I couldn't even use a pair of Vernier callipers to accurately assess the mess I had made.

No wonder my tutor openly prayed that, had he been killed in the ill-fated WWII Dieppe raid, he could have escaped ever coming into contact with me!

Ironically though, not a single moment of this time was wasted. On the contrary, when I began writing professionally I did have a grasp of industrial techniques and, in an embarrassingly incompetent fashion, I can weld and use a lathe. Most importantly, I developed a tremendous respect and admiration for engineers and, later, this was to prove hugely useful.

If only we could learn to admire what we can't do, or even understand, then Britain would be a happier and more successful place in which to live.

The engineering training was tough. We had to be at Warrington Tech. College at half past eight in the morning and then it was pretty well flat out in the classroom and workshop until nine at night. Afterwards, we had a mountain of homework. The idea of "me-time" and "work/life balance" just did not come into the equation.

After lunch, we had one short session which for me was the highlight of the day: this was called "General Studies 2". The group filed into a classroom for a session in which we were supposed to discuss what might loosely be called "Current Affairs."

We were given a mini lecture, asked to write notes, and then make an extremely short presentation. I loved it for a number of reasons. First, instead of being the class idiot I was the star. Producing a 150 word précis from a lecture was so simple that I had it done in the same time as it had taken everyone else to interpret an engineering drawing. This was great.

I also had a very wide ranging knowledge of current affairs and could understand them. When we discussed the war in Vietnam, not only did I know what was happening in south-east Asia in general terms, but I also knew what Dien Bien Phu was and how it led directly to the partitioning of Vietnam.

To be honest, this degree of knowledge and awareness did not go down well with the engineers. Reading for "nothing", and having a knowledge outside of your work requirements, was considered to be very suspect.

Enjoying a "Chinky" takeaway on a Friday night was one thing. Knowing the difference between Mao Zedong and Chiang Kai-shek was very different.

Things came to a head during a discussion about the Police, and whether they were biased against working class young men and turned a blind eye to the well-connected and middle class. We were asked to define justice and the group came up with the normal range of: "Not getting picked on"; "Not getting done just because you have been on the pop" and "What's wrong with taking a bit of scrap home to do a foreigner?"

I wrote: "Justice is the perfect judgement of man by man." My lecturer made no comment.

At the end of the session, when the group was streaming out for tea break, my lecturer called me to his desk. He was blunt and demanded to know where I had "copied" my definition of justice from.

I explained that I hadn't but that it was my own work. He paused for a few seconds before saying: "You're wasting your time here. Get yourself out and into somewhere where you can use your brain."

And that was that: Careers' Guidance, Warrington Tech style.

It was another case of the baby penguin perching in the wrong bird's nest - but getting myself out was going to be easier said than done.

However, escape had to wait because I discovered that I could do the motorcycling equivalent of patting my head whilst rubbing my tummy and this little trick was going to have a major impact on my life – as was getting to know King Orry.

3

Getting to Know King Orry
and the Greatest TT ever

WITH my motorcycle licence came an unquenchable thirst to explore my world. Whenever I had money for fuel, I rode. In fact, very often I would choose to ride rather than eat and I would infinitely have preferred to spend what little cash I had on petrol, rather than the normal teenage interests of "beer and fags." Truly, I was a hard core, no holds barred, motorcycling fanatic.

I soon discovered two things. First, I had a real ability when it came to motorcycling. Later, I would find out how limited this talent actually was when it came to world class riders but, within my peer group, I was good.

Because I could ride, and wouldn't take no for an answer when it came to borrowing bikes, I rode a vast range of motorcycles ranging from pre-Second World War vintage bikes to the very latest Hondas, Suzukis and Yamahas.

This was not as straightforward as it seems. For example, a pre-war Norton not only had completely different handling and power characteristics from the new Hondas but most of the controls were different too.

The gear change lever on a Norton was on the right-hand side of the bike and on the Honda it was on the left. The Norton had manual ignition adjustment – and you had to know how to use it accurately or the bike wouldn't start – and the Honda was completely automatic. The Norton demanded, again with great skill, the rider to adjust the fuel mixture before the bike would start, whilst the Honda did the job for you.

And these were just simple examples. The earlier bikes I rode had a hand-gear change and no brakes worth mentioning in even a Tweet!

I also rode two-stroke and four-stroke machines turn and about. Single cylinder and twin cylinder machines – each one as different as chalk and cheese – posed no problems. I discovered that I had a God given knack that was going to be a true Golden Goose when it came to being a freelance journalist: I could ride anything, confidently and instantly.

I need to explain how important this skill is. Even on an official manufacturer's launch you are given a bike and expected to be able to ride it. That's all there is to it. Here's the bike now get on it and perform. If you take more than a mile to familiarise yourself with the machine, then you are considered to be having a bad day at the office.

When it comes to the freelancer, the situation is even more demanding than this. Usually, the owner of the bike you are riding doesn't actually want you to be on his motorcycle. That's the first problem. Then he is deeply sceptical of your riding ability. Finally, the clock is ticking in terms of the minutes and seconds you are allowed to have the bike so it's no use expecting a couple of hours patient tuition followed by an afternoon to play about.

Sometimes, this state of affairs can be extreme. I once had the great honour, the very great honour, of riding the National Motorcycle Museum's 1907 TT winning Norton. This bike has no clutch, no gears, 98% of no brakes and fully manually controlled air, fuel and ignition. It is also worth about £10 zillion.

The bike is started by reducing the engine's compression with a lever – manually again – and pushing. If the myriad of fine adjustments is absolutely perfect, the bike fires and off it goes. And, as a special thrill, despite being over 100 years old it is quick and takes off like a scalded cat!

When I came to ride the bike, I was given a few minutes tuition and then expected to get on with the job. Of course, the additional fun is that the photographer wants her shots to be award winning and she expects you to ride precisely on a pre-agreed arc around the corner – and then do it again another fifteen times!

So, the bike's owner wants it back without you actually riding it because he's convinced that you're an incompetent Muppet who shouldn't be there in the first place, whilst the photographer is asking for three days to shoot the job so that she can get the perfect pic.

Meanwhile, you are trying to work out what all these strange levers do and whether the bike has some hidden foible which will kill you.

Clearly, the bike has a mind of its own and it isn't going to help at all.

In the midst of all this fun, you have another job. You have to write the article as you go along. It's all well and good riding the bike but you have to seek out the heart and soul of the machine because your readers want to know what it was like to actually be on the motorcycle. You are not being paid to play about on the bike but to tell others what it was like to be in the saddle: what makes this machine special – what makes it magic?

If you can do all this, then you will make a freelance journalist. If you can do it really well then you will be allowed to ride some really exotic machines.

I don't see being able to juggle all these balls as anything to do with riding ability and certainly not any indication of intelligence. Rather it is a knack, like being able to pat your head whilst rubbing your tummy. You can either do it or not, and I'm not sure whether the basket of skills can ever be learned.

Perhaps some brains are wired differently because almost from the first moment I rode motorcycles there was no bike which fazed me. This is really odd because I know riders who are much better than me but who panic about a different gearshift pattern and who would be horrified at the thought of having a gear lever on the right-hand side of the bike. For me, it makes no difference. As I tell the young riders, I simply put a different chip in my brain and off I go.

***

This hunger for constantly changing bikes did get me into trouble. One of the key areas of friction was insurance. Although I challenged the finer points of law in terms of speed limits, I was generally law abiding and so my bikes were insured most of the time. I wasn't an angel in white leathers so I would frequently try someone else's machine for an hour without checking the minutiae of insurance – "Don't ask and don't know" was the cardinal rule – or ride a bike home which I had just purchased, but my own machines were, invariably, properly insured and legal.

The problem was that, in these pre-computer days, all the records were kept on paper and my file in the insurance broker's office was huge – and I do mean immense! I would go into the office on a Monday with a change of bike to the latest machine I had bought at the weekend and then, two days later, I would be back in again for another revision.

I mention this in detail because the person I dealt with was a full on bully – a clerical thug. He was, maybe, ten years older than me and he had a real job, with real power and delighted in using it. By contrast, I invariably arrived looking very second-hand and, to begin with, rather diffident and unsure.

I would come in with details of the latest purchase I had made and he would have to get my file out of the back office – a real Health and Safety issue since it weighed a ton – amend the details and either take a tiny sum from me or, because the new machine was cheaper to insure, make an equally miniscule refund.

He hated the job and he hated me, so he would shout and rage and do his best to humiliate me in front of the "grown-ups" who were being sensible and making their one, annual, payment for insurance.

At first, I found this process very stressful. In fact, I used to wait on the pavement outside the office trying to build up the courage to take the barrage of insults which I knew for certain awaited me.

However, a very interesting thing happened as the months rolled by. Very, very slowly, because I really was extremely nervous and lacking in confidence, the effects of the tirade diminished. The force and venom remained but, like snow melting after a particularly long winter, I realised that they meant nothing. He could shout and mock and sneer but I still walked out of the office intact, with my bike insured, and rode away. In tiny steps, I was learning that officialdom, in all its forms, really was a giant confidence trick. Nothing was going to happen – and nothing did. It was a life-changing lesson.

★★★

With that week's bike properly insured, I had the travel itch – and very badly too. I fell, a little tiny bit, in love with a Vicar's daughter near Rhosneigr, which is in Anglesey. How this passion developed is a useful window on my rather distorted view of life.

It was about 110 miles to Rhosneigr from Warrington but the great attraction was that I could ride through the Clocaenog forest. This was fifteen miles of completely and totally deserted public road, snaking and twisting through the pine trees.

I rode from apex to apex on each corner, just like a race track and never saw another vehicle. It was sublime.

After the Clocaenog, it was down on to the A5 and another 35 miles of breath-taking mountain roads before the final run across Anglesey to Rhosneigr.

There was no traffic, no radar cameras, and Police were unknown so it was motorcycling heaven.

In Rhosneigr, we would sit on the grass outside her Dad's Church and sometimes even share a Mars bar but, other than briefly holding hands, that was the limit of our intimacy. She was shy and unsure of what she should do next and, by contrast, I did know what to do – and that was ride through the mountains again.

★★★

I was just seventeen years old when I went to the TT in the Isle of Man for the first time. It was only an hour's ride to Liverpool and the TT was considered to be very much a local event for those of us living in the North-West of England.

As a writer, I should tell you stories about how great was the 1965 TT and what wonderful memories I have of the experience. However, I am trying to be honest throughout this book and so I have to say that the TT was too much for me in almost every way. It was like going out for a fine quality Indian meal and then, by accident, ordering a Vindaloo Extra Special which is just so hot and strong that you only feel the heat rather than taste the flavours.

I knew, and felt, that I was very much at the bottom of the motorcycling ecological ladder – and in every way too – and the TT only served to clarify this idea of my place in the biking world.

First, I had a really awful 350 Velocette which was rusty and leaked oil and so I had no status in terms of a bike.

I did not know any of the insiders' jokes about the riders and their bikes so I just sat at the back of every group and listened and watched.

25

Clearly, I had almost no money and so only the bare necessities could be afforded.

To save every penny, I caught the midnight boat from Liverpool which was by far the cheapest way to reach the Isle of Man. I slept on the deck using my Dad's ex-Navy gas mask bag containing my tools, and the essential spares for the Velo, as a pillow whilst the beer fuelled singing and cigarette smoke drifted up from the saloon beneath.

It is important to remember that I didn't feel that this was anything but completely normal. I had no money and no contacts so where else would I be, other than on the deck of the King Orry with my gas mask bag? The sun is hot, water is wet and poor kids slept on the deck – or didn't get to see the TT at all!

Before the War, my Mum used to go to the Isle of Man for a week's holiday and to dance every day at the Villa Marina. When I was ten years old she had taken me to the Isle of Man too and I had been entranced by the racing. From her dancing days, she got me a cheap deal in a boarding house in one of the small streets at the back of the Villa Marina.

The King Orry docked at dawn and I wasn't allowed to go to the boarding house, on pain of death, before 8am so I sat on the wall at Douglas Promenade and let this new world wash over me.

I smelled the sea air and the Castrol "R" from the "Ton Up Boys" who ran their sports bikes on this exotic lubricant. I listened to the calls of the seagulls and the crackle and boom of barely silenced BSA Gold Stars as they headed out for a lap of the TT circuit. I felt the rough stone cutting in to me as I sat on the sea wall and I tasted the sweet salt of the sea mist - and I felt alive, in a way I never was in Warrington.

It was very much like leaving a dense forest and entering a new world and, like some human sponge, I sat and I looked and I listened and I soaked up everything.

I also smelled the frying bacon from the café at the Pier Head and looked forward to breakfast because last night's tea at home seemed a long, long time ago.

I travelled very light for the simple reason that I owned almost nothing. It's surprising how little luggage you carry if you don't have anything. All that I needed for a week was in a small, plaid, fabric duffle bag and my gas mask tool bag contained everything else.

I waited until a little after 8am because I didn't want to seem bad mannered by rushing in as the doors opened. My "digs" were a perfect parody of every boarding house that was ever satirised. This was a 1930s boarding house par excellence!

The Camp Commandant, who owned the establishment, greeted me at the door with a pair of cold, narrow eyes which had been machined from two blocks of case hardened steel.

Interestingly, she was dressed entirely in a range of industrial greys.

The first things to catch my attention were her surprisingly large feet. These were wrapped in a pair of heavy shoes which were close relatives of working boots – but, surprisingly, without the steel toe caps. She had clearly missed a trick there!

The shoe-boots had once been black but the leather was scuffed and now reflected a faint, grey half-light worthy of any newly awoken vampire.

Her skirt was an interesting mix of light grey, mid grey, dark grey and black tweed and what had once been a white blouse was now another shade of grey - probably in an attempt to show solidarity with the rest of the ensemble.

She wore a grey cardigan which carried the only touch of lightness in her whole outfit: a piece of worn, black jet formed into a flower.

The Commandant's skin was a lighter shade of grey than either her blouse or her cardigan and, to be fair, her teeth were hardly grey at all – they were a rather threatening arc of brown tints.

At the very top was a bundle of grey hair, tied back into a tight bun.

Liverpool and London might have been swinging to the rock 'n' roll beat of the sixties but hotel trade in the Isle of Man certainly wasn't!

She showed me to my room - but not before we passed the dining room which was awash with the smell of frying bacon, hot beans and burning toast. It was all that I could do to avoid drooling on the corridor floor.

To describe where I was to stay as a bedroom is being rather unfair to hotel rooms throughout the world. In fact, to give it the status of a cupboard is a bit cupboardist too: it was tiny. There was just sufficient space for a small single bed and a bare, cracked, wooden chair. The chair was a true, multi-purpose piece of equipment which served as a wardrobe, bedside table and clothes hanger too.

A small window looked out over the back of the house. There were herring gulls foraging in the yard below so I knew that I must be near to the seaside and therefore on holiday.

After taking several seconds to settle me in, the Camp Commandant showed me the bathroom. It was shared by a good number of residents and so was always busy. This was not a place for the faint of bottom.

I was given a brusque explanation of the rules. I was allowed a single bath in the week and, to avoid excessive queuing, I should take this mid-week because things got busy towards Friday evening. As the Junior resident, I had to show deference to my elders and betters.

There was a mark etched on to the bath enamel showing how much water could be used. No more than two inches (that's about 50mm) was permitted because of the cost of heating the water.

Even by my incredibly low standards this was harsh but I accepted the strictures in silence, counting the seconds before I could tuck into toast and hot tea.

We descended the near vertical stairs and, using my most obsequious voice, I asked if it was okay to have breakfast now. The scene which followed was straight from Oliver Twist. "Breakfast? B-r-e-a-k-f-a-s-t? B-R-E-A-K-F-A-S-T?" The volume increased with each repetition of the word.

Did I realise that it was only as a token of respect for my Mum that I was even allowed to enter her boarding house before mid-day and now I wanted breakfast as well?

Didn't I realise that B-E-D and B-R-E-A-K-F-A-ST mean that breakfast followed bed?

The first breakfast to which I was entitled came the following morning and I should be ashamed of my weak and cruel attempts to exploit a kind, gentle lady who was providing me with such lovely accommodation.

Every eye in the tiny dining room turned on me and if I had been cast into a fiery lake of molten lava, managed by devils with pitchforks, it would have been a good swap. I turned from deep red to some teenage shade of purple and visibly shrunk in size.

Still, it wasn't all bad. Occasionally the Velo started first kick, as it did on this occasion, and I was soon on the TT course following the road out to Ramsey.

Strangely, I can remember nothing of the ride. I say strangely because I have a near photographic memory of almost every trip I have ever done. I can recall not only what I have seen and heard but what I tasted and smelled too. Yet, the enormity of my first few miles on the TT course was so great that I must have gone into some form of sensory overload. There was just so much to see, hear, taste and smell that my brain simply gave up and shut down.

It must have re-started in Ramsey, because I found a little café and bought a round of toast and a big cup of tea for a shilling (5p). I asked the smiling lady if I could have the crust end of the loaf because this was thicker and she was happy to oblige. A shilling was a big spend but I was starving and I knew that I could cut out a couple of meals later in the week and claw back the money.

My memories of the week are mainly based on sounds. The swinging sixties was at its peak and I feel sure that there must have been some great bands playing at the TT but of them I remember nothing. I had no money to pay for a ticket, and no clothes to wear, so the bands held no interest for me and nor did they have any impact on my life.

Are you concerned what Prince William is doing today? His life is so far removed from yours that it is beyond a waste of time and energy to even contemplate his day. So it was with me and the TT social scene.

Grown-ups with money did things, whilst I survived each day and that was that. I viewed this state of affairs as neither unfair, nor cruel nor unjust. It just was.

So I sat on the wall at the end of Sulby Straight for free and let the harsh, melodic scream of the works Hondas wash over me and penetrate every molecule of my body.

As I write this now, I can still hear, and feel, the gear changes as Jim Redman slowed his factory Honda from maybe 140mph to 60mph. The Hondas made a torn, almost mournful, wail as they braked and then accelerated away around me and past the Ginger Hall pub.

Jim battled with Phil Read riding a two-stroke Yamaha and this had a vicious, aggressive, tortured scream.

These two were the lead soloists in the orchestra - the First Violins of the show. But the rest of the musicians were just as important. There was the deep braaaah, braaaah, braaaah as the British Norton and AJS machines came down through the gears and the slightly harsher, higher pitched and more urgent notes of the Aermacchis.

These sounds were to stay with me all my life. In fact, these were the sounds which would become my life.

Jim won that race and was my hero. As I sat on the wall at Sulby, I could never have imagined that Jim would later ride for me and become a family friend.

After the 350cc race, I headed back to Ramsey and the little café again. The lovely lady must have sensed that I was at the bottom of the financial ladder and so she gave me two rounds of cheese on toast for the price of one. I stuttered a mumbled thanks and blushed deeply again but I was so grateful. I was fully fed and under budget. Could life be any better?

When I went to back to the Velo, there were three people stood looking at it – an older man, a well-dressed rider in black leathers and a teenage boy, about my age. We chatted and as things transpired they were all Velocette fans. I bluffed and waffled and dredged up Velocette information from the dozens of articles I had read about the marque and, since they didn't walk away, I guessed that I was doing rather well.

What made them really interesting was that, not only were they Velo enthusiasts, they were Dutch.

At this point in the story I need to digress. I had lived abroad but as part of the military because, for a brief period, my Dad had worked for the Air Ministry.

However, being part of British military life at what was, in effect, the end of the Empire was an odd experience. I went to a British Army school staffed entirely by British teachers using British books, British pens, British rulers, and even British toilet paper. My Mum shopped at the British Naafi and we ate exclusively British food. In practical terms, we were in Britain – just in another country.

The rest of the world was a bit of a hazy blob. I thought that I knew that they had dykes and cheese and clogs in Holland; that Germany had started the War and that the Romans had originated in Italy.

Then there was Britain, a bit of Europe, the rest of the world and America. I could never have found Luxembourg on a map and wouldn't have been much better with Austria, Hungary, Finland or Sweden. They were all "foreign" where people spoke something which wasn't English.

America really wasn't a country – it was a different world. I knew more about America than the vast majority of the British population because we had lived near an American air base and I had an American friend. I had ridden in his Dad's 1958 Chevrolet and I had been a baby sitter for American kids – which was well paid, if horrendously hard work.

I had eaten turkey at Thanksgiving and toasted marshmallows with Robbie on the beach but these were more like cultural postcards of America – useful and interesting but lacking any detail or real information.

But as for America the country, I could only guess. It wasn't quite the equivalent of a Cargo Cult acolyte trying to work out what the Stock Exchange in London did, from looking at some postcards of Tower Bridge and the Houses of Parliament, but it was certainly along those lines.

With Holland, I just didn't have the vaguest hint of a clue. If someone had said that every Friday night the Dutch painted themselves blue and threw bananas at each other then I would have shrugged my shoulders and accepted the story as fact. After all, it was foreign and foreigners did odd things.

The teenager was Jorg Van Beek, the older chap was his lovely Dad and the well-dressed rider his cousin.

Jorg spoke superb English and told me about the Dutch TT, held on the public roads around Assen, and said how much I would enjoy the event. I liked Jorg a lot and his Dad was great. During the week, we met several times and exchanged addresses.

The one place I didn't visit was the TT paddock in the centre of Douglas. I knew where the paddock was, and I knew what it was, but I was just too shy to go there. I was frightened of doing or saying the wrong thing or being out of place, so I just stayed away. This was a shame because it was a memorable time in the history of motorcycling.

On the Friday of TT Week was the Senior TT – the most important race in the motorcycling world at the time. To win the Senior was the equivalent of being a World Champion and it was the one race that everyone on the Island looked forward to.

I ate well that morning. If you were careful, you could scam two extra rounds of toast for breakfast by eating the first two very quickly and then pretending that they hadn't arrived so this was a good start to the day.

It was pouring down with rain and so I rode to Ramsey along the coast road through Laxey rather than over the mountain road to Snaefell.

In Ramsey, fast becoming my favourite place in the Isle of Man, I bought a ham roll, filled up my ex-Army water bottle from the tap in the public toilets and headed up the mountain to the Gooseneck Corner – one of the slowest parts of the 37¾ mile course.

The TT circuit is very fast – riders were regularly averaging over 100mph even in 1965 – and so spectator viewing can be somewhat restricted. It is spectacular to see a bike pass a few inches away from you at 150mph but you don't get long to study the finer details of the bikes or riders.

By contrast, at the Gooseneck, the riders climb uphill directly towards the spectators, brake hard and then accelerate slowly away towards the Guthrie Memorial.

The only problem is that you are trapped there for the entire duration of the race because there is no access road, other than the public road which is part of the actual TT circuit.

Viewing is also surprisingly restricted. The best spot is just on the apex of the corner from where it is possible to see all the way down the track, almost to Waterworks Corner, and then uphill towards the summit of Snaefell.

I was there early and settled down to watch in the driving rain. Things weren't as bad as they might seem at first glance. I had my old cycling cape to sit on and since the grass was wet it wasn't too hard.

I had put a good coat of dubbin on my boots so they weren't going to let any moisture in. My waxed cotton Belstaff jacket and trousers truly were waterproof – and would remain so all day. My Mum had knitted a really thick bobble hat for me and this was waterproof too. Other than smelling strongly of sheep lanolin, because this kept the water out, things were good.

In my gas mask bag was my ham roll for lunch, there was water in my bottle and my hero Mike Hailwood was riding in the Senior TT. What could be better?

The rain hammered down and, as a result, the road was flooded. It was quite literally a full flowing stream, running all the way across the road at almost 90 degrees and also down towards Ramsey. There was that much water!

The TT riders, all stars in their own right and with huge amounts of experience of racing in the wet, came almost to a halt in front of me and then coaxed away their Grand Prix Norton and Matchless single cylinder bikes with just hints of throttle and timorous use of the clutch.

The couple next to me had a little transistor radio and I stole the words of the commentary from them as they squeaked out of the tiny black box and into the lashing rain.

There were only two real contenders for the race – Hailwood and Agostini. Ago crashed at the notoriously difficult Sarah's Cottage section of the course, in conditions which would have had the race abandoned at any circuit in the world today.

Hailwood swept on past me with his MV Agusta throwing up clouds of steam as he drove through the streams of water.

On lap three, Mike crashed at the same place as Giacomo. He was cut and bleeding and his MV Agusta was badly damaged with a smashed windscreen and flattened exhausts. Retirement was inevitable.

Then came one of the great moments of motorcycle racing history. First, it was completely and totally illegal, not to say dangerous, to re-start a bike against the direction of the course – to head into oncoming traffic.

Sarah's Cottage is on a steep climb and there was no way of push starting the MV uphill. Who was going to be the marshal to tell Hailwood, the people's hero, that he couldn't run his bike downhill? Who in Race Control was going to wave a black flag and ban him from competing? In all seriousness, there would have been a full scale riot.

The weather took on a Wagnerian majesty. Looking down to Ramsey, the sheets of rain were so heavy that they marched solidly across the moors in tight, grey-black battalions. The wind howled and bent the trees near horizontal. All that was needed were three Rhinemaidens in black leathers and the Ring Cycle could have had another couple of hours.

Mike reached the Gooseneck with his face protector hanging loose and the MV looking a real wreck. Even to my amateur ear the bike sounded dreadful, popping and banging as he accelerated away.

Later on Mike had a carburettor slide, which had been damaged in the crash, completely removed from the MV so that one of the four cylinders would not shut off – on a treacherous track and in torrential rain. That is what makes a winner. That is the mark of a champion and a hero.

Hailwood's TT win dominated the whole week and on the midnight ferry back to Liverpool there was no other topic of conversation. There simply were no adjectives sufficiently superlative to describe it.

I sat on the floor at the back of the Saloon bar with a bottle of ginger beer and a bag of crisps and listened, as my elders and betters analysed the win in minute detail. There was no dissension. This was the greatest TT win ever.

For me it was more – far more. Hailwood was the son of a multi-millionaire, he was playboy rich and public school educated but none of this mattered when he raced.

In the driving rain and the howling wind, through the blood and the pain his only companion was courage. Ride harder, be braver, be stronger, be more determined and you win.

That is the purity of motorcycle racing and nothing was ever purer than Hailwood in the 1965 TT.

Back in life's cheap seats, my life was bursting into action on every front but I'm going to keep to just one path for the moment, because a page torn from my old school atlas and a blessing from a Catholic priest were going to have a long lasting effect on my life.

4

Excuse Me, Where is Germany Please?

EVEN after spending twenty-five years with me, and not even a trophy to show for it, my lovely wife Carol is still stunned by my child like naivety. She can't understand how someone with a modest degree of intelligence, and who has spent a lot of the government's money on being educated, can be so simple minded.

I can't understand it either for that matter and for much of my life I have felt rather like the little chrome ball in a pin ball machine, ricocheting off things which made loud noises and startled me, whilst I occasionally scored a point.

Not quite understanding what the grown-ups were talking about has often got me into trouble but never more so than when I was selling poppies for the British Legion, outside Warrington Market.

I had been rather conned into this activity. The week before, a very, very attractive mid-20s daughter of a British Legionnaire had been selling poppies and, as I chipped up my sixpence, said that she would be so incredibly impressed, and personally highly excited, yes e-x-c-i-t-e-d, if I would take up a collecting box and flog some of the paper flowers the following Saturday.

I'm sure that her job wasn't so much selling poppies but recruiting dummies like me who fantasised that a tall, impeccably dressed, curvy ash blonde was actually going to drop everything, and in my fantasies I really did dream of everything, merely for standing outside Market Gate for a couple of hours off-loading her Dad's poppies. As I have noted, Santa and the Tooth Fairy were dead certs in my eyes.

Regardless, the following Saturday did find me with my tray of poppies and a collecting box, with, surprisingly, no sign of the recruiting seductress - but still quite enjoying myself.

I was in sympathy with the British Legion's admirable work, and I still am for that matter, and there was no rain so collecting wasn't an onerous job. It was also nice to be treated with courtesy and kindness which made a very pleasant change. If I could have had a few Villiers' spare parts on the pavement as well, and turned an honest shilling or two whilst working for the British Legion, then life would have been perfect.

Warrington on a Saturday was a very busy place, not only for shopping but socially too, so I wasn't surprised to see a group of lads I had known from school come ambling into view. There were a few comments about my poppy selling but nothing nasty or overly facetious: just a bit of good hearted ribbing.

The boys were older than me and sounded so much more sophisticated and grown up. One had been accepted into the Army and was looking forward to shooting guns and blowing things up. Another had a good job with Barclay's Bank as a trainee clerk and a third had been taken on by a big insurance broker in Manchester to become a professional insurance person or something. Clearly, I didn't mention anything about my haphazard bouncing from one job failure to another.

The baby soldier was the pack leader and he explained to me that I really did need to get a grip of myself and join the real world. After all, the three of them had been to Spain that summer, without their parents, and they were therefore fully qualified international travellers.

I was wide eyed with wonder and admiration. There weren't enough "Wow" related expletives in the English language to express how incredibly, utterly "Wowed" I was. Wow, travel to Spain, wherever that was, without your Mum and Dad and explore. That couldn't possibly be more wow if you had just won the wow bank at Monte Carlo!

This is where the child-like innocence kicked in. I translated: "We have been to Spain without our Mums and Dads" as:

"We got on our bikes, rode to Spain, explored the country and then rode back again."

Now that was proper adventuring.

In fact, I later found out that what had actually happened was that a coach had collected them at the end of their road and taken them to Manchester Airport for a charter flight to Spain. On arrival, they had been disgorged from the plane, another bus had scooped them up and dumped them at their hotel in Torremolinos.

The three of them shared a room, had "Full English Meals" every day, got heavily drunk on Sangria and failed to have sex with three girls from Bury who were in the adjacent room - all whilst never straying outside of their hotel complex.

It was the "Swinging '60s" but the bottom of the social ladder was a far cry from the sex, drugs and rock 'n' roll of the glamorous end of the scale.

Regardless, I considered their adventure as a true call to arms and went home with a foreign trip very high on my mind.

***

Following the acquisition of my car driving licence I raced as often I could afford. The Morris Oxford van was surprisingly roomy and I could just fit a bike in the back if it was put in at an angle. I added some luxury touches like a big interior light and a hand pumped windscreen washer and rode at both scrambles and grass track meetings.

The problem was the bikes – a cry which I am sure has been heard ever since the first Neanderthal hunters came back to the cave empty handed and moaned about the quality of the flint on the spears they had been given.

However, in my case there was more than a hint of justification. Immediately following the utterly inauspicious birth of my racing career at Oswestry, where I didn't actually complete a lap, I swapped the BSA for a 1950s, three-speed DOT. Both me and the owner of the DOT occupied the same part of the primordial sludge in the racing cesspit and we both thought that we had got one over on the other.

He got a grossly overweight road bike with tyres useless for motocross and I became the owner of a genuine scrambles bike that was so fragile it would break merely by looking at it.

I took the DOT to my second event which was at a farm just outside Whitchurch in South Cheshire, now, interestingly, a very posh golf club. How the world has changed…

I made a stunning start on the DOT and went into the first corner only just in last place and alongside another racing amoeba of equal incompetence. We battled wheel for wheel for five laps and I finished an amazing next to last - by dismounting and running next to the DOT for the last fifty yards and so out accelerating my opposition. I had beaten someone – fair and square! What a result!

I dealt my way through half a dozen equally bad 250cc bikes all powered by ancient, and incredibly fragile, Villiers engines. They were all useless and I was getting really fed up with going to a race meeting and having something break on every occasion. Even by my very low standards, this was no fun.

Then I saw a Tribsa scrambler advertised in Motorcycle News. A Tribsa was a home built special using a BSA frame, Norton front forks and wheel, a BSA gearbox and a Triumph engine. The bike had been put together very well by a mechanical fitter who worked for GKN - a huge, prestigious engineering group. This was an important factor because the bike had been built largely as a "foreigner" at GKN.

The lovely expression "foreigner" needs some explanation. There was a lot of high quality engineering being done in the North-West of England and one of the unwritten rules of the relationship between the management and the workforce was that a reasonable amount of foreigners could be undertaken in the factory. A foreigner was an unofficial job which was done on works premises but, at best, not on works time.

For example, you might need a broken footrest welding. You would seek out a skilled welder and ask him to repair the part as a foreigner. He would take the footrest into work with him along with his snap, or lunch, and instead of taking his half hour lunch break he would repair the footrest, return it to you and be "squared off."

It might be payment in cash for services rendered or it might be a swap for something you could do. Very often, it would just be a favour with nothing in return.

The unwritten contract also included the use of scrap materials. When I climbed further up the ecological racing ladder, I became a strong advocate of Britain's nuclear submarine fleet for two incredibly important reasons. First, these wonders of aquatic technology used lots of titanium – a wonderful metal alloy which is both super strong and very light: simply perfect for racing motorcycles.

Second, the tradesmen who worked this tough metal were absolutely top drawer – the best of the best. If you got some "ti" bolts from Vickers, you could guarantee that they were of nuclear quality - for the simple reason that they were.

The nuclear boats – submarines are always called boats – were made at Cammell Laird's yard in Birkenhead, just across the Mersey from Liverpool, and Vickers in Barrow-in-Furness. Both were hot beds of the motorcycle racing industry.

My Mum had drummed into me that stealing was morally wrong and so I carried a rather puritan set of rules around in my head – and still do for that matter. I was happy to accept a bit of scrap titanium, and equally happy to agree that, philosophically, a turner had stolen, for this is what it was in practice, some of his employer's time and equipment to make a bolt or wheel spindle for me. Viewed properly, this was wrong and it is stealing.

However, doing foreigners did have a huge effect in terms of keeping everyone happy. The welder or turner got a few pounds in his back pocket and the loss to the employer of a tiny amount of scrap metal was truly negligible

Teachers were using school notebooks and pens to write down their shopping lists and bank managers were enjoying free drinks in the golf club with clients. Why should manual workers be any different? Treated sensibly and fairly, doing the occasional foreigner hurt no-one.

The fatal flaw was that the system, if this is what it could be called, was sometimes mortally abused. The Ford plant, at Speke on the outskirts of Liverpool, became a by-word for mass theft. Quite literally whole engines, gearboxes and even car body shells were stolen to order.

This was a galaxy removed from a welder doing a five minute job in his lunch break. Theft at Speke reached a truly commercial scale and was wrong on every level, both moral and legal. Like all good things, the few spoiled things for the many.

However, in the case of the Tribsa scrambler GKN had made an unknowing donation of some lathe time to turn out some really nice little bits and pieces for the bike, a few high tensile fasteners and a few hours of welding time spread over four months: that was it.

The problem was the cost. The price was a non-negotiable £55 and this was almost double what I was paying for the Greeves and DOT scramblers which were giving me so much heartache.

The vendor let me test ride the bike on the tip at the back of the CWS margarine works at Urmston - and I immediately fell in love with it. The Triumph engine had been tuned and produced three times the power of the Villiers engined machines which I had been riding. With a lovely snarl from the unsilenced, siamesed exhaust the bike dismissed the steep climbs on the tip with contempt.

It handled well too. The BSA frame was renowned for excellent handling and the Norton front forks weren't bad either. Here was a bike on which I could actually compete rather than just trying to finish a race.

I went home very dejected because I couldn't afford the bike - and being sad was an unusual state of affairs for me.

My Dad kept my Mum on a very short leash financially. There was a distinct pecking order in his list of priorities, the first of which was supporting Greenalls' brewery. In fact, the next 98 most important things were also predicated on keeping Greenalls in profit!

To help things along, my Mum had found a job as a dinner lady at the local Primary school. I don't know what this paid but I would be surprised if it was more than £4 a week. This money was the difference between her being able to merely survive on the miserable stipend my Dad allowed her and having a tiny amount of flexibility, in terms of what food or clothes she could buy.

In an act of incredible generosity, she "loaned" £25 to me – in the certain knowledge, I feel sure, that it would never be re-paid. As things transpired she was wrong but, at the time, I certainly wouldn't have loaned £25 to me!

So the DOT went for £30 and, with my Mum's £25, the Tribsa purchase was on.

I collected the bike and brought it home with the same degree of pride as if I had just bought a brand new Rolls Royce. At last, I had a bike on which I could truly race.

The problem was that the bike was physically too big and heavy for me and this was later going to have a huge impact, literally and metaphorically, on my life but at the time nothing mattered except having a real race bike. Now, I had a motorcycle on which I could pass other riders. Open the throttle, hang on - and the Tribsa took off like a rocket.

Like all racers, the moment I had the Tribsa I immediately raised my expectations. The first thing I needed was a replacement front rim to replace the dented one which had come with the bike. Inevitably, the standard problem of money arose.

At Sandiway, on the edge of Winsford, was Spanns' Garage. This was operated by Fred Spann, who really should have been a registered charity because he helped so many impecunious racers so often and always with a smiling mixture of kindness and credit.

***

Fred agreed to lace a "new" second-hand rim – a brand new item was impossibly beyond my budget - on to the front hub and four days later I set off to Spann's shop, after work, to collect the wheel.

The rim was like new, and he had made a beautiful job of the building. So I lashed the wheel to the side of my Matchless road bike using Bungee cord elastics top and bottom, with the pillion footrest as a support and set off for home a very happy litte racer.

The return journey went beautifully, with the Matchless humming along and the smell of burning oil from the leaking rocker box wafting up to me like nectar on the breeze. Life was looking good again as I hurtled down the dark road which runs parallel with Warrington Technical College, as it was then called.

A combination of my highly illegal speed – a good 20mph above the limit for a built up area – and a badly fitted manhole cover, caused the Matchless to jump slightly. When it landed, it was with some surprise that I saw I had now been joined by what looked awfully like a Norton 21" wheel, complete with scrambles tyre.

The wheel, being a friendly sort, hovered alongside me for a moment before accelerating away whilst I mused that it looked identical to the wheel I was carrying on the bike, "was" being the operative word.

The wheel bowled away purposefully whilst I set off in pursuit, the Dam Buster's "Bouncing Bomb" signature tune ringing in my ears.

Unfortunately, heading towards me was a Vauxhall Cresta. This car was a dreadful parody of the '50s Chevrolets. It had vestigial fins on the back and was constructed from tracing paper thin, mild steel sheet. The wheel knew this as well as I did, and locked on to its target with ruthless efficiency.

The impact was impressive. Since Fred had put about 40 psi in the tyre to blow the bead out, it had an excellent profile for maximum penetration and it cut through the rusted bumper with ease, finally lodging itself up against the radiator.

The car slewed to a halt and out leapt the driver. Purple with rage he dragged the wheel missile loose and hurled it on to the grass verge. I was not pleased with this, not pleased at all, and I told him so in no uncertain terms.

I also told him that it was bad enough contemplating the damage which his car might have done to my wheel, without subjecting my property to further abuse. Whether it was the shock of being faced with this line of reasoning, or merely that he had calmed down somewhat, I am not sure but he released my Belstaff jacket and put me down again without actually hitting me. In fact, we were both distracted by the sight of the car's passenger who had disembarked and was lurching up and down the grass verge, gasping for breath and looking quite ill.

Mr. Vauxhall was nearly in tears and after the briefest exchange of addresses I re-loaded the wheel and left the two of them there. The key thing was that the wheel wasn't damaged.

It was only when I went round to Mr. Vauxhall's home, to confirm that I accepted responsibility for the wayward behaviour of my wheel and that I forgave him for his bad temper, that I realised how serious the situation could have been.

The poorly passenger who had been lurching up and down, ashen faced and gasping, was the driver's father who had just been released from hospital after suffering a mammoth heart attack. Above all else, he was under strict instruction that he must not suffer any excitement or stress or else the results could be fatal. And, in all seriousness, they very nearly were.

But he didn't die, and my precious wheel was undamaged, so all was well. I knew that the following day would bring a fresh tranche of troubles so there was no point in worrying about what could have happened when it hadn't.

***

During the winter, the idea of a foreign trip weighed heavily on my mind. I was in correspondence with one of the Dutch boys I had met at the Isle of Man TT. Jorg Van Beek invited me to stay with his family at their house in Hengelo, in the eastern part of the Netherlands near to the German border, and I became obsessed with this trip. Jorg had told me stories of the Dutch TT at Assen and I was determined to see this race in real life.

It was only because I had so little idea of what I was doing that the scheme went ahead at all. First, I was desperately short of money so my nascent social life was brought to a full stop. As I have said, the "Beautiful People" might well have been in full flow in London and Liverpool but, for me, their life was just an unattainable blur inhabited by other people from a different planet.

Not only did I carry on with my various "day jobs" but the spares' business was doing well, although erratically so because of a lack of capital. I was also working at anything else which brought in a few pounds, such as delivering paraffin at weekends.

I wasn't too bothered about a lack of social life because I had bigger things on my mind!

In terms of road bikes, things were looking up – or more accurately, down. In short, I had been conned into buying a 500cc Velocette Venom. At its best, this was a formidable sports bike and, since I had red, white and blue blood running through my veins and a Union Jack etched on the inside of my brain, I was a real sucker for the smooth talking salesman at Bill Hannah Motorcycles in Liverpool – and goodness me, did I get a real spanking!

I only hope that he enjoyed his bonus money from the sale because the misery he caused to a near penniless teenager should have him cast into the depths of perdition, to be forever pelted with broken and oil soaked Velocette bits.

It really is a waste of time discussing the bike because simply everything on it failed – and continued to break - until I, quite literally, sold it for scrap.

However, despite the Venom's best efforts, I was utterly determined to plough on with the Assen trip. Even as a self-taught businessman, I could make decent guesstimates at profit and loss and this is what allowed the spares business to survive. When I did the sums for Assen the figures revealed that the trip was impossible. It just couldn't be done with the money I had, no matter how careful I was.

Drastic measures were required. I worked out that if I had a really big breakfast when I left our house in Warrington, I wouldn't be desperately hungry until I reached Hengelo, where Jorg lived, and that was only two days later. I would fill up my ex-Army canteen with water at home and there had to be equally free water on the ferry so it was only a matter of skipping food on the outward and inbound legs of the journey, and not eating anything at the race, then there would be sufficient money to get me to Assen. Money problems? What problems?

My Mum did what she could to help and she promised a £5 loan, another oxymoron, which I could repay to her later. She also helped with my packing. All my spare clothes were stuffed into a small, ex-Army knapsack – this really was minimalist touring – and into my Dad's gas mask bag went a range of Velocette spares including spare clutch plates, the vital clutch adjusting tool, cylinder head and rocker box gaskets, two spare valves, spare valve springs and collets, valve spring compressor and four pints of oil because the Venom used lubricant like a two-stroke. Not only in terms of weight, but also bulk, I carried more spares and tools than I did clothes!

I came home from work and had a final check over the Venom as my Mum fussed around and did what she could to help. It was at this point that disaster struck or, perhaps more accurately, got ready to strike.

I have almost zero mechanical ability but not even I could mistake the smell of petrol dripping on to the concrete at the back of our Council House. This alerted me to the fact that the bottom left-hand seam of the Venom's fuel tank was starting to split.

My Mum was heartbroken for me and tears started to fill her eyes. Tears were coming to me too but the ferry from Hull to Rotterdam was still twenty hours away and I wasn't going to be beaten.

Unusually for a family of our income, we had our own phone – I had begged my Mum to get one installed primarily for the spares business – and so I spent the next hour trying to hunt down a Velocette fuel tank. There was no chance of buying one so not only did I have to find a tank but I also had to persuade the owner to lend it to me free of charge.

How it happened I don't know but a much older man living on the far side of Warrington said he would lend me a Velocette tank – but warned me that it was almost scrap and had been outside all winter.

I rode to his house on the Venom - naturally with petrol dripping over the hot cylinder head. I remembered that one of my Chemistry teachers at school had shown us that it was possible to pour petrol over a very hot surface and all that happened was that it evaporated. Only when a spark was added would it burst into flames. I just hoped that he hadn't scammed the experiment to impress us and that the petrol fumes would get blown away before blowing me up!

The tank I had come to see was in a bad way, being both heavily rusted externally and dented, but it looked okay internally so I balanced it between my knees, held it in place with my left elbow and rode home.

My Mum switched the lights on in the kitchen and I worked on into the night, cleaning out the replacement tank by swilling copious amounts of fuel around inside it. This was then dumped into the drains - I wasn't very environmentally friendly in those days – and then I fitted the petrol taps from the leaking tank and sealed them with thread tape.

Late into the night, the new – and very rusty – tank was on the bike. I filled it up with fuel and my Mum held our torch to check for leaks: there were none and I was going to Assen!

I didn't sleep that night and so it was no problem to be up at dawn. I had even done some route planning. I was a careful boy at school and didn't lose books. This meant that at the end of every term, unlike my compatriots, I always had a surplus of text books. Most of these I dutifully returned but a couple I "re-homed", as the euphemistic expression goes.

One of the re-homed books was a large world atlas and in this was a map of North-Western Europe. What could be better? Not only was Britain shown, and it's always handy to know your starting position, but so were Holland, Germany, Denmark and some other strange and wonderful places.

I simply removed the page of Western Europe from the atlas and taped it to the Velo's rusting fuel tank and that was that: a full, route planning guide.

My Mum gave me a really huge breakfast and also made me an enormous pile of sandwiches for lunch, with really thick "door stopper" rounds of bread. I hadn't told her about the idea of skipping food for two days but I think that she had a good idea of what was happening so she was doing her best to help.

The M62 motorway from Lancashire to Yorkshire was only open in a few parts so mainly it was a case of plodding across the Pennines to Hull on the old roads. The Venom was actually being well-behaved for once and it sounded lovely as I dropped down into Huddersfield, with the braaahhhh, braaahhhh, braaahhhh from the barely silenced fishtail exhaust bouncing off the limestone walls of the terraced houses.

I ate my Mum's sandwiches by the side of the road as the Velo cooled down and crackled in the June heat. The sun was shining and I had a full stomach. The fuel tank wasn't leaking and I was on my way to Assen. Truly, I was blessed in every way.

There was more good news to come. Because the Velo was being so well-behaved I arrived in Hull early. With time to spare, I wandered around a street market and came across a green grocer who was packing up for the day. On one side of his stand was an enormous pile of strawberries. I loved strawberries, and still do, but they were far beyond my budget. I was chatting away to the stallholder and he made me an offer I couldn't refuse. For a few pence, I really can't remember how much, I could have all the soggy strawberries on his counter. In truth, they were probably heading for the bin but beauty was in the eye of the beholder and I saw not only that evening's meal but tomorrow's breakfast and lunch. Okay, the strawberries weren't pristine – but they were a lot better than the alternative which was nothing!

He loaded the strawberries into a big, double thickness, brown paper sack and I balanced it between my knees and rode to the dock.

The overnight ferry was huge compared to the Isle of Man ships and looked and felt like a palace. There were spacious passenger lounges and restaurants, although these were clearly off limits to me, and everything looked so luxurious. I had never seen so many well-dressed, and clearly wealthy, people in my life.

When everyone went for their evening meals, I headed for the upper deck and sat watching the sunset with a cup of water from my canteen and all the strawberries I could eat! What could be better in the whole wide world?

I had purchased the cheapest possible ticket and this meant no cabin but I wasn't too bothered. I was used to sleeping rough, although I didn't like the experience, so it was just another inconvenience on the way to Assen.

I was about to pack up when I had an interesting experience and one which was to remain with me for a long time – even to this day. I got chatting to a Catholic priest who came on to the outer deck to see the last fragments of the sunset. At the time, I was quite a devout Anglican and had read, and was reading, the Bible extensively.

We gossiped about a range of topics, religious and secular, and he found out that I had no-where to sleep and, strawberries apart, hadn't eaten. He smiled and nodded knowingly, then blessed me before he left - which was very nice of him.

The following morning, by a sheer fluke, I happened to see him leave his four bed cabin – three beds in which had been unoccupied. The blessing was a very good thing to receive - but a bed would have been even better!

I went into the passenger lounge and tried one of the seats. They didn't look too comfortable so, following standard practice, I settled down on the floor with my Velocette tools between my legs and my duffle bag as a pillow.

As the lights dimmed, one of the stewards came across to see if I was ill. I explained that I was fine and this was how I travelled. A few minutes later, he returned with a blanket, laid it across me quite tenderly and wished me a good night's sleep.

Perhaps that was the difference between an amateur Christian and a professional one.

Another kind thing happened. I woke up bright and early, just as dawn was streaming through the lounge windows, and another steward came across to see me and check on my welfare. This was getting embarrassing but I was very grateful.

She went on to say that they had a spare breakfast if I would like it. I explained that I couldn't pay for a breakfast but the lovely lady was at pains to point out that it was going to be thrown away if I didn't eat it so I was actually helping the crew. So, I did help them out – fried eggs, bacon, sausages, beans, toast, tea and all.

Now, I had a full tummy, a good night's sleep and the Dutch coast was in sight. Things were going better than exceedingly well.

The Velo started easily, well fairly easily because I bump started it down the loading ramp to the dock, and there, stretching away in the distance, lay the world. I was in awe and my mouth ran dry with anticipation. I owed so much to bikes. My passion for motorcycles had brought me to the brink of a wonderful new adventure and I just couldn't wait to get going.

There was one slight problem: I didn't know how to get going! Europort in Rotterdam is almost a country in its own right and stretching away in every direction were infinite ribbons of tarmac – and not a single sign for Hengelo.

After half an hour of groping around, and becoming ever more lost, I realised that things were going very badly wrong so I did what all right thinking Englishmen would do, I stopped and asked a Policeman for help. The Officer hadn't heard of Hengelo. There was no reason why he should have known because Hengelo was a small town, 120 miles distant from Europort.

He asked for a few clues and of course I couldn't provide any additional information except to say that I knew that Hengelo was near to Germany. I didn't pick up the irony of his next statement. "Well, that's no problem," he opined, pointing to the dual carriageway. "Germany is down there on the right."

I thanked him, kicked the Velo into life and set off for an adventure which I am still following today.

5

Sleep Well - the Girls
Won't Bother You

I took the Police Officer at his word, pointed the Velocette towards Germany and rode on through the warm, cloudy, Dutch landscape in a near trance. I just could not believe how lucky I was.

After a couple of hours I stopped at a Service Station and dined on what was now strawberry mush. I had to admit defeat with the last quarter of the bag which really did look in a bad way and was starting to develop an aroma a bit more than just strawberry!

The ride across Holland was completely uneventful and I arrived in Hengelo, where the Van Beek family lived, in the late afternoon. Jorg lived in a small, neat house on an equally neat street - and I immediately felt uncomfortable. This was a long way further up the wealth ladder from our Council House and I was very nervous and unsure of myself. However, Mr and Mrs Van Beek could not have been kinder, or more welcoming, and they did everything possible to make me, quite literally, feel at home.

The following day, we all set off for Assen which was 90 miles north of Hengelo. The first part of the journey was very ordinary and to my eyes, used to riding in the twisting country lanes of Cheshire and the Welsh mountain roads, deadly dull. For sure, the Netherlands really is flat and the roads are straight!

Things changed when we came within 20 miles of Assen. There were bikes everywhere – and a much more eclectic mix than I was used to in Britain.

At this point in the story, it is important to mention just how kind Mr. Van Beek was to me – and how much his generosity was appreciated and needed! Jorg was still at school so Mr. Van Beek treated me like a second son. I offered to pay my own way, and he did accept the entrance money for Assen, but for everything else, he picked up the tab. You may imagine just how grateful I was for this when I was, quite literally, watching every single penny.

We arrived at Assen bright and early for practice which was on Friday. I didn't have a clue just how big an event the Dutch TT was and there must have been 150,000 fans in the area.

Clearly, accommodation was non-existent but somehow Mr. Van Beek found space in an old farm house – not commercial accommodation but rather the sort of home stay which the Isle of Man specialises in.

Mr. Van Beek took the tiny box room and Jorg and I shared an equally miniscule attic. It wasn't exactly 5* accommodation but it was vastly better than sleeping on the deck of the "King Orry" so I was more than happy.

Assen was wonderful and I learned so much from that trip in so many ways. Looking back, what is really interesting is how quickly and happily I adapted. I ate, drank and enjoyed whatever Mr. Van Beek put before me and I never felt out of place with anything. On the contrary, I took to the different culture instantly and never tried to take an English bubble with me.

From my background, it might have been reasonably expected that I would have wanted to cling to my working class Warrington roots with "proper" English meals and an insistence on driving on the "right" side of the road. In fact, the contrary was true. I simply wanted to dive in and through and over and round - to experience everything as I still do today.

I already knew that I was a fully paid up member of the Self Preservation Society. So, after practice finished, I persuaded Jorg to walk across the track with me and up to the pit boxes. When we were challenged by the security staff I simply looked the guard in the eye, pointed casually to one of the Aermacchi factory mechanics who was pushing a bike back into the paddock and confidently said: "We're with him." And that was that. We were in the paddock at the Dutch TT.

Almost five decades later, I can still remember the colours, sounds, smells, faces and bikes. I can see, as clearly as if it were yesterday, Luigi Taveri's tense look as the Honda mechanics started the five cylinder 125cc bike by spinning the back wheel.

I can smell the acrid cigarettes as I watched the Italian mechanics work on Renzo Pasolini's works Aermacchis and can feel, in my mind and heart and soul, the boom and rasp of the British AJS and Norton singles being checked by their riders and mechanics.

I was not an outsider but swam like an amoeba in this wonderful racing soup and, for a short time, I forgot who I was and where I came from.

Later, much later, I discovered that God had given me what is called a writer's eye. It's nothing to do with intelligence or perception but rather that I see and hear and smell things around me - just because I do. A fish doesn't think about swimming, nor a bird about flying and so I never try to see what is around me – the information simply arrives in my brain. But what a useful skill this is for a writer!

My only regret is that I don't have any photographs of the visit. I only had a very cheap camera, could only afford one roll of film, and so took very few images and even these have been lost. It's a shame but many more have survived over the years so it's not too great a loss.

At the time I could only think that tomorrow was race day and even more doors were going to open.

Mr. Van Beek got us to the track very early and so we set up our informal camp right next to a low fence on a lovely left hand corner. In those happy days, we were perhaps only 30 yards (27m) back from the track itself so not only could we hear everything but we could, quite literally, smell the castor racing oil baking on the engines.

The waves of noise crashed over us in deafening aural surges of screaming two-strokes and wailing Honda 4s, 5s and 6s. We were inside the GP almost as much as the riders were and in a way which is unimaginable today, when riders are as physically distant from spectators as they are.

In many ways, the 1966 season was the apogee of GP racing. There was an immense depth of talent, with some of the finest motorcycle racers of all time, and a technical interest which has never been surpassed.

It's worth looking at some of the statistics because they are breath taking. Bill Ivy won the 125cc class at Assen – and the next three places were filled by previous World Champions in the form of Hugh Anderson, Luigi Taveri and Phil Read.

The range of manufacturers represented across the classes was incredible and is worth listing. There were works bikes from MV Agusta, Honda, Suzuki, Yamaha, MZ, BMW, Bridgestone, Bultaco, Aermacchi and Jawa. And there are probably some that I have omitted even with a list as long as this one.

Today's riders truly are motorcycling deities but for interest and excitement, modern racing cannot match the Golden Age of the late 1960s.

And the one moment which dominates my memory of the whole weekend? Mike Hailwood, the people's champion, arguably the greatest motorcycle racer of all time but still one of us in terms of his modesty and utterly amateurish approach to racing. He passed MZ factory rider Derek Woodman right in front of us – and pulled his tongue out in play.

Hailwood, carrying the weight of Honda's World Championship expectations on his shoulders, still found the time to do what we did when we were out riding with our friends – pull out our tongues and mess about. Truly, the People's Champion.

Assen was over all too quickly. We rode back through the tens of thousands of our tribe united in the joy, and there is no other word to describe it, of motorcycles and motorcycling. For me, the experience was all the more intense because I lived in a grey world of penny pinching and corner cutting, where only one room in the house was heated because there was no money to warm any more.

I ate soggy strawberries not through choice but to put food in my stomach and I rode a derelict bike because this was all that I could afford. But here, in the mass of my fellow tribe members, I could smell and hear and taste and feel the glamour of another world. There was something better out there – I just had to reach it.

I said my goodbyes and my thanks to the Van Beek family, and set off for home. The Venom fired up first kick and I blipped the throttle so that the braaahhhh of the exhaust note bounced off all the houses in the immaculate, Dutch suburban street. I was poor, and the journey back was not going to be easy, but I was riding a 500cc sporting single so braaahhhh, braaahhhh, braaahhhh to the whole world!

Best of all, thanks to Mr. Van Beek's generosity, there was money in my cheap little leather wallet so things were looking more than very good.

I am trying to be honest in this story so, rather than claim that I set off to Amsterdam with the planned intention of exploring this magnificent city, I have to admit that I got confused between Rotterdam, which was the ferry port, and Amsterdam because, to my untutored English ear and eye, they both looked and sounded about the same. It really was as simple as this.

So as the sun set I found myself in a small, urban Amsterdam street. I parked the Velo outside what looked like a modest hotel and asked the rather attractive young lady, who was standing by the door, if they had any rooms and how much they were.

After considerable hesitation she asked me to follow her and I was introduced to another, much older, lady. I explained that I was on a tight budget but wondered if she had any budget rooms.

By this time, three or four other pretty girls had joined us which I thought was bit odd but reasoned that the hotel must specialise in providing accommodation for young ladies on holiday in Amsterdam – a sort of upmarket youth hostel.

I told the older lady what a wonderful time I'd had at Assen and how tonight was my last night in Holland before I returned home.

The ladies giggled but she was very kind and said yes, she could help. She showed me to a very large cubicle with a big bed, made up with immaculate white sheets. One of the girls returned a few minutes later with a blanket. This, the senior lady said, would be my bedroom.

The girls looked through the door, had another giggle and then the older woman wished me goodnight with the comforting words that I still remember today: "Sleep well. The girls won't bother you - they're all busy working."

I couldn't imagine what they could have been doing this late at night but I did sleep very well and the following morning the girls gave me a really nice breakfast of bread, cheese, ham, pickled vegetables and very strong coffee. I set off for Rotterdam, and the ferry home, with a full tummy.

The journey was uneventful. Because of Mr. Van Beek's kindness I was able to have a hot meal in the cheapest of the ship's restaurants and I slept well on the lounge floor.

The highlight of the trip home was a pretty girl from Manchester. Our initial meeting was fairly dramatic in that she nearly tripped over me in the lounge as I settled down for the night but, the following morning, we were starting to become friendly as the English coastline appeared on the horizon. Any hopes of future progress were well and truly brought to a halt when her Dad appeared.

She was pretty, smartly dressed and spoke well. By contrast I failed on all three counts and, in those days, Dads didn't take any nonsense. She was ushered away, her Dad gave me a look which would have drilled holes in titanium and I was reminded of my place in the world and what would happen if I tried to exceed it.

Negotiating the streets of Amsterdam and Rotterdam had destroyed the Velo's clutch and the engine had also become very hot and was leaking oil copiously. I rode home with a mist of oil blowing on to my waxed cotton trousers and without stopping once, for fear of the clutch simply giving up and leaving me stranded.

I struggled across town to return the petrol tank, and sold the Venom there and then for salvage. I walked back across Warrington - glad to see the back of the wreck.

★★★

Things were moving fast on every front and one of the big changes was that my Mum found a new job for me. The Post Office were recruiting clerical staff for their huge administration centre in Manchester and my Mum was excited at the thought of me wearing clean clothes for work - and earning a regular wage.

Not surprisingly, I wrote a literate letter of application. My Mum dressed me smartly and I went off to Manchester, interviewed well and was appointed as a trainee Executive Officer in Post Office House.

It is difficult to articulate just how much I hated this job.

I loathed catching the Manchester train from Warrington's Central Station. I choked on the caged smells of the wage slaves, locked in the carriages on the way to their empty lives and I felt like an animal trapped in an office where everything, from the number of times workers used the toilets to the precise length of tea-break, was noted, monitored and controlled.

I used to tremble as I dried my hands after using the toilet, just at the thought of walking past the lines of desks back to my own tiny space.

Almost everything was tightly controlled and regulated. The adverb "almost" is a key one.

First, every letter and communication was pre-written and stored in a huge file from which the appropriate text was copied with the most minimal modifications: really, only the recipient's name and the current date were allowed to be added.

No-one was permitted to send out anything which was not already in the file. No clever use of language. No metaphor or analogy. A total ban on humour or kindness. Only approved letters left the grey, concrete, faceless brain of the Post Office.

I was in a windowless literary cell, chained to a wall of mediocrity in the damp darkness.

There were almost no outside phone lines so all calls had to be applied for. However, there were a very few exceptions – and one was me!

The reason was the quality of my interview. It must have been thought that I had potential as a Post Office apparatchik so, after two weeks' training, I was put in charge of discretionary sick leave.

I am not sure if this was even the correct title for the job but it went something like this. A Post Office engineer – and remember that there were thousands of them because the Post Office was the Grandad of British Telecom – would phone up and give me some sad story about his Great Auntie dying and please could he have half a day off to attend the funeral.

I hated the Post Office, and all its choking bureaucracy, so I always approved the request. With the same consistency, I also made a complete mess of the supporting paper work.

Soon, it became known that there was this bloke in Telephone House who really was helpful/stupid/an easy touch – the adjective didn't really matter – so the requests became ever more bizarre and the length of time away began to increase dramatically. I was clearly heading for disaster.

I am hard wired to be happy and outward looking but the Post Office made me quite ill. There was a large clock which ticked in whole minutes. I used to try to count in my head when the minute hand would advance. Tick. 72 minutes until I could escape. Tick. 71 minutes to freedom. Tick. Now only an hour plus ten minutes. The clock was eating my life.

After six months, matters came to a head. I had become a legend in my own lunch-time in terms of generosity and the poor Clerical Officer who was supposed to be helping me was in despair.

I was called into a private office, on the floor above my workstation, and there a surprisingly kind and tolerant senior manager asked me if I was really happy in my work. I was incredulous. Happy? I hated even thinking about Telephone House, with a loathing which is normally reserved for war criminals who have committed mass murder!

However, I wasn't being shouted at or threatened or getting ready to duck in case someone threw something at me. Maybe there was a way out.

I explained that I really did love my job and really, really, really loved working for the Post Office even more but I found the daily travelling stressful. Me, who rode the length and breadth of the country for fun, now found the 30 minute commute too much to handle physically and mentally!

The three wise men sat opposite and nodded sagaciously. Yes, it was a challenge travelling all the way from Warrington to Manchester and they could understand how this would affect the standard of my work.

Yes – nod, nod, nod – it was a real challenge – nod, nod, nod – but, even so, they were not quite wholly happy with my performance – nod, nod, nod – and so my position was, how can we say this, not as rosy as it might otherwise be – nod, nod, nod, nod and a final nod.

Had I perhaps thought of other careers which did not involve all this dreadful travelling?

I could have fallen on the floor and licked their polished shoes clean, I was so overjoyed. Yes! I was going to be sacked. Greater joy did not exist in the world.

What was even better was that they were prepared, willingly, to avoid the truth. How about: "Melling, you are a mindless, irresponsible moron with the administrative skills of a bored gibbon.

"We are now going to beat you senseless and then sue you for the return of your wages."

But no, they were too civilised, too gentile and probably too kind as well. From their point of view, I had thrown away a brilliant job with paid holidays, a sick pay scheme and a pension in only forty two years' time. I truly deserved their every sympathy.

So I took Vol Res. Voluntary Resignation; the Post Office equivalent of Seppuku - the Japanese ritual suicide undertaken by a Samurai who had dishonored his Master. I would be forever without a Lord – without company status or protection, and left to wander the world depending only on my own wits for survival. In fact, although I didn't know it at the time, I was going to be a freelance writer and what in the world could be better than that?

I quite literally skipped and jumped all the way to Manchester's Central Station with a smile which was positively manic.

The saga wasn't over though. First, I was given a reference. It was a masterpiece of obfuscation and ambiguity. Much was made of my happy personality and my willingness to help people. The fact that I was barely capable of signing a letter in the correct space at the bottom of the page was tactfully glossed over. I looked at the reference and was more than a little proud of myself – a fine case of believing your own PR!

I will mention the last month at the Post Office because it shows how, if you take a happy young man who would help anyone even to his own detriment, and trap him in an intensely unhappy situation strange things will occur.

I was transferred from Discretionary Sick Leave to another desk, a long way from my original section, to fill in meaningless statistics. They had to be utterly valueless because my clerical incompetence had become legendary in Telephone House. Equally, I had to work my month's notice.

The smart thing would have been just to show me the door and get me off the premises as soon as possible. This would have made me incredibly happy and the Post Office would have benefitted too by getting rid of what was very toxic administrative waste.

However, the system meant that this couldn't happen so I was given a mountain of paper returns and told to fill in the number of pencils used by one depot and the amount of Tippex ordered by another.

I didn't record these details with a malicious lack of care but I could only do my best – and my best was never very good in tasks like this. Not that it mattered. I was a pariah. I had taken Vol Res and everyone knew this.

So, I set myself alternative tasks. I invented a new game. Every single time I had to make a phone call to check some meaningless, and valueless, bit of data – and now I had to ask for an outside line on every occasion – I used my ball point pen on the dialing ring with the intention of wearing it through in the one month left to me.

The game had a stringent set of rules. I was only permitted to use a standard issue, black, Post Office pen and I could not press extra hard or make fake use of the dial. Every use had to be legitimate and there could be no redials.

However, the pen was allowed to rest inside on both the inward and outward journeys round the dial.

I spent a long time in heated debates with myself regarding the legitimacy of a move and whether the Post Office had earned a free penalty in the form of a dial without the pen being used.

As it happens, the Post Office won because although the dialing ring was severely damaged it didn't quite break through – and this was despite pen dialing right up until the very last phone call.

There was a very poignant moment towards the end of my incarceration. A fifty something Officer came across to me and pointed out that I seemed to be deliberately trying to damage Post Office equipment. I explained the pen game to him and he paused for a few seconds and then said: "Well done lad. I wish I'd have had your balls when I started here – but now I'm trapped for life."

With that, he squeezed my shoulder and went back to his desk space.

★★★

I was still struggling dreadfully in terms of falling in love. I ached for someone to love and it wasn't just hormone driven lust. The problem was that although I had been out with girls for dates I had never had a girlfriend – and there was no wonder either!

There were three problems. First, I was achingly, deep purple blushingly shy in the company of girls. The second thing was that I re-defined boy/girl ineptitude. Finally, I had something less than zero social skills.

Here's an example of a typical chat up line which I would deliver at supersonic speed – and in one breath:

"I'vegotapenknife.AndaTribsa.AndIracedatWhitchurchlastweek.AndI qualifiedforthe500final.Andmydog'snameisKim.AndhehadaBoniowithhis tea.AnddoyoulikeMikeHailwood?AndIreadBeowulf.AndI'vegottogotothe toiletnow."

At best, the poor young ladies looked utterly confused - not to say bemused!

I still remained deeply enamored of the lovely "S" but struggled dreadfully in terms of establishing any form of even a beginner's relationship.

The Morris van had gone by now and in its place I had a Wolseley 444 ex-Police car which my Dad had bought for £55 from the car auction at Queensferry and I was paying him back at £5 a week. It was a lovely thing with jet black paintwork and a brown leather interior. I much preferred this to the so called sports cars which my compatriots drove. The Wolseley also had an enormous, electrically operated, chrome plated brass bell on the front bumper which was no end of fun.

Not quite knowing how to ask "S" out formally on a date, I used to try to drive along one of the roads she walked down when I knew that she was returning from work. I would then casually offer her a lift and we could talk for a short time. Sometimes, we would stop outside her house and we would chat for longer.

To be honest, "S" wasn't much better than me and so we both blundered around ending up in one social cul de sac after another as we tried to make sense of our new adult world.

"S" was pretty and every time I was with her I felt a different person. The feelings weren't just sexual. Eighteen year old boys have no problems with being sexually aroused by anything and everything. There wasn't a minute in the day, or night, when I wasn't excited by something, no matter how loosely connected with girls!

But with "S", another door opened. The vast majority of my experience of women came through my Mum whose hands were rough through manual work and her face was lined. She was never dirty but if I recognised any scent it was of carbolic soap or bleach.

I used to try very hard not to make eye contact with "S" for fear of her thinking that I was staring at her – which I always was. Her skin was tight and firm and wrinkle free. Her lips were pale pink and smooth, without any make-up, and there were lovely hints of delicate pink roses in her cheeks.

When I was permitted to kiss her, it was like entering another world of softness and the very essence of her womanliness. I could have spent hours doing nothing more than just gently touching her cheeks and wondering in awe at them.

When we held hands it was a particularly wonderful experience. My hands were large and strong with callouses from work and racing. Her hands were small and soft and fitted inside mine in a way which made me feel very protective and very manly. She was definitely pure woman and, in my own baby way, I was beginning to feel equally male.

There were many huge changes happening inside my adolescent brain and so very fast that I felt as if was being tumbled upside down every time I was with "S".

Eventually, I made some clumsy attempt to move on from kissing. She was angry and tearful but not crying. I still remember what she said: "You're like all men. You want to have sex with every girlfriend – but then marry a virgin!"

But I didn't want to have sex with "S". I wanted to hold her hand and to meet after work and for her to ask me if it had been a good day.

I wanted to stroke her hair and tell her that she was lovely.

I wanted to walk with her round a race circuit and for her to be excited about racing.

I wanted her to be my special friend and for me to feel proud when I walked alongside her.

That's what I really wanted. Sex was not even on the wish list!

We drove back in silence and exchanged the briefest of goodbyes outside her house.

It was a black day so I went straight into my shed when I got back home and cleaned the Tribsa. I couldn't work out girls - but I was getting quicker and quicker on my motocross bike.

6

This is 1B.
They'll be Good for You

I suppose that I should have been a lot more distraught about the end of the relationship with "S" but big things were happening in a blur all around me so my love life got shunted to one side whilst more important things took precedence.

There were four equally huge moments at this time of my life and when I looked at my notes for this book I had to decide which I would put first. My choice is interesting.

As you may have gathered, I didn't have the happiest relationship with my Dad. He was never physically cruel to me but I didn't respect him for a vast range of reasons.

He was drunk all day every day, and violent towards my Mum, so there remained an unbridgeable gulf between us – even when he tried to be kind.

One of the occasions when he did try to help was when he found an Adler portable typewriter for me. Nothing can describe the joy of owning this wonderful machine. It was stove enamelled in a soft, cream colour and lived in a fake leatherette carrying case and was, even more than my bikes, my most prized possession. Now, slowly and hesitantly with two fingers, I could type out adverts and write to club newsletters. I had a fully functioning literary nuclear weapon!

The first task for the Adler was writing to bike magazines asking for a job. I didn't understand the concept of being a freelance contributor and therefore could only ask for full-time, paid employment. The two big players in the motorcycling industry at the time were the venerable, and by this time combined, Motorcycling and Motorcycle published by the equally establishment Iliffe Specialist Publications. The other major magazine was EMAP's Motorcycle News.

The merger of the venerable Motorcycling and Motorcycle magazines was aimed at taking on the new and commercially aggressive Motorcycle News - but they always carried their 64 years of history with them in everything they did.

*Working on a customer's bike. Amazingly, there were baby racers
even less competent mechanically than me.
My first garage was made from old packing cases. Palatial it wasn't!*

*The BSA after my first race at the Oswestry debacle.
There were many better bikes available at the time – but
none as cheap as the BSA.*

"Tiger" Tom Leadbitter with me and the 250cc Cheney Suzuki.
Tom was not only a fantastic rider but also very kind and a real gentleman.

My second article was a world exclusive about the fabulous Cheney Suzuki.
You can see from the concentration that crashing Suzuki GB's only factory
bike wouldn't have made me flavour of the month!

My beloved Tribsa – the mighty steed which gave me my first prize money - and a permanently damaged knee.

Jorg Van Beek outside his immaculate house in Hengelo. The duffle coat and "pudding basin" helmet were high fashion at the time!

Getting ready to board the midnight boat to the TT.
This is the only picture I have of that first, epic trip.

Malcolm Davis, on his works Bultaco, showing me how to really ride — as he
did on many occasions.
Malcolm should have been World Champion at least three times.

Desperately trying to avoid hypothermia and still look as if I can ride
Malcolm Davis' factory Bultaco.
Malcolm, as always, was full of smiles — despite the weather!

This picture is of my own Bultaco Pursang (#303) in a club scramble,
probably in Wales, with Malcolm's works barrel. It was a quick 250!

I took this picture of Ago at Oulton Park after the Scouse dockers had given us all free entry to the paddock.

Post Teaching Practice at S.Kaths.
You can see the relief!

The works BSA was so unbelievably beautiful that I wanted to get undressed on Warrington station platform and make love with it.

The factory B.50 convinced me once and for all that I would never be a decent motocross rider – but it did give me a fleeting taste of fame at Fluke Hall.

This was a posed picture taken for Reg Dancer at BSA. I am still embarrassed to say that I was the factory's last works rider. But goodness me, I did love the B.50!

Getting ready for one of the long continental trips on my favourite BMW R75.
Note the Griffin helmets. We're both wearing the illustrious "seconds".

This is Eddie Crooks in the Isle of Man with the 250cc Production Racer.
I rode this bike several times but never liked it nearly so much as the 490cc
T500 which kept my brand new journalism career alive!

It wasn't too much of a surprise when I received a very curt, "Dear Sir/Madam" letter from a secretary a long way down the Iliffe food chain telling me not to waste any more of their time until I was a professional journalist.

Motorcycle News was much better. The editor was Robin Miller, who went on to be Chief Executive of MCN's parent company EMAP. He replied to me personally, and in the warmest possible terms, but he also said that I would need a National Union of Journalists' training before I could join the magazine.

It's worth noting that, at the time, almost every skilled occupation was Union controlled – and the NUJ really did have a strangle hold on professional writing.

To be fair, their training was excellent and covered many useful skills which I have never mastered such as Pitman Script shorthand.

The problem was that to get on to an NUJ course it was essential to have "A" levels and my CV of scrap metal burning, second hand car sales and being sacked by the Post Office did not quite match up to their criteria.

Nor did writing for notice boards and being rejected by club magazines. I needed a proper education in order to be a real journalist and that, young man, is that – don't you ever forget it!

Ironically, not being a real journalist turned out to be a wonderful attribute when I did start to write professionally.

★★★

If things weren't looking too rosy on the journalism front there were vast improvements with racing. The Tribsa wasn't exactly a GP bike but it was a quantum leap better than anything I had previously raced. It was far too heavy for me and did not handle well against the modern, lighter bikes. Against this it was fast and, when I removed my brain and left it at home, the results were starting to come.

At the time, entries for motocross races in the Cheshire Centre were huge and the standards were high with a good sprinkling of works riders at every event. There were usually two, or even three, heats for the 500cc races and so you had to finish in the top ten or twelve, depending on the entries, to qualify for the main races. Race by race, I was beginning to qualify for finals more often.

A lot of my success, such as it was, came down to one thing: I was a demon starter with the reactions of a fit rattle snake. At school I had always been the despair of my PE teachers until, one snowy session in winter, a bored teacher got out a ruler to play the game of releasing it from a height and then seeing how many inches it was before anyone could catch it between their fingers.

I beat everyone in the class by such a huge margin that he was certain I had found some cunning way of cheating. I don't blame him for having this view because I was generally so bad at sport but, in this one case, he was wrong. I really did have extremely fast reactions.

In those days, races were started with a long, tightly stretched length of elastic. This was released from a central pin, usually hidden behind some sacking. Most riders stared at the elastic in front of them but I always looked inside the sacking or at the rope attached to the release pin or, if I could, even at the starter himself.

I also always watched a few races before mine and studied the starter. Did he hesitate before pulling on the release rope? Was he nervous with the noise of the revving engines? Perhaps he liked his moment of power and would keep the riders tensed up before starting them. All this was vital knowledge if I was to second guess the starter when it came to my race. The homework before my race was essential.

If he was consistent and reliable then the moment the starter's arm tightened, before the pin had even moved, I dropped the clutch and often made some brilliant starts. A little later, this skill was going to cost me dearly.

As well as motocross, the Cheshire Centre was a hotbed for grass track racing with some of the best grass racers in the world competing regularly. The truth was that no motocross bike could compete with a dedicated grass track machine on a proper, smooth grass oval. Grass track bikes are first cousins of speedway machines and with a decent rider on board, they would broad slide round corners almost flat out and leave any 'crosser for dead.

But there is always a caveat in any sport and, in this case, it was that a minority of grass track courses were quite unsuitable for proper grass machines. The tracks might be so rough that the restricted suspension of a grass bike couldn't cope or there could be very tight corners which required heavy braking and caused problems for grassers.

I always ride better in nice weather and the June sun beat down on a lovely grass field, south of Oswestry, when I pulled the Wolseley into the paddock towing the trailer with my Tribsa on board.

The Welsh grass courses were often what might kindly be described as rather ethnic, and this one was as good an example of sheep pasture as you could hope to see. The track was the shape of a Norman knight's shield with a fast, broad curve at the top, leading downhill to an ultra-tight point. The two linking straights were pock marked with sheep scrapes where the animals had dug holes to shelter against the bitter, winter winds.

Best of all, the start was downhill so none of the grass track bikes could go flat out and be totally committed into the tight, first corner - for fear of over shooting it.

After practice, I knew that I was in with a chance of being in completely unknown territory. I could actually make the top four in a race. Why was this important? Prize money was paid all the way down to fourth place. It was an impossible dream. The kid who hadn't completed a single lap in his first race, and who had to run alongside his bike to finish his second event, was now looking at prize money.

I rode well in my heat and qualified for the final. The tapes, as the elastic is called, flew back, I launched the Tribsa off the line and led into the first corner.

It was a strange place to be and more than a bit unnerving. Having a completely empty track in front of me wasn't a new experience. In my first few races, I was so far behind that there was often no-one in sight. But this was totally different. Fifteen seconds after the start I still couldn't see another rider – but the roar of the Jawa and JAP grassers on my shoulder told me that the rest of the field was well and truly there!

There couldn't have been a Christian anywhere in the world babbling more prayers as I tipped the Tribsa into the first corner. Please God, don't let me fall off. Please God, don't let everyone pass me so I end up last. Please God, don't let me make some other horrendous mistake which I can't quite conceive but which will ruin this wonderful moment. P-L-E-A-S-E G-O-D!!!

To be competitive on a motocross machine in a grass track you have to "ride the pegs". This means that you ride right up to the edge of the white, track boundary marker pegs so that there is no room for a grass bike to slide up the inside and then out accelerate you on the exit to the corner.

However, if you knock the pegs over – they are only tiny wooden stakes no higher than a jar of coffee – you will get penalised. The knack is to ride with your foot actually over the pegs but the left-hand side of the bike still a tiny distance from them.

I placed the Tribsa to perfection and the grass bikes had to swing wide, way round the outside of me. The result was not only that I led into the first corner but out of it too. I was beginning to like this!

On the climb uphill the grass bikes, with their huge power and weight advantages, simply pulled away and left me in a lonely fourth place – a good distance behind the leading three but with the same advantage over the other eight riders chasing.

The yellow and black flag came out to indicate the final lap and I concentrated like I had never done in my life. Not exams, writing, job interviews or being sacked could match what was running through my mind.

I sat outside myself and talked to the riding Frank constantly. Brake just there. Tip the bike in here. Ease the throttle on now. A touch of opposite lock to correct the tiny slide. And then the chequered flag came out and I had finished fourth.

I rode through the paddock and back to my trailer recklessly fast and dived into the car for the paperwork for the event – the "regs" (regulations) as the entry forms are known. Yes, it was true. There was prize money paid down to fourth place in the 500cc final. I had won prize money. I had lost my amateur racing virginity and was now a paid rider. I sat back against the trailer in a daze and took deep breaths. This is the world of the amateur racer where success is an unusual experience.

The next stage in the process was almost as hard: I had to collect my prize money – and I was a virgin once again.

After the last race, I went across to the Event Secretary's caravan and stood in line. All the stars chatted informally with him and took their little brown envelopes with a coolness which made the North Pole look like a sauna.

I shuffled nervously up the line until I was by the window of the caravan. The Secretary was busy checking the results with the girls who did the lap scoring.

The wait was interminable and I felt a burning desire to visit the toilet. How bad would this be? I was going to wet myself with fear waiting to collect my first ever prize money.

The Secretary looked up: "Yeah?"

Gulp. Swallow saliva in desert dry mouth. "Frank Melling. I finished fourth in the 500 final."

Silence.

Infinitely extended silence whilst he consults his results' sheet.

Deafening silence. Has there been a mistake? Perhaps I wasn't fourth. I must have been lapped and couldn't remember. Maybe I had knocked a peg over and they've excluded me. I know, it's all a dream and I'm still at Telephone House dialling out with a Post Office pen.

Oh God, please don't let me die. Not now. Not here. Not with ten shillings prize money on offer. Please God.

"Here."

He slides a small brown envelope to me. On it is scrawled "Melling 4/500" in blue biro. In the envelope is a crumpled, pink ten shilling note – 50p. I have won prize money. I am a professional rider. My life is complete. It is a seminal moment in my life – and I still have the very same ten shilling note.

That ten shilling note also swung open a huge door and what it revealed initially took me by surprise. Motorcycle racing is an intensely selfish activity because it is a truly naked place to be.

Make a mistake and you will get hurt. The injury, or death, you suffer will be a result of your own error and you will pay the price.

Ride well and the success will be yours. Yes, at the highest levels you will need a good team behind you but in the area of the racing universe I inhabited, there was no support.

I prepared the bike. I loaded it on to the trailer. I drove to the meeting. I made the good start and I won ten shillings.

It would have been wonderful to have my Mum or Dad or "S" stood track side sharing my success but they weren't and so I made my own way and stood, or fell, by my own efforts.

What this showed to me is that I could change my life. I didn't have to be tied to my family background and a Council House. I could rely on me to make things different and this was an immense shift in my mind set. From now on, I was going to become a player in life's game – not a spectator reacting to circumstances which were thrust upon me.

This is the purity and joy of racing. You either win or lose on your own merits with your own skill, your own tenacity and your own courage. Or, you don't win and this will be your responsibility too with no valid excuses and no-where to hide. I loved the idea.

The lesson was a gift from God in terms of every aspect of my life.

***

But there was another side to the coin. Racing is a demanding mistress if you make a mistake.

My starts were bringing results which put me regularly in the top dozen or so in local motocross meetings and this attracted the interest of a local car accessories firm who gave me a bit of discount on things like oil.

The owner expressed an interest in sponsoring me to a greater level – and, maybe, even buying a bike for me to ride.

Even a nice, but still cheap, second-hand 250cc machine like a DOT or Greeves would have been wonderful but he was talking about the ultimate motocross machine of the day – a 250cc Husqvarna.

I entered the Cheshire Centre meeting at Hatherton Hall and my prospective sponsor said that he would come and watch me race. The day was hot and dry and I liked the course. Things were looking good.

I qualified well in my heat and then made an excellent start in the 500 final. I was in the chasing pack behind the leaders so this must have put me around fifth, sixth or something like this.

I have a very clear memory of the accident even today. I rode hard downhill towards the stream crossing which was near to the end of the lap. The Tribsa was simply too big and heavy for my strength and I couldn't hold on. The front wheel dug in a hole with such force that the forks were snapped clean off. My ankle caught in a rut and I felt my knee tear apart. It wasn't good.

The first lesson was that sponsors have a short attention span. My would-be benefactor never even came to see if I was injured. I crashed and failed to deliver the results so that was that. It's the honesty of racing. Never complain. Never explain. Just deliver.

It was a big accident and I lost consciousness for a short time but, in those easy-come-easy-go days, if you came round after a few minutes the First Aiders considered you to be fit and well.

It was a doubly hard blow because a really nice lad called Lew Garner had been coming with me to some races. Lew was good company but he wasn't really a racing person and so only came with me intermittently.

Unfortunately, this was one of the times he decided to stay at home and that day I really did someone's help!

I tried to laugh off the accident but the truth was different. I knew I was hurt. Some of the other lads gave me a hand to load the Tribsa, minus its front wheel and forks, on to the trailer and I drove back pressing the car's clutch in with my right foot because my left leg was useless.

It wasn't much fun driving back home but I got there, unloaded the bike and then drove myself to Warrington Infirmary.

It would be easy to criticise the medical care there but the Nigerian doctor who saw me was tired out and the waiting room was like a scene from a First World War casualty clearing station, there were so many patients waiting to be treated.

Late at night, he declared me to be injured and sent me up to a ward for review in the morning.

I limped to the pay phone and told my Mum that I was in hospital but not to worry because everything was okay.

My primary concern was that I was filthy. I hadn't washed since coming back from Nantwich and I was sweaty and covered in dust. It was always a major concern of the working classes that they would be rushed into hospital in a dirty condition and that the doctors would treat them harshly. Now here I was, grubby and sweat stained.

I told the doctor I would find my own way to the ward and he shrugged his shoulders and moved on to the next casualty. My eccentricities were my concern and, rightly and properly, he had bigger problems on his mind.

I limped round the corridors, in some serious pain by now, and found a deserted toilet. There I stripped off naked, sloshed myself down with water and then dried myself on the roller towel machine and my shirt. The brown stains on the towel showed that it had been a smart move.

Climbing the stairs was not easy but I eventually made it to the ward and was given a hospital gown with as much bad grace as the unsmiling nurse could summon. She then ordered me into bed, turned her back and walked away.

I was raging thirsty and so slid out of bed but by this time the skin around my knee was drum tight and my knee was very sore. Even so, I was desperate for a drink and limped across the ward, holding on to each bed, until I reached the toilet. I drank out of my hands, propped up against the wall and standing on one leg. The water was delicious and the trip had been well worthwhile.

I had just discovered two more important life lessons. First, motorcycle racing is dangerous and you can get hurt.

Second, don't expect any sympathy when you present yourself with a motorcycle racing injury at an NHS Accident and Emergency department.

The following morning, the Specialist came to see me. He showed no interest or kindness but I wasn't surprised or disappointed. This is how it was on every occasion I had come into contact with the medical profession and he behaved no differently from all the other doctors I had met.

He sent me for an x-ray which showed that no bones were broken so he discharged me.

Again, it's not a criticism because there wasn't the technology available to doctors that there is today but even so, he was somewhat peremptory in his diagnosis. I hadn't broken my leg but the medial ligament had been snapped in two and the cartilage badly torn.

Many years later, I had the cartilage improved but it was decades afterwards that a CT scan showed I had lived all my life with the ligament in two pieces. Yes, this was a nuisance in that my knee has always been prone to popping out of joint but it's not really stopped me from doing anything that I have wanted to do so it was probably a good thing that I didn't know how badly I was injured.

The hospital had strapped my leg tightly into a splint and told me to rest. The first problem was getting home with this long, stiff strip of aluminium bandaged to the back of my leg. It was going to be something of a challenge and the solution required some real creative thinking.

First, I got a pair of vice grips from the toolbox which was always in the boot of the car and used these to clamp down the left hand side of the driver's seat so that my leg could rest straight.

Then, it was only a matter of using one of the crutches, which the Infirmary had kindly supplied, to press the clutch in and I could drive home. It has to be admitted that gear changes weren't quite as smooth as normal but I made it and so everything was good.

I can't remember what job I had at the time but, after my departure from the Post Office, I was doing all sorts of bits and pieces from selling second-hand cars to labouring for a local farmer.

It must have been one of these minor jobs at the time because my Mum wouldn't let me go to work. Not that I could anyway because I was in some considerable pain.

The first task was to get hold of Sammy Green and put him on to sourcing new, second-hand, front forks for the bike. To his everlasting credit, Sam came up with a pair of Norton forks and we began re-building the bike so that I could make a racing come back at the earliest possible opportunity. Whatever the problem with my leg, it couldn't possibly be permanent so the Tribsa had to be race ready as soon as I could walk.

A third lesson had been learned. I was a full on, hard core racing addict and, for better or for worse, remain so to this day.

***

I recovered amazingly quickly. I was young, ultra-fit and with a high pain tolerance. These three things did more to get me better than any amount of medical care. However, before I could return to the track, the Warrington Guardian display ads rode into my life again.

My Mum showed me a small advertisement for Unqualified Teachers at a school in Runcorn. I had never imagined being a teacher no more than I could conceive of not always living in a Council House or not sleeping on the floor of ferries. Still, the ad. was interesting. The school was asking for someone with an interest in English and a minimum of five "O" Levels. I qualified easily on both fronts and my Mum was very encouraging. The she played the ace card. "Think of the holidays when you can work on your bike and still get paid."

Now that really was a desirable fringe benefit...

I wrote a very literate letter of application - but skated deftly over my previous work experience. An invitation to attend for interview came back by return post. First, my Mum checked my clothes, as she always did when I was applying for a serious job. I had a decent sports jacket which Mum had bought for me. She had ironed a nice white shirt and pressed my brown trousers. My shoes were clean and my hair combed. In fact, I looked quite presentable - and not a bit like a still injured motorcycle racer.

I was interviewed by Mr. Edgar Parsonage – a patrician, ex-Army Major who had drifted into education post war and was almost instantly promoted to Head Teacher. It's worth mentioning just how different things were at the time. Later, I worked for another Head whose Uncle had been Chairman of an Education Authority. This gentleman had done one year's teacher training at the end of the war. His second year was as a classroom teacher; the third as a Deputy Head and, in the fourth year, his Uncle had parachuted him into a school as Headmaster. This is how much schools needed teachers at the end of hostilities.

Mr. Parsonage faced the same problem down at the bottom of the teaching ladder. He was simply desperate for bodies to put in front of classes. Attracting teachers to a Secondary Modern school, located in a not very fashionable town, was not easy.

I sat up, ram rod straight, in my chair and called Mr. Parsonage "Sir". I had no illusions about my place in the universe and Mr. Parsonage was not only a Major – I never felt that the word "ex" ever applied to him – but he was also a Headmaster. In truth, he was a form of double deity and I was sat alone in his presence and within arm's reach.

He read my typed letter of application and asked me who had written it. I explained that it was entirely my own work – including the typing. Then he moved on to the questions of what books I had read recently. This was so easy for me. I rolled off a list of them from Arthur C. Clarke to Dickens and tossed in some Graham Greene by way of flavouring and a bit of Great War poetry. I was on home ground when it came to reading.

Mr. Parsonage played with his pen, had another long look at my letter of application. Then he looked up and said: "When can you start?"

I stuttered and blushed – I was always blushing in any social situation during this period of my life – and coughed out: "On Monday, Sir?"

Today was Wednesday – a consistently lucky and auspicious day of the week because Motorcycle News was on sale – and so, six days from now I would be a teacher.

I was excited at the prospect but not over-awed at the thought of standing up in front of a class. The real excitement came from having a regular wage again. Although the salary for an untrained teacher was modest, the hours were good and this enabled me to continue very much with my private enterprise businesses.

The lack of concern about the new challenges came for two reasons. First, I had been employed, and sacked, from so many jobs that I had developed a fairly thick skin and a very adaptable frame of mind. Whatever it was, I would – usually at least – roll up my sleeves and get stuck in.

The second reason was that I had so little idea of what teaching was or how to do it. Two years earlier, I had been in school so I knew what I liked and didn't like in a teacher but as for any professional skills, I had zero knowledge. Better still, in terms of not going catatonic with fear, I had no idea of what I didn't know and so ambled along in blissful ignorance.

The following Monday, my Mum turned me out in pristine condition as I set off for Balfour Road Boys Secondary School in Runcorn.

I arrived early and was introduced to the staff. There was the strong sense that I was like the new pilot being introduced to hardened veterans in a Battle of Britain Squadron.

All the teacher-pilots had seen more combat than they cared to remember and they lounged around the crew room, lolled in their own chairs and drank strong tea from their personal mugs.

I was the new boy and the Jerries (the kids) would have me shot down in flames before the week was over.

What these tough teacher-flyers didn't know was that I thought it all looked incredibly friendly and a truly lovely place to be. I wasn't perched on top of a steel beam with an oxy-acetylene torch and nor was I chasing a farm trailer humping 55lb (25kg) bags of potatoes into the back. No-one was shouting at me and I wasn't watching the minutes tick away until 5pm. In fact, everything seemed very pleasant.

The morning flew by. I had a short briefing from Mr. Parsonage and then a tour of the small school and finally an introduction to a real battle hardened veteran of close combat teaching – Mr Jim Chadwick.

Jim had seen and done everything in the teaching world and he was in charge of what was lovingly known as "The Annexe". This was a wonderful collection of buildings which, I was told, used to be the Fever Annexe for the local Cottage Hospital. I don't know the truth of this tale but the buildings were magnificent

– large, bright and airy, and perched on the hill at Weston Point facing west and south and overlooking the Mersey Estuary.

Jim drove me up to the Annexe and I thought I had arrived in Heaven. The sun was shining, the kids were playing in the quadrangle between the buildings and the Annexe teaching staff were so laid back that they were almost horizontal.

On the drive up to the Annexe, Jim quizzed me about my teaching experience. He had been hoping for a pilot with at least some training, and a few hours of battle experience in the classroom, and instead he had me. His attitude was that I was better than having to double classes up – but only just.

We sat down in the staffroom and I was given a cursory introduction to my colleagues who showed very little interest in the new arrival. I think that the feeling was, just as it had been in the main school, I would only last a few days so why bother wasting breath on someone who wasn't going to be around?

Jim was busy with a million other things and so it was only as the lunch-break came to an end that he turned to me and said: "You'll be taking 1B for English."

It was only then that the full realisation of what was about to happen hit me. In a couple of minutes, I was going to be left with 34 eleven and twelve year old boys to control and maybe even teach – and so far I hadn't had ten seconds' training or even a particle of guidance.

It was blushing time again. "What shall I do with them?" I asked Mr. Chadwick's back - as he marched out of the staffroom on his latest mission.

But Jim was long gone. Help came by way of Stan Williams, a truly larger than life character in the teaching profession who was also extremely kind to me. Stan gave me my first tuition in teaching, scribbled on a page torn from an exercise book.

"Look, here's how to do it. Tell them a story about getting shipwrecked on a desert island where there's buried treasure and they have find their way to it and describe what they see on the way – you know, marshes and jungles and wild animals and natives with spears and all that."

The miracle was that I did know and I did understand the "…and all that." And I didn't need any more explanation. Everything made sense instantly and, in a few seconds, I could see a lesson forming in my head.

Mr. Chadwick returned and Stan gave me a big smile and a pat on the back.

We walked across the corridor and out into the wooden floored classroom, housing the neat lines of desks. Looking out expectantly was a sea of faces – anticipating, distracted, disinterested and, a few, even eager.

Jim spoke in his most commanding voice: "This is 1B. They'll be good for you. Won't you 1B?"

With that, he turned his back, closed the door and, true to his word, 1B really were good for me and in many, many ways.

7

Time for the Penguin Chick
to Leave the Nest

TEACHING was great. There was no other word for it. I couldn't wait to go to school in the morning and I didn't like leaving Balfour Road in the evening. Every day was a good day and many were absolutely excellent.

First, I got on well with the kids. In some ways this wasn't surprising because I was only a few years older than the fifteen year olds so they had a real sense of empathy with me.

The other thing was that I was invariably given the bottom set children. Secondary Moderns were for those children who had failed the 11+ examination whilst in Junior School and had therefore not gone on to Grammar School. However, there was a considerable spread of ability within the Secondary Moderns and many of the kids there were only a sliver away from Grammar School standards.

In a school like Balfour Road, these bright children were cherished and pushed hard with the kids being funnelled into the "A" stream. Below them was a "B" stream and then what was called a "Progress Group".

It is wrong to think of the Progress groups as being sink classes - unwanted and neglected. I am angry when I hear this current, politically correct description of such kids. At Balfour Road, the Progress classes had small numbers of children and were well equipped and highly regarded by the staff. They were not third rate in any way.

Even so, as an unqualified teacher, I was given a lot of the Progress classes because the school was very ambitious for its most able pupils. I can understand and empathise with the thinking. Our best kids needed academic qualifications to go, mainly, into engineering as skilled tradesmen and middle managers. The school had a moral obligation to serve these young people.

By contrast, our Progress kids had real problems with basic numeracy and literacy and the key aim was to serve these core needs. The idea of sixteen year olds leaving school illiterate or innumerate just wasn't acceptable.

It wasn't that the most experienced teachers didn't want to teach the Progress groups but simply that the priority had to be serving our brightest students. This meant that Heads of Department, and experienced teachers, came into contact with these bottom set kids only infrequently whilst a lot of my timetable was spent with them.

I found the experience very moving. For the first time in my life I was doing a paid job for some other reason than just getting money - and it provided a unique satisfaction. I prepared my lessons well and thoroughly, taught to the best of my nascent ability and then marked the kids' work thoroughly. Little by little, I saw the children I taught actually make progress and I found this a truly wonderful thing.

Because I was teaching bottom set children I had a vast amount of freedom in terms of lesson content so I was like a kid at Christmas when it came to the literature we used. I found that if it was presented properly then these lovely children could be as interested in great literature as the most able students.

So, out came Shakespeare and we read winter sonnets. We wrote spells along with the witches from Macbeth. We compared the Bridgewater Canal with Mr. Polly's Inn and we charged through the Valley of Death with Lord Byron and the "Light Brigade." In short, we had a fantastic time.

It was also a very odd experience to be given a wage for doing something which, in truth, I would have done for free. What could be better than sharing my love of literature with young people and then getting paid for it? Compared with my earlier jobs, this was like taking money under false pretences.

Another reason for my happiness was that I was popular. If any of the staff, the real teachers, wanted anything doing then I was the first, and usually the only, volunteer. I fetched and carried with enthusiasm and was willing to help anyone do anything.

In staff meetings, I sat against the wall and said nothing unless I was specifically asked. I never disagreed, or offered an opinion, but simply joined in with the consensus. Truly, this was the calm before the storm which was to follow my later career!

All the time, I was like a giant, intellectual sponge simply soaking up information and experience.

Quite quickly, I became a trusted colleague. Soon, I was no longer a mere child minder but a member of the teaching staff – albeit the one at the very end of the food chain.

This shift in status was quite important. There was another unqualified teacher in the school at the same time as me but he didn't last long before resigning. Standing up in front of a class of kids wasn't for everyone.

There was one more important benefit. I had status on my Council Estate. Now, I was no longer Flo Melling's lad who had just been sacked or who was a farm labourer or a scrap metal burner. Now, Flo Melling's son was a teacher.

In the current social climate, it is difficult to explain just how high was the standing of teachers in the community. In terms of social status, they were in the same general area as doctors, solicitors and bank managers. Teachers could sign passport photographs and act as bank referees. They were solid, dependable, highly respected members of the professional community and I liked the experience of being one of them very much.

I used to park my car in a little Council garage about half a mile from our house. This was rented by my Uncle Frank who sub-let it to me for a pittance. I would walk back down the road to our house with clean hands and polished shoes, instead of working boots with steel toe protectors. I carried a second-hand leather briefcase with books in it, instead of my Dad's khaki gas mask bag containing a battered flask. Curtains would flicker as I walked past: Flo Melling's lad and he's a teacher. Who'd have thought it?

It gave me a very warm feeling inside and as these wonderful new doors opened, the ones on my old life were closing fast.

Not quite everything was perfect though. I was taking teaching so seriously that my business interests were suffering. There is an expression used about soldiers who fall in love with Army life. It's called "Army Barmy". I was in the educational version of this state of mind.

The key problem was that as an unqualified teacher I wasn't paid very much money at all. By the time I had commuted to and from Runcorn, and not made any money from selling bike bits, the financial cupboard was very bare indeed.

This is why the next lesson in my life skills' class was so galling – and at the same time so incredibly valuable.

***

First, I parted company with the Tribsa. I had a great affection for the bike because of the prize money we had won together. Also, thanks to the Tribsa, the first trophies were starting to clutter my bedroom.

I wasn't so much frightened of riding the bike as worried about racing it hard. Any decent rider can take a motorcycle to 95% of its performance without any concern. The problem is that results come not from 95% commitment but 101% and I didn't have confidence in my ability to master the Tribsa at the ragged edge of its performance envelope.

With a good deal of sadness, I swapped the Tribsa for a Greeves Challenger – and what a retrograde step that was! The Greeves Challenger was the top British 250cc machine of the day but the bike I got was an old and badly used version. I think that if I had thrown it in a skip, the bin would have projectile vomited it out again as being too horrendous even for a pile of rubbish.

I bought the Greeves because it was much lighter than the Tribsa and in this respect it was better than the big, heavy 500cc machine. By every other measure it was hugely worse.

The engine had been highly tuned, and made plenty of power, but was prone to seizures and the handling, compared with the stability of the Tribsa's BSA frame, was dreadful.

Regardless, I worked away steadily improving the bike - more because there was no other option than through any sense of commitment.

I really wanted to improve my riding and so, despite the cost, I signed up for one of the new motocross schools which were then coming into vogue. I was determined that, regardless of what else I had to do without, I would take part in one.

I duly arrived one cold, foggy Saturday at a training ground in Derbyshire hosted by one of the star riders of the day. Even now, I wouldn't honour him with a mention by name.

The initial presentation was amateurish in the extreme and despite being in awe of his status, I remember thinking that he wouldn't get a job teaching at Balfour Road.

It was also interesting to see how he surrounded himself with sycophantic acolytes just like the school bully strutting round the playground.

At each section, he told us how he tackled this part of the track and there is no doubt that the advice was first class - coming, as it was, straight from the mouth of one of the best racers of his generation.

One rider from the group was then asked to ride the section so that we could see how the techniques worked out in practice.

Despite hanging back, or maybe because of it, I was singled out and told what to do whilst everyone else watched. I was given a set of steep undulations to ride and this immediately set my heart pounding. I was never good on this sort of going and the Greeves, with its peculiar leading link forks, hated it so I couldn't expect any help from the bike.

I was also back in my normal, blushing state and mortally concerned about what everyone else would see – and then say. The result was inevitable. I got everything wrong, crashed heavily and ended up in a heap right in front of the Great Man. His reaction was interesting and taught me a lot.

He never moved a muscle - except to laugh out loud and then walk off, with his coterie of toadies in tow.

I was left under the bike until one of the other lads gave me a hand to escape.

I didn't break any bones but I had the mother of all bruises on my thigh and shoulder. I was in so much pain that I loaded the bike on the trailer and got changed to go home.

As I was leaving, the Superstar walked past me. I told him I was going home because I was sore. Again, his reaction has stayed with me to this day. There was another guffaw for the benefit of the bottom licking team and then: "You shouldn't have fallen off then."

That was it.

There and then I promised myself to try to use whatever power I might be given in the future as wisely and as kindly as could. I have failed in following this mantra on multiple occasions but I have never lost the belief that if you have power you should use it gently and not selfishly.

Although I didn't know anything formally about customer care, I also vowed that when someone paid me for doing something I would treat them with respect. Again, I would never win any awards for being an angel but the aspiration has always been there.

***

If you were in love with motorcycles, and particularly motorcycle sport, Warrington was a wonderful place to be in the late 1960s. In the town centre, we had two large motorcycle dealers – Jack Frodsham Motorcycles and Bill Pope Motorcycles – just a few hundred yards apart.

There was also a host of smaller dealers doing everything from simple repairs to race tuning.

One of these was Sankey Bridge Motorcycles which was owned by a very talented road racer, and a truly gifted mechanic, called Colin Wilkinson. The premises were not exactly at the palatial end of the retail premises market. Without wishing to be discourteous, Sankey Bridge Motorcycles was a wooden shed – and not a very good one at that – sitting next to the very tired Sankey Bridge which spanned the derelict Sankey – St. Helen's Canal. Mayfair it was not!

Even so, the work which Colin turned out was outstanding and Sankey Bridge Motorcycles became a destination for young motorcyclists in Warrington.

As a teenager, a couple of years' difference in age is a vast gulf and Colin was also much more grown up than me. He had real girlfriends and had been to nightclubs in Manchester and drunk alcohol. In every way, he was a real adult sophisticate and I really looked up to him.

At this point, it is worth saying how much the different arms of motorcycle sport were integrated at the time. Today, few motocross fans would ever be seen near a road race meeting but, at the time, hard core bike enthusiasts flitted from one discipline to another.

Colin was a good off-road rider and an international quality road racer. For my part, I took every chance to ride road racing machines as well as off road bikes. If it had two wheels, I would be on – and often off – it!

Later on, this Jack-of-all-Trades ability was to prove a key asset when I was writing about motorcycles but, at the time, it was simply the chance to try another bike and have even more fun.

It was the promise of a ride on Colin's road race machine which persuaded me to help with some testing of his home built Norton Domiracer. This was a copy of the works Nortons which had a tuned, twin cylinder Dominator engine housed in the legendary Norton "Featherbed" frame. Thanks to Colin's skill as an engineer, the bike was really quick.

A couple of miles away from Sankey Bridges were the remains of the huge American airbase at Burtonwood and, in those relaxed times, access to miles of empty tarmac was easy. You simply arrived, lifted a bit of very nominal fencing to one side, and drove in. It was no more difficult than that.

We unloaded the Domiracer from Colin's van – he was so posh he actually had a big van dedicated to racing – and after some checks, the Norton was ready to go. Before the days of electric starting rollers, which is how race bikes are fired up today, the only way of starting a racing motorcycle was by pushing.

Colin duly tickled the Domi's carburettors – a lovely expression which means that extra fuel was put into the carbs to help cold starting – nodded to me to push and off we went. Colin leaned across the fuel tank to bring his weight on to the rear wheel while I pushed flat out on the rear frame loop. In an instant, he dropped the Norton's clutch and accelerated away.

The problem was that my thumb had slipped down between the rear frame loop and the mudguard, and I was trapped. It was like one of those "Road Runner" cartoons as I screamed at Colin to stop, with my legs wind-milling like an Olympic sprinter. If nothing else, it proved that my damaged leg was better – severed ligament or not.

Of course, I got no sympathy from Colin – only utter, derisory contempt for interfering with his test session. This was exactly what I expected. At a time when the idea of personal responsibility was still dominant, I should have taken more care – and I accepted this.

Colin was as good as his word and did let me ride the Domi – despite the inconvenience I had caused by trapping my thumb. This was the second thrill of the day. I had no problem with the power of the Domi, or the speed, but it was stopped by an enormous 10" (250mm), twin leading shoe, Münch front brake. These racing drum brakes are quite unlike discs, which have a very progressive feel. Even on racing discs, the more pressure you apply the greater the braking effect. It is simple and predictable.

A racing drum brake works very differently. Once the brake shoes make contact with the drum, there is a self-servo effect which increases the brake force. The knack is to apply some pressure to start the slowing down process – but not to keep blithely squeezing or the wheel will lock and you will go sliding down the track in a flash.

The giant size of the Münch brake exacerbated these problems to an enormous degree. Just how much, I was about to discover.

After a few laps of the informal track which Colin had laid out, I was becoming ever more confident. I accelerated hard down the improvised straight, tipped the Domi into the bumpy right hand bend and took a big handful of the Münch brake. In half a blink the front wheel had locked and Colin's Domi was heading for the tarmac.

It's interesting how one's mind reacts in these situations. My primary concern was not falling off and getting hurt but rather the loss of status within the Warrington biking community. Goodness me, the shame of borrowing a race bike and then falling off it would have stayed with me for life. A Nepalese, mountain top monastery wouldn't have been far enough away to escape the disgrace!

At the same time, the hundreds of hours of dirt racing I had done kicked in and I put so much opposite lock on to the Norton that it was surprising I didn't break off the handlebars. The slide corrected and I rode back to Colin - chastened but still trying desperately to look cool and relaxed. Now I knew how to stop a bike with a big, drum race brake!

★★★

Today, motorcycling is very fragmented. There are clearly defined sectors for everything from custom bikes to touring, and racing is sub-divided into micro categories. Road racers do use dirt bikes for training but you will rarely see a British Superbike fan at an off-road event or vice versa for that matter.

In the 1960s, things were very different - probably because we all felt part of a single tribal community. We were motorcyclists, and lived for bikes, and so naturally everyone went to Oulton Park and often the TT too. But we also spectated at motocross meetings and trials – and not just those of us who were riding in these disciplines.

I have ridden in every form of motorcycle sport from desert racing to the Daytona road races but the one discipline which I have never really taken to is trials. This is, or more accurately was, the art of riding a motorcycle very slowly, and without stopping, over rocks and through mud and is, in many ways, the most skillful and artistic of all the forms of motorcycle competition.

These days, Trials are a much more athletic and aggressive form of riding with unthinkably difficult obstacles which demand super-human courage and skill. In the late 1960s, the sport was on the cusp of huge changes and therefore it was a very interesting time to be a spectator.

Our favourite event of the year was the Northern Experts Trial which was held deep in the Pennine Hills, between Macclesfield and Buxton. The sections, as each test was known, were spread out for miles through rugged limestone, bogs and wild torrents.

What made the event so good was that we spectators rode round with the competitors, from section to section on public roads, and so felt very much part of the event.

The section I loved the best was Dane Bower – a lovely name for a long line of enormous rocks just below the Cat and Fiddle Pub near Buxton, on the border between Cheshire and Derbyshire. The legend was that the name referred to very start of the River Dane, which flows through Cheshire, but the reality is that the river starts a bit further up on Axe Edge. Dane Bower is the start of one of the thousands of small streams which are in every depression of the area and provided so many stiff, wet tests for the Northern Experts riders. The section was laid out through the limestone boulders which make up the first couple of hundred yards of the stream's life.

Although the lightweight two-strokes were coming to dominate trials, there were still some of the old fashioned, heavyweight British bikes competing. It was wonderful to see the big, single cylinder machines from AJS, Matchless and Ariel being threaded through the giant lumps of limestone.

It was good that we did see them too because these dinosaurs were in the very last gasps of their existence. They were quickly being replaced by lightweight two-strokes from Bultaco and Greeves and, being the Northern Experts Trial, the Manchester built DOT machines.

The British singles made a soft chuffing noise, almost like steam engines, and their riders had to ease them over the rocks in a spirit of anthropomorphic co-operation. They gave off a soft aroma of engine oil and baking mud, smelling more like a kitchen than motorcycle sport. The bass note exhausts, the warm scents and the gentle bond between man and bike came from a different age – and one which was almost at an end.

By contrast, the riders of the two-strokes were tomorrow's world. These barely silenced engines had harsh, urgent, tearing cloth crackles accompanied by the acrid stench of two-stroke oil mixed with petrol. Their riders hunched over the bikes, forcing them through sections with the first hints of aggression and athleticism which epitomizes off road sport today.

These young riders, some hardly older than me and a few even younger, were the new guard marching into a world of technology and energy and relentless commitment.

I sat on the very edge of the divide between these two eras and soaked up every sound, every smell and every sight.

Despite the cold of the Pennines in November, I perched on the rocks in my waxed cotton Belstaff jacket and pants, with the thick cheese and tomato sandwich and a flask of soup my Mum had made for me, and was content. I had all that I wanted and, interestingly, all that I could ever imagine wanting. Sitting on the rocks at Dane Bower in the cold November drizzle, my life was complete.

For better or for worse, Fate was not nearly as satisfied with my life as I was and had other things in mind for me.

***

Just before Christmas, Mr. Parsonage summoned me to his study. I couldn't think what I had done wrong but I was still dry mouthed and nervous. I liked Mr. Parsonage, and was grateful for the opportunity he had given to me, and the thought of displeasing him was terrible.

He was smiling but firm. Directly and simply, very much in a military style, he explained my current situation. First, I couldn't go on as I was, teaching without qualifications. Yes, I was doing well but I was also wasting my time when I could be doing better.

Second, and he really did read down his impeccably precise, fountain pen written list, I would have to apply for teacher training.

Third, I was to report back to him within seven days telling him what progress I had made.

I drove home that night in a state of near terror. I was being thrown out of the familiar nest where I was happy, successful and liked, into the strange, new world of higher education.

Only a fraction more than 8% of eligible young people completed a Higher Education degree in 1970, compared with 30% in the year 2000 – and even more now. Kids from my background were rarely seen in tertiary education.

No-one I came into contact with knew anything about University. The idea of studying merely for the sake of acquiring knowledge would have been completely baffling to everyone in my circle. It would have been like offering a tax return form to a dolphin. Not only would they not know what it was, they wouldn't see the value of filling it in either.

Knowledge was highly prized in my community - but it had to be useful knowledge which was going to get you better trade skills and so more money.

Learning new welding techniques was worthwhile and, if you were clever, attending Day Release and Night School to obtain a Higher National Certificate in Engineering was also worth doing.

By contrast, wasting three years learning about pictures, old ruins or languages like Ancient Greek or Latin, which no-one even spoke now, would have been considered to be frivolous to the point of being silly.

Teacher Training was much better. You went to College, got your piece of paper and then you had a good job which was clean, safe and had long paid holidays. Yes, Teacher Training made sense.

Even so, I was flying solo in terms of making an application.

I chose to apply to S.Katherine's College of Education in Childwall - a very upmarket suburb of Liverpool. I never visited the college before I applied and nor did I have the slightest clue whether it was good, bad or indifferent. My main thought was that if I was thrown out after a few weeks, something which I thought was quite likely, then there was nothing much lost and I would be near enough to Warrington to find work again in an area I knew well.

As well as being conveniently near to a known escape route, S. Kaths also had another strong attraction. At a time of rapid change in the criteria for teacher training admission, it still accepted students with five good "O" levels when many other colleges were beginning to demand two "A" levels as a minimum.

The urban myth, or it may have even been true, was that if you put S. Kaths down as your first choice of College, and were suitably enthusiastic, then you would be accepted on the grounds that the regime was so tough that you would either succeed or die trying!

I knew that my letter of application was going to be a deal maker, or breaker, and I toiled at it for days. Before the advent of electronic word processing, re-drafts were time consuming and tiresome but I didn't care. I somehow had to explain away the time between leaving school and joining Balfour Road Boys Secondary Modern School. This task demanded some real creative writing, involving a lot of re-arranging the facts - and the occasional manufacturing of new evidence.

I was helped hugely by what I was told was a very strong reference written by Mr. Parsonage. I think he must have told S.Kaths that he approved of me - and so should they.

In the Spring, a letter arrived asking me to attend the College for interview. I was overawed by S.Katherine's and fell instantly in love with the place. The College had been built in 1844 and, except for the New Teaching block which was an ugly and graceless building, oozed history and tradition.

Instead of the urban Liverpool which I had imagined, S.Kaths was set in huge grounds with formal gardens and enormous sports fields: it was so gracious that it could have been one of the Oxbridge Colleges.

I wasn't given a tour of the College or even a hint of welcome or hospitality. Instead, I was shown immediately into a large, wood panelled room lit by a lovely, dappled light streaming in through the mullioned windows.

The centre piece of the room was an immense wooden table which seemed to stretch out forever, like an airport runway. There was a chair at one end and I was directed to it. On the table was a stack of lined paper. I was told to write why I wanted to be a teacher and why S.Katherine's College of Education should accept me for teacher training. With that, the clerk left the room and the heavy, wooden door clicked purposefully closed behind him.

Outside, I heard a BSA twin being kicked into life. It coughed at first and then caught and ran sweetly on two cylinders. After a few moments, I heard the harsh click of first gear going into place and then the bike pulling away. Then there was silence - and I was left to my own fate.

It was another case of: "When the flag drops – the bull**** stops."

It's very true - and very apposite for many situations I have faced.

Now, the flag had dropped and I was writing for my life. On one side of the chasm was an endless succession of worthless jobs which I hated. I knew about this existence all too well.

On the other side was a real profession which I loved.

All that I had to do was walk across the tightrope from my past to my future life.

Strangely, I had no doubts or concerns. I wrote furiously, for fear of running out of time, but with skill, accuracy and passion. Expressing ideas in good, clear, standard English held no fears for me.

After a long time, the clerk returned and asked me if I was finished. The timing was good because I had just concluded the final re-draft. The pages were covered in corrections and addenda but they did show that the writer understood how to improve his work.

He took the essay and told me to report back at 2pm.

I didn't know where to get any food but eating wasn't much of a concern so I drank some water out of my hands from the men's toilets and then went back to my car and read Motorcycle News.

In the afternoon, I met three tutors who had all read my essay. They were pleasant enough and chatted about the points I had raised in the essay and, surprisingly, only very little about what I had done at Balfour Road. I think that their view was that I wasn't much more than a child minder and that I had everything still to learn about the teaching profession.

I answered their questions with confidence and enthusiasm and, when I left, even a sliver of hope that perhaps I had not made a complete mess of things.

Three weeks later, a stiff, formal letter arrived informing me when and where I was to report for Teacher Training – along with a terrifyingly long list of books I was expected to have read before October. Three years at S.Kaths was not going to be a paid holiday!

8

Please Don't Let Bikes Ruin Your Life, Love

I arrived at S.Kaths on a lovely Autumn day, keen, eager and desperate to see what this brave new world had to offer me.

By 4pm I wanted to give up, go home and die.

There were posh kids, with bags full of good "A" levels, everywhere. My fellow students were relaxed and confident. They smiled and tripped off their successes and backgrounds. Yes, "A" levels – some of them even three. Grammar School, minor Public Schools, Dad owns his own company, Mum's a Headmistress at a Girls Grammar…

And now Frank, tell us about how you won 10 shillings at a grass track – we'll all be fascinated to hear about that – NOT!

I went into full blushing mode and stammered and tripped over my own tongue and generally sounded like some medieval village idiot who had just been dragged before the Manor Court.

My first day finished on a really spectacular high. I went into the toilets, gave the roller towel machine a sharp tug to dry my hands and it crashed down on my ankles leaving me in a heap on the floor.

The only question was whether I was going to get thrown out of College for being stupid in a public place, wrecking their towel machine – or both.

The following day, I went in to see Mr. Leyland, my English tutor, in his small office in the English block overlooking the Junior Common Room. I told him that I was too thick to be at College and I was going to leave.

At this point, I learned another invaluable lesson. Geoff Leyland didn't like me much personally. I never did discover why this was but it didn't matter in the wider view because he offered me something far more important than kindness. Geoff was the consummate, dedicated educationist and his behaviour had a huge influence on me as my career progressed.

Despite a lack of affinity with me, he behaved as the complete caring professional and for this I admire him tremendously. He listened, carefully and patiently, to all I had to say and then explained that every first year student in every college in the world was finding it tough in some way or another in these first few days.

He didn't make any silly or patronising statements about me being as bright as the other students, or even being able to manage the rigours of tertiary education but, in his strong Liverpool accent, he said that it was too early to say what was going to happen and that I should forget what the other students could, or could not, do and stick it out for a couple of weeks.

After two weeks, I could come back and see him and then we would decide, together, what to do next. In the interim, he would be my only contact with the English department and, for two weeks at least, he wasn't going to throw me out.

Mr. Leyland lifted an immense load from my shoulders by giving me a tiny breathing space and fourteen days to find a solution. If I was running dead last, at least I was still in the race!

The following week, Geoff's Tutor Group crammed into his small study and we were given our first assignment. The brief was simple: "Write a critique of a play, or even a film, book or poem. Write as much, or little, as you want. Don't worry about anything. Just write what you feel comfortable with."

With that, there were smiles all round and we filed out. I really was between a very big sledgehammer and an extremely large anvil with this one. I was far too shy and embarrassed to ask any of the other students for help and equally reluctant to say to Geoff that I really didn't have the vaguest clue about what to do.

Clearly, I had read thousands of books but what sort of literature was acceptable for the assignment? Did it have to be very high brow, serious material or could it be science fiction? Were fun poems good or did they have to be the metaphysical stuff I never liked and couldn't much understand? The alarm bells rang loud and clear.

More out of desperation, and a complete lack of alternative ideas, I decided to take myself off to the cinema in the Old Swan district of Liverpool, and review a film that was currently making national news and receiving rave critical reviews. It was "The Graduate" – the story of young man a little older than me, who is first seduced by an older woman and then falls in love with her daughter.

The film received a ton of Academy Award nominations for Best Picture, Best Actor and many more and Mike Nichols won the Academy Award for Best Director. With this sort of success, I thought that the film might pass the worthiness benchmark.

I sat in the semi-darkness of the cinema and wrote like a fiend from hell. It was a surreal experience. Around me, popcorn was being munched, Kia-Ora orange was slurped through straws and contented sighs came from happy couples.

Meanwhile, I sat on the edge of my seat and wrote for my life. If the roof had fallen in, or tigers had appeared in the aisles and eaten viewers, I wouldn't have noticed. The flag had dropped and I was on a mission.

Essays at S.Kaths were graded in five levels. At the top was an A grade. No-one ever thought about A grades in English because they were impossible to obtain. Not only would the grammar, spelling, syntax and vocabulary have to be perfect but the arguments presented in the essay would have to be subtle, accurate and convincing. A grades were pure fantasy and didn't exist in the real world.

Good students got Bs. Anyone with a B+ was celebrating. A good, sound essay was a C. On a bad day, and they had better not be too often, a D+ would do. Don't even think about an E because this was hyper dangerous territory. A metaphorical yellow card was shown and a re-write was needed.

I handed in my "Graduate" essay and retired to a safe place to await the incoming fire. With luck, I would get a straight "D" grade or even perhaps a D+ if things went astonishingly well.

Surprisingly I hadn't found either the research for the critique very hard, or the writing of the essay itself. The characters in the film were clearly drawn, and unambiguous, and the plot was straightforward and episodic. Even the music, by Simon and Garfunkel, was strong and easy to analyse.

A week later, Geoff marked quickly out of courtesy to students, I was sent a note asking me to see him. Maybe out of kindness for my state of extreme angst, he immediately slid the essay across his desk to me. There, in the top right hand corner was a C+. I gulped. The expression, "I couldn't believe my eyes…" is much mis-used but in this case, I couldn't. I was utterly speechless. I had written a film critique and achieved a C+. This was the equivalent of a podium finish at an international motocross meeting.

Geoff paused to let me savour the moment – another thoughtful act - and then said: "It's a good attempt - but it's not right. Let me show you."

And then, with a smile and infinite care, he unpicked my essay word by word by word. He showed me where I had mis-used a semi-colon because a colon was more accurate punctuation. Then he demonstrated how to add weight to an argument by putting an additional idea in parenthesis, and when to avoid using the vernacular when Standard English was essential. He was teaching me to write accurately and succinctly, and it was a truly wonderful experience.

I listened in near silence. Geoff explained. A light came on in my brain and we moved on. Another explanation and another light. Yes, that's obvious. More explanation. Now I see. It was like opening up a mothballed factory. All the information was there in my head, it just needed Geoff to show me where it was stored and what to do with it.

After the tutorial, I skipped down the slatted wooden steps with a smile which nearly split my face. I had been wrong. I could do this College thing.

Geoff's kindness and professionalism wasn't over yet - because my Auntie had been on holiday to America.

★★★

My Auntie Edie wasn't really my Auntie but my Mum's cousin. However, she and my Mum were very close and so I always referred to her as Auntie – and was always the recipient of very wet, and somewhat effusively intimate, kisses. Still, contact sports apart, I liked Auntie Edie a lot.

For some reason I can't remember, she was going to America on holiday. This was a big deal within our community because no-one had ever been to the USA. I saw a golden opportunity coming out of her trip. The Americans speak English so please Auntie Edie, would you bring an American motorcycle magazine back for me? And I had more than just reading the mag in mind…

My lovely Auntie Edie did not bring back one magazine, as I had asked, but fourteen. Goodness only knows where she got this number from but I went down to her house and collected them – along with a tsunami of wet, sloppy kisses and long hugs.

The mags were the most eclectic mix of motorcycle literature I had ever seen. At one end of the market were very serious, main stream magazines like Cycle World and Motorcyclist and, at the other, some seriously hard core Chopper publications featuring riders you wouldn't want to meet even at mid-day in bright sunlight!

The Greeves had gone – what a delight that was - and, for the first time in three years, I was without a race bike. This was no hardship because my mind was focussed 100% on making my new career work in education. Well, perhaps not actually a whole 100%.

Every time I read a motorcycling magazine I did so with a lust and aching which matched any biological urge. I really thought that I could write about bikes but there was no way this was going to happen in Britain – so what about America? After all, the Americans spoke English, sort of, and they rode bikes so the big bits of the project were already in place. All that was needed was for me to get hired.

It was time for another creative writing session. Taking the core facts that I knew about bikes and could write, I then gave the truth a little bit of a massage in terms of my experience and work which had already been published.

Finally, I bet the kitchen sink - £5 actually - on buying some really nice headed notepaper.

That weekend, I toiled over fourteen individual letters. My two-fingered typing wasn't bad but each letter had to be perfect so I pecked away, letter by letter, like a cypher clerk operating one of those Second World War code machines – terrified of making a mistake and having the message mis-read.

The next problem was posting them to America. Air mail letters were expensive and normally sent on tissue thin, blue paper. My missives were big, heavy, clonky things and weren't cheap. The saviour appeared in the form of another clubman racer who knew that I was in a state of semi-retirement and came sniffing around for a bargain, like a hyena circling a wounded wildebeest.

He went away with a gallon of Castrol "R", some Greeves' sprockets and my lightly used motocross boots – and I headed to the Post Office with the capital for an international sales pitch.

As the Postmistress took the letters, I felt like kissing bon voyage to each one individually but, instead, maintained a stoic face. Now came the waiting.

Two air mail letters arrived almost simultaneously. The first, from Cycle World, was meticulously polite in a very "Dear Sir or Madam" way. It thanked me for my letter and said that they had no requirement for my work.

The second came on notepaper much worse than mine. It was from Motorcycle World in New York and, in a couple of sentences, asked me to send them a story and some photographs and they would consider the piece.

I must have re-read the letter a thousand times expecting the text to change to, "No, we don't want you and don't bother us ever again."

But the words wouldn't change, nor did they try to escape from the notepaper. They did say send us story and they did say we will consider it.

I was rolling down the runway for take-off.

I should add that Motorcycle World was not only the big bet to launch my journalistic career – there was no "Plan B" since the other twelve magazines never even bothered to reply!

I couldn't wait to tell my Mum the good news but the reaction wasn't what I expected. Two big, fat tears quite literally rolled slowly down her cheeks. She held both my hands and said, in a very soft, quavering voice: "Please don't let bikes ruin your life, love. You've done so well getting into College and you'll be a teacher and have a good job and not be like me and your Dad.

"Don't waste all this just for bikes."

It was the best of advice, given with all a Mother's love. Both my Mum and Dad had left school at fourteen years of age and no-one in our wider family had even stayed on at school to do "A" levels. Now, here I was at College and succeeding - with an incredibly high status job waiting for me.

Motorcycles were working class. They were dirty, and dangerous, and noisy, and belonged to my old life which I should leave behind. By every measure of common sense and logic she was right and her advice could not have been more accurate and kind.

The problem was that I was in love again and when I turned over the pages of Motorcycle World I could see my name there. If I had to swim the Atlantic to deliver the story to New York by hand, I was going to write it.

The big question was what to write about. The motorcycling season was coming to a close and although I had made some rather optimistic promises about my contacts, the truth is that I knew no-one of even minor importance in the bike world.

I was involved in a high stakes game of poker with Fate and Destiny and I had just been asked to show my hand of cards.

At the time, the Wirral 100 Club ran sand races on an oval track laid out between the high and low waterline on the beach at the end of New Brighton Promenade. I had been to the races with Sammy Green and found them interesting because of the range of bikes competing. There was everything, from small capacity 250s all the way through to the biggest 650cc machines from the British factories - and road racing, motocross and even trials bikes raced against each other.

I thought that maybe this odd mix of machines just might make an interesting feature – but for a rather odd reason: I wanted to write a story that I would like. This needs a little explanation. The sensible thing would have been to go down to New Brighton Prom and write a feature in the same vein as those which I had read so many times before.

It would say that the conditions were like this and Joe "X" won the 250cc race on a Yamaha, and Brian "Y" battled from a poor start to take the 350 class on his BSA and so on. This was motorcycle magazine reporting.

The problem was that I didn't much enjoy this sort of writing. I wanted to know how it felt to be there – to see the races and hear the bikes. Also, I wanted to know what it was like for me, the clubman racer with no contacts, to be at the event.

This was a very naïve view of life because ordinary riders didn't, and don't, influence affairs. Teenagers with rubbish bikes were spectators in the world of motorcycling – not players. Regardless, I decided that I would go down to New Brighton and write what I saw, heard and smelled.

In taking this approach, I had one enormous advantage. Because of a lack of "A" levels, I hadn't followed an NUJ course and therefore I hadn't been taught to write "properly". Further, I had never worked in a newspaper or magazine and therefore had not been influenced by established writers around me. Because I didn't know what was right or wrong I wrote what, and how, I wanted.

Without knowing it at the time, I had just exposed the mother lode in what was to be a very rich goldmine over the next 40 years.

I was my readers in that first article and I remain my readers today.

I might have dinner with some senior executive from a bike company, or sit in the motorhome of a World Champion who rides at one of the events Carol and I organise, but I always do so as an outsider.

First by accident, and now by design and intent, I am the eyes and ears of the ordinary motorcyclist – and I am incredibly proud to be so!

Down at New Brighton Prom I sat on the sea-wall and wrote what I saw and heard. I didn't deliberately choose to write in a very literary style but I simply used the language which I felt best described what was happening. It really was as simple as a decent tradesman using the correct tool for the job. At the time, I saw myself as a literary tradesman – and still do for that matter.

If I needed a verb, I chose the verb which best explained the action. When the verb needed qualifying, I used an adverb – and that was that. It wasn't a case of being clever or pretentious but just getting the correct spanner for the right literary nut and then using it properly.

Today, much is made of the need to avoid "difficult" language in a story for fear of alienating the reader. I think that this is a most pernicious form of political correctness which is patronising in the extreme to readers who have not had the same range of literary experience as the writer.

What gives the author of a piece of writing the right to say whether it will be too challenging for the reader? To do so is an act of supreme intellectual arrogance and I will have nothing to do with the idea.

So, in a manner which came naturally to me, I chose to treat my readers as my equals. I wrote about the piercing screams of the unsilenced two-strokes, battling with the angry calls of the gulls which had been driven away from their beach. I told the reader about the rich, near narcotic smell of the sea water burnt on to hot exhausts and mixed with the soft aroma of racing "R".

I took them down onto the beach and, through my words, let them feel the wet sand clinging to my boots and, most of all, I said what a great time I was having and how much I loved being there.

It wasn't a difficult job. I saw and heard and smelled everything easily, made a few, a very few, notes - and then had an ice-cream. I really liked this journalism business!

Before I had even left the beach, there was a fuzzy outline of the article's structure in my mind and, back in my room, I tapped away at the Adler and things came fairly easily.

I still work in exactly the same way today. First, there appears a mist – never a fog – from which people, structures and smells poke out so that I can see the first hint of what they look like. As the concept progresses, the mist clears away and there is a story plan in front of me. After this, it's just a matter of filling in the spaces – rather like a literary "painting by numbers."

I finished the article in one long afternoon and a bit of an evening, and then made an appointment to see Geoff. Again, I must praise his professionalism towards a student with whom he had no real empathy.

I explained that I had a commission, here was the story I had written and would he please have a look at it for me?

A couple of days later, Geoff was always prompt with work, there was a note in my pigeon hole to go up to his study.

I had barely eaten or slept for fear of the results and, as each hour passed, it was becoming ever clearer just how much this story meant to me. There was literally nothing – physically, mentally or intellectually – that I wouldn't do to see my story in print. Truthfully, if Motorcycle World had said that I had to eat a bowl of broken glass, washed down with a glass of concentrated acid, my only question would have been: "What do you want me to drink – nitric or sulphuric?"

I had to see that story in print.

Geoff was all smiles. "It's not bad, not bad at all."

I nearly fainted with joy.

"Let's have a look at it."

And so we did.

"This was a bit pretentious – just ease it back a little.

"Here, you have over written it slightly – give the reader space to join in the story without choking them with detail.

"Look, if you use a dash you can join those two sentences into one and make the story tighter. See what I mean?"

And I could see what he meant – and instantly too. Everything made sense and I couldn't wait to do another draft.

What was also exciting was that Mr. Leyland spoke to me in a manner which said that I was a writer and that he was completely confident that I would understand the points he was making. This made me very proud.

And then came some truly memorable words – and these are verbatim because they have been burned into my brain for four decades.

"You know, that article is okay. You might even get some sort of fame writing about motorbikes with a story like this." At the time, I thought that it was a very odd thing to say.

I carefully put the precious manuscript into an envelope with a batch of 10" x 8" photographs. The pics were okay, because I had taught myself photography as a young teenager, but they were not brilliant. Today, they would be rejected out of hand but, because the print quality of Motorcycle World was so bad, you could get away with a lot more.

If there had been a God of aspiring journalists, her shrine would have been in my bedroom and covered in votive offerings. I was desperate.

I took the package to the Post Office near our house but was reluctant to hand it over when my turn came at the counter. It reminded me of how I used to be with our daughter Elizabeth when she was a baby going to toddler group. "No, that's my baby – be careful with her!"

Eventually, mainly because a very big bloke was behind me waiting to post his "Pools" entry, I gave in and passed the envelope over. More prayers:

Please God, don't let there be a fire in the Post Office.

Please God, don't let the plane crash going to America.

Please God, don't let the Viet Kong invade New York and machine gun everyone at Motorcycle World.

The following morning, I was waiting for a reply – whilst the letter probably still hadn't left Warrington!

Three weeks passed. I had failed. The River Mersey was helpfully close, just a couple of miles from College. All that I had to do was find a suitable block of concrete and a piece of rope, wait until high tide and then chuck myself off the "Iron Promenade."

The only thing which kept me from ending it all was the frantic pace of work at S.Kaths. The College viewed the first year as a weeding-out process and the workload was absolutely non-stop. We literally jogged from one seminar, tutorial or lecture to the next and in between we barely stopped for breath. It was truly a case of what doesn't kill you will cure you and the college was determined to find out how much we really wanted to be teachers.

Eventually, a white envelope bearing an American stamp and an air mail sticker arrived. Yes, the piece was very good and they wanted to publish it. Would I accept $75?

I couldn't believe my good fortune. I was going to be published. I sat and re-read the letter over and over again, letting the words wash over me like a warm shower after a winter ride. I had done it. No more notice board adverts and club magazine rejections: I was a professional writer.

I didn't have any idea how much $75 was worth so a day later I went into Thomas Cooks, the travel agents in Warrington, and asked them if I had $75 what would it be worth? The clerk behind the glass dabbed at his mechanical comptometer and said: "A bit less than £30 after our commission."

This was another shock. £30 was an immense amount of money at a time when a skilled tradesman was earning an identical amount for a week's work. I was being offered a whole week's wages for sitting on a sea wall, licking ice-cream and then having a fantastic time writing a story. How could anyone be this fortunate?

The time flew by until a large, mid-brown envelope arrived from America. In it were two copies of Motorcycle World. One magazine I kept for many years until, very sadly, it got lost when we moved house.

I cut my article out of the other and kept the pages with me all day and every day. As we were waiting for a lecture or tutorial to start, I would melt into a corner and look at the by line: "By Frank Melling" it said. Frank Melling's name was written under a piece of real journalism, in a real magazine. Nothing in the world could make me this happy.

I was so ecstatic that I actually forgot about the cheque. The by line on the story was of far more importance. A week later, I took the cheque into Thomas Cooks. The clerk asked me to sign on the rear and then counted out five £5 notes and some change.

In those happy days, there were no passports to present or ID checks. Instead, trust was everywhere. I had presented a cheque and Thomas Cook believed it to be honest and so bought it from me.

I walked out with my wallet fatter than it had been for many months. It was a wonderful feeling.

But the envelope from my new employers also contained a letter – and this was a real good news/ bad news communication. It was another case of when the flag drops…

9

I'm Frank Melling and
I'm a Journalist

ON many occasions, perhaps invariably, I have felt that I have been a spectator in my life -watching as it raced away from me whilst I tried to catch up. The first few months at S.Kaths were like this. Every first year student complains about the workload in tertiary education but at S. Katherine's College of Education the pace really was savage.

I recently watched a programme about becoming a Royal Marines Commando and I was continually jumping up and down and saying to Carol: "It was like that at S.Kaths!"

It seemed that, every day, some student or other was called in for "a chat" - and then advised that there were many other fine careers and really, teaching was not for them.

There was a particular rash of these "chats" after our first school visit. Most of the other students had been pupils just a few months earlier and at very top of the food chain in Upper Sixth. Now they were down at the bottom again, as first year students at College. S.Kaths job was to ferry these baby students safely across the Rubicon from being the taught to doing the teaching.

In theory, Small Group Teaching Sessions were a trainee teacher's version of those wildlife films where Mummy Bear takes her cubs to the water's edge and lets them play at catching salmon whilst she stands guard: a safe, fun experience for the little ones whilst the grown-ups look after them and beam happily at their progress.

The reality was very different.

Six of us were given a Primary school in the toughest part of Liverpool 8, right on the docks. It's not fair to name the school because it will be much better now but, at the time, it really was a tough draw – and with a capital T.

Sadly, the Wolseley had given up the ghost and now I had a Standard Ensign van. It was a desperately dull example of a motor vehicle but it could, just about, fit four students in the back and one in the passenger seat.

I duly loaded up everyone and we set off for our Small Group Teaching Sessions with a real sense of anticipation and excitement.

Waiting for us was a class of nine year olds arranged in groups of four, five or six around tables. The idea was that we should meet them, chat, and do a bit of art and language work. Afterwards, we would write up our impressions about how we had got on.

I smelled an enormous rat the moment we walked in. The Deputy Head gave us the briefest of introductions - and then did a runner. We were left with the kids and the class teacher - and he looked as if he had just come out of a First World War trench, having been shelled continuously for 24 hours. This felt seriously wrong.

It was literally minutes before the chaos kicked in. I had brought in a book about dogs which I felt was safe ground, in terms of a non-controversial subject which the kids might like. We could talk about the different kinds of dog, draw one and then write a sentence underneath. What's not to like?

Other students had been more ambitious. One of the girls arrived with some lovely pictures of flowery, hippy dresses with the idea that the kids would then design their own. Lads in Liverpool 8 drawing pictures of girls' frocks? Well, it didn't seem like a sound bet to me…

Within five minutes, there were kids everywhere and anarchy was beginning its inexorable march towards a full blown disaster. Two lads from my table got ready to join the fray but, in those happy days, a more direct and unequivocal form of communication could be employed than would be acceptable today.

Me: Sit down. Now.

Nine Year Old Would-Be Rioter: Why? You can't make me. You're only a student.

Me: Listen to me Sunshine. I'm not a Student. I'm a real teacher. I'm just here to watch what the students do.

Nine Year Old Would-Be Rioter: So…

Me: So, if you move an inch I'll nail your hands to the desk and leave you there until next week.

Nine Year Old Would-Be Rioter: (Long pause as he makes eye contact and undertakes a thorough risk assessment). Okay then Sir.

Me: Good lad. Now, let's draw a dog.

At the conclusion of the three weeks there was a flood of students seeking other careers.

★★★

Things were going well at College but the letter which had arrived from Motorcycle World sat in my briefcase, throbbing like a lump of extremely toxic plutonium.

First, the good news. In essence, the story was fine but now they wanted an exclusive story – something which was unique to Motorcycle World.

It's worth providing some background on Motorcycle World because I was really fortunate in terms of being in the right place at the right time when I wrote to this magazine asking for a job.

Motorcycle World was part of the Countrywide Publications' empire which published as many as fifty titles each month, from soft porn to science fiction plus a myriad of gun magazines. In the late 1960s, motorcycling was becoming huge in America and Myron Fass, the owner of Countrywide Publications, would publish anything which would sell 20,000 copies. Bikes were an obvious target.

Given the immense interest in motorcycles at the time, the 20,000 figure was well achievable and a lot of publishers thought so: hence the number of magazines Auntie Edie was able to gather for me.

The problem for Motorcycle World was that they were based in New York – when everything of any importance in American motorcycling happened on the West Coast of America, with the epi-centre being Los Angeles.

With me, they just might possibly have something a little bit different which could help sales along towards the magic 20,000 target – if I could deliver.

It was a lot to ask of a teenager with no journalistic experience and the responsibility weighed very heavily on me. Yes, I had been published but now my career was coming to a total, crashing halt. This was the end. It was only the frantic pace of work at S. Kaths that prevented me from becoming really depressed.

Regardless, I was still in the journalism race and that was everything.

There was a televised motocross meeting at Nantwich and so I duly turned up, blagged my way in (that was a matter of pride) and approached twice World Champion Jeff Smith, who was riding a works BSA. I explained what had happened and threw myself on his mercy. The result was interesting. He was contemptuous and dismissive. No, there was no chance of me ever writing about a works BSA. How wrong he was to be…

Tom Leadbitter was riding in the meeting and I knew him from riding at the same Cheshire Centre events – although Tom was a much better rider than I was. He said I looked fed up so I told him the tale of woe and how my brand-new journalism career was already over before it was started. Tom smiled – he was always happy – and said there might be a solution.

He had been offered a ride on a unique bike with a British built, Cheney chassis housing a works Suzuki engine. It was the only one in the world and he would put a good word in for me with Suzuki GB and perhaps they would let me ride it.

At Monday lunch-time, I took two pockets full of change to the phone booth and rang Suzuki. Tom had been as good as his word and yes, I could ride the bike a week on Wednesday.

Almost before I had put the phone down, I was writing to my editor in New York telling him the good news: they were going to have their world exclusive.

I wasn't overawed at the thought of riding a factory bike. Freelancers have an odd mind set in which the article dominates everything. No story – no wages: it tends to bring the real issues into focus very clearly.

My big concern was how to get the photographs which would accompany the story. Clearly, I couldn't take pictures of myself riding the bike and so, for the first time, I needed to hire a photographer. Once more, Fate intervened by flicking a really good card to my side of the table.

On my first day at S.Kaths, I had gone to the dining room for a coffee and there, lolled against the wall, was a much older man reading Motorcycle News. I was desperate for some companionship and so I went across to say hello.

Even with someone who clearly liked bikes I was all blushes and tongue-tied shyness.

I began: "Hiya. I've got a bike." This was actually not true because the Greeves had gone but I have never let facts interfere with a good story.

The reader didn't even look up.

"So?"

"Well, you know, you were reading MCN and…"

The words ground to a halt and then suffocated in the silence.

The paper was laid on the table. "What've you got?"

I lied about the Greeves, his eyes twinkled and a grin appeared - and from that day on we became friends.

The man was Peter Wilson. He was a good road racer and eight years older than me – which is an awful lot when you are teenager.

Pete was doing a neat piece of job-juggling – and one which took cojones the size of a fit Hereford bull. Pete was actually employed as a staff photographer for British Sidac, in St. Helens, but had already started at S.Kaths. Somehow, he juggled College and his day job for a few weeks and so kept his grant and his wage. Clever - if you can pull it off!

I explained what I needed and Pete agreed that we would work together on the Suzuki job.

Once more not knowing how to do things properly, as a mainstream magazine would have done, was a huge advantage.

The Cheney was also the perfect article to start with. First, there were middle management staff from Suzuki GB at the test and they were sufficiently senior for me to have to learn how to interview them as I went along.

I continued in just the same way as I had done with the sand-racing article. I asked them the questions I wanted answering as a clubman racer. I didn't try to be clever or cunning but just went straight in and talked about motocross bikes and racing.

Tom was a star rider but he was also extremely modest and a truly lovely person. Instead of the dismissive curtness shown by Jeff Smith, Tom was encouraging and chatty and told me what I wanted to know without me even asking.

I didn't crash the bike – always an advantage when you are riding someone else's motorcycle – and Pete got some decent pics.

Best of all, the story had a real edge. The chassis was built by Eric Cheney, in Fleet, Hampshire. Eric was a pure, unadulterated genius. In fact, even this does not do him justice. He was better than merely brilliant. Good as he was as a chassis designer and builder, his business skills lagged far behind. Eric told me that he built the chassis for Suzuki, with the promise that the Japanese factory would order a further 200 if they liked the prototype.

As it happens, Eric would never have built 200 units of anything because he became bored very quickly and was always looking for a new challenge. Regardless, Suzuki never placed the order.

However Eric swore that the following year's factory Suzuki, used so successfully in motocross GPs, was a copy of the Cheney and that Suzuki had stolen his design and then reneged on the deal. Whether this was true no-one will ever know but this is what Eric always maintained.

I sent the story off to New York with a lot more confidence than the sand-racing piece and by return, I got another letter. Yes, they loved the article and would $100 be okay? This was catch your breath time. The bottom line profit wasn't any greater than the sand racing article, because I had to pay Peter and there was the cost of getting to Staffordshire to ride the bike, but the nett was £40 – more than a week's wages for a skilled mechanic or welder. I could really get to like journalism. How to keep my journalism job dominated every spare thinking moment.

***

I have already explained how all hard core motorcyclists at the time were interested in every form of motorcycling, and this meant that Oulton Park was an absolute shrine for us. The track is one of the most beautiful in Britain, and twists and turns through sandy parkland for almost two and three quarter miles of glorious drops and climbs.

At the time, Grands Prix paid appalling prize money. There is no doubt that the organisers of World Championship events exploited the fact that riders were forced to compete in their events by the manufacturers who employed them.

The motorcycling factories knew the score just as much as the riders and so a compromise was reached. Throughout Europe, there were numerous international meetings which attracted huge crowds. To get these big spectator numbers, the promoters paid good money to star riders.

For their part, many of the riders were contracted to compete on a particular make of motorcycle. It would have been impossible to have a Honda team rider use a Yamaha or vice versa. The solution was to let contracted riders use second string works bikes.

The 1960s was the most glorious era for exotic motorcycles and so, at an international meeting, you would see everything from the classic British Manx Norton and AJS 7R machines, through to Spanish Bultacos and Derbis, the "fire engine" red, works Italian MV Agustas, Morini singles, Bianchi twins, German BMW engined sidecars and the fast but fragile MZ two-strokes. Then there were the dream time twin and four cylinder bikes from Honda, Yamaha, Suzuki, Bridgestone and Tohatsu.

All these machines were to be seen at Oulton Park being ridden by World Champions such as Mike Hailwood, Jim Redman, Luigi Taveri, Phil Read, Bill Ivy and Hugh Anderson – and that's by no means the full list! In short, just fifteen miles from home was everything a road racing fan could wish to see and, being completely unsilenced, hear!

The attendance at these meetings was huge – absolutely enormous. Even leaving home at seven in the morning, the queues to get in started a good four miles from the circuit.

The problem was just as bad in terms of getting out so I always preferred to park outside the circuit in the woods opposite. There was nothing wrong with doing this and, at a major international meeting, there would be thousands of bikes dotted around the sandy woodlands.

Parking there also had a secondary benefit – at least in my early days when I was in a state of utter, abject poverty. I don't condone dishonesty so I'm not proud of what I did to get into Oulton. However, I put my criminality in the same category as those refugees scraping a handful of rice from the bottom of an aid lorry as it drives off. No, they shouldn't be stealing rice - but they are desperate. I was just as desperate to have my racing hunger sated.

The more athletic poor people climbed over the wall at Oulton. It was ten feet high and covered with broken glass along the top and I just wasn't capable of getting in this way.

My method required a cool nerve under pressure – and that was it. No physical prowess was required – just the ability to look very ordinary and nondescript whilst staying calm.

Entry to the track was via the Bailey Bridge. Spectators walked up and over the bridge and paid for their tickets at the end. The queue was always very tense because the crowds were desperate to get in and see the action.

All that was required was to walk boldly up to the pay booth, point confidently behind and say: "He's getting 'em."

Then walk through. That was it - but the strategy did require a total confidence in delivering the line.

By the time the bloke in the booth had worked out that there was actually no-one going to buy the tickets he had an invidious choice. The first, as happened rarely, was to leave his post to chase me. At this point, a couple of hundred equally dishonest spectators rushed past his pay booth and he had to return soonest – or face even more loss of income.

What usually happened was that he would shout abuse, requests that I be arrested or death threats as I walked calmly into the circuit.

There was only one fix for this because the last thing I wanted was to be collared by one of the Cheshire Police Bobbies patrolling the egress to the foot bridge. I would instantly find someone who looked scruffier and even more of a vagrant than I did, fix them with a horrified stare and then move away in fear and disgust. All eyes would then be focussed on the supposed criminal – whilst I melted quietly into the crowd. The whole exercise worked a treat but did require a very clear head under pressure.

It wasn't the best way to start the day – but it did provide a cheap route in and was better than dropping ten feet down a wall - and right into the embrace of a waiting policeman!

Once inside, Oulton was heaven. The racing was intense and the atmosphere sublime. I would stand at the bottom of Knicker Brook and hear the wailing Hondas come down through the gears for the ferociously fast right hand bend, and then accelerate uphill and away towards Druids.

It is right and proper that motorcycling today should be environmentally aware, and good neighbours to everyone else in the community, but the raw, barely tamed cries of these wonderful bikes are still etched into my heart and soul as if it were today.

It's a shame that there can't be some compromise in a modern society, so that residents next to race tracks show tolerance to noise on a few days in the year. Yes, the sound of these fabulous engines scorched across the Cheshire countryside for miles, almost stripping the leaves from the trees, but the bikes spoke of greatness and glamour and glory and all the things which were missing from the life of a working class teenager in a Northern town. Those wonderful bikes, and the music their exhausts made, were as inspirational to me as any rendition of Handel's Messiah or Mozart's Marriage of Figaro.

Spectating was wonderful but the cherry on the very top of the cake was paddock access - and this was invariably missing. The problem was that you had pay to get into the paddock and since I didn't have enough money even to get into the circuit, there was less than no chance of funding a paddock pass.

The pay booths were also a lot tighter controlled than the Bailey Bridge and circuit staff patrolled the inside of the wooden fencing to ensure that athletic miscreants didn't attempt a three feet (1m) high vault into the paddock.

If things were tight normally, they were absolutely crazy when Giacomo Agostini rode at Oulton and this, ironically, got me into the paddock – and free of charge too.

A large, very large indeed, Liverpool docker arrived at the pay gate with his ten year old, or thereabouts, lad. The ticket vendor explained, with an unfortunate brusqueness and lack of sympathy, that the boy, as well as the Dad, needed a ticket before the pair would be allowed in.

The docker argued that the day was expensive enough without having to pay for a minor to get into the paddock. Fortunately, or perhaps unfortunately depending on where you stood regarding what followed, the docker was accompanied by four of his equally large and muscle bound mates.

I stood back because I knew that this was going to be one heck of a floor show. The ticket seller made some pointedly racist comments something along the lines of, "Thieving Scousers (the nickname for residents of Liverpool) shouldn't even be allowed in to the track…" and from that moment on, something spectacular was certain to happen.

The Liverpudlians did no more than rip the chestnut paling fence from the ground and began jumping up and down on it and, as it flattened, five hundred of us poured into the paddock free of charge. So, free track admission and free paddock entry – a true bargain for the impecunious race fan.

★★★

My interest in, and passion for, every form of motorcycle sport was about to become vitally important because the increasingly familiar air mail letter arrived - and it was yet another good news/bad news missive.

Yes, my editor liked my work and yes he wanted some more of it. So, happy days.

The bad news was that Motorcycle World wanted a test report on the bike which would win the Isle of Man TT races.

Although the USA had very little tarmac racing at the time, the TT was still the most important event in the road racing calendar and was therefore known to my American editor. Hence his instructions for the article.

At the same time, because it was the most important road race in the world, getting a ride on a bike which won a TT was quite simply impossible.

When I speak to young journalists who want to be freelancers, I try to explain to them that perhaps the single greatest asset you can have is the ability to deliver. Always accede to an editor's request - and then work out how to do the job later!

Editors don't want to know if you are feeling sick, whether your dog has just died, or if you've been run over by a hippo which has escaped from your local zoo. Their attitude is that they have commissioned the work, they're prepared to pay you, so deliver - or get out of the game.

This black and white attitude was what I loved most about working for the Americans – and still do. America truly is the most democratic nation in the world. No-one at Motorcycle World asked me about my family background, my "A" levels – or lack of them – or my total absence of professional training. Everything was wonderfully, beautifully simple. Write the story and if we like it we'll pay you. If we don't, you're fired. What could be fairer than that? You could have all the qualifications in the world, but if you couldn't deliver you weren't going to get hired and certainly not paid.

I thought that this was great so I did what all good freelancers do – I lied. Yes, I would test a bike which won a TT and yes it would be an exclusive. What could be easier?

The answer was almost anything in the motorcycling world.

For a start, the main classes were simply beyond reach – even with my fevered and desperate imagination. Giacomo Agostini and the works MVs looked to be certain winners in the two Premier classes and things weren't much easier in the 250cc and 125cc divisions. I just was not going to get a ride on any of these bikes.

My only hope was the Production TT. Production Racing is a class for what are, supposedly, standard road machines and at the time there was a huge amount of interest in the idea of racing machines which, in theory at least, the general public could buy.

Production Racing attracted factory entries from Triumph, BSA, BMW, Velocette, Bultaco and Norton all striving for race results which would help sell bikes so, in theory at least, I was in with a chance.

I headed off to the phone booth with another pocket full of coins. I started with BSA. "Hello, I'm Frank Melling and I'm a journalist writing for Motorcycle World…"

I didn't get much further until the much loved "Dear Sir or Madam" response kicked in and I was asked to send my CV in to the Press Department for consideration.

The lady on reception at Triumph was a little less brusque – but not much.

Two down and no scores so far.

Norton was no better and the British BMW office had no idea what the parent factory were doing and no interest in me whatsoever.

Geoff Dodkin, who ran the works Velocettes, was polite but Velocette were on their last legs as a motorcycle factory - he doubted if there would be any bikes at the 1970 TT.

I had run out of ammunition and the enemy was swarming over the hill with fixed bayonets. This was the end. My two article journalism career had been a wonderful experience but, thank goodness I had taken College seriously. At least I wasn't going back to scrap metal burning!

Then I read an article in Motorcycle News. Eddie Crooks, the owner of Crooks-Suzuki, was going to enter the Production TT with a 500cc Suzuki. It was the final dregs in the almost empty bottle of the terminal order in the Last Chance Saloon. This was it. One last bet - and then I would be thrown out on to the street as a failure.

I loaded up with loose change, headed for the phone booth again and dialled the Crooks' shop in Barrow-in-Furness.

"I'm Frank Melling. I'm a journalist. May I speak to Mr. Crooks, please?"

"Yes, this is Eddie. What's up?"

I was in shock. Instead of a distant secretary or receptionist I was talking to the man who could, just possibly, save my head from the noose.

I need to digress at this point to explain about Eddie. He had no training or experience in marketing or PR but intuitively knew more about the subject than anyone in the motorcycling business, and probably any other profession for that matter. I am sure that he left his mother's womb looking for a photo opportunity because he was quite simply a natural, and gifted, marketing genius.

He also took to me immediately and we were instantly on the same wave length. In some respects, Ed was not always a paragon of virtue but with me he was wonderful and, as the years passed, we were to become ever closer.

Ed's aim was to make Crooks-Suzuki, located right at the end of the Furness Peninsula and in a deeply unfashionable part of the country, one of the biggest Suzuki dealers in the world. To do this, he needed publicity and here was what at least sounded like a journalist offering him five pages of it.

Yes, I could ride the T500. Yes, I would be the only journalist allowed to ride the bike regardless of whether it finished first or last.

For my part, I promised that I would write the story regardless of the results and we shook hands over the phone.

I wrote another letter to America with an interesting interpretation of the facts. I had got a bike and for 101% certain it was going to win the TT – I skated over which TT – so all was good. Trust me, I will deliver.

The two sentence reply was beaming and confirmed that they had reserved five pages in the next issue for the TT winning machine.

There was another spot of good fortune. The Production TT was on the Saturday of TT week and I was scheduled to ride the bike on the Sunday morning. You could cut lectures and tutorials at S.Kaths but your absence was noted. Too many "poorly tummies" and you would be called in for the dreaded "chat."

I worked all day Friday and then drove down to the Pier Head in my van and caught the midnight boat.

It was back to sleeping on the deck, but it didn't matter in the slightest. I was so wound up that I couldn't have gone to sleep even if I had been in a palace. This one had to go right.

Eddie's rider was Frank Whiteway, who was also the Crooks Suzuki workshop foreman. Frank was a good rider and had already won the Manx Grand Prix, the amateur version of the TT, and so knew the course well. He was also a clever mechanic who had prepared the bike he was riding personally and understood the machine inside out.

After we docked the following morning, I walked from the Pier Head at Douglas to Bradden Bridge and sat and cheered - and thanked God when Frank won the race. Against all the odds, I had my TT winner.

It was another sleepless night but the following morning I turned up at Eddie's Mum's house at Marathon Avenue, near to the TT paddock, to ride the bike.

In some ways, Ed was hard work – even with me. By the time I arrived, his mind was clearly on other things, as it often was, and me riding the bike wasn't one of them. The Suzuki was in the front garden of the modest house and was exactly how it had finished the TT the day before, thick with flies and still carrying the race numbers.

The keys were in the bike and the conversation was very short. "Here you are. Bring it back when you want. Gotta go."

And, with that, he left me on my own with the very motorcycle which had just won a TT.

It was a bike I came to know, and admire, over the years but at that time I was both perplexed and very unsure about what to do next. With no-one else there, I simply kicked the big Suzuki into life and rode it out on to the TT course.

I loved the T500 right from the first moment and I was having a great time until I arrived at Parliament Square in Ramsey. The Sunday of TT week is always known as "Mad Sunday" because all the spectators go bonkers riding the TT course which, when it is not being used for racing, is a normal public road.

Mad Sunday really is a crazy period - and I have always been very cautious of it.

So there we are, with the roads knee deep in wannabee TT stars, I rock up at Ramsey on a bike carrying race numbers and looking as if it has just finished a TT – which it had!

The white helmeted Constable holds up a hand vertically and pulls me over. The next bit is absolutely verbatim: "Okay son, what do you think you are doing? Riding in the TT?"

A calm response was needed. "Actually, no Officer. I am the official test rider for the Crooks Suzuki team and this is the bike which won yesterday's Production TT."

And then, looking as cool and nonchalant as I could: "I'm just doing some carburettor testing before the Senior." (the week's premier race)

The reaction was instant and the whole of the Ramsey Constabulary gathered round as I talked them through the finer points of the bike – some of which were accurate and many more a product of my desperate imagination.

"Well, you'd better get on with the testing then, Sir." And with that, the lovely Officer strode boldly out into the road, stopped all the traffic and waved me regally on my way.

The more I did of this journalism job the more I liked it.

I actually wrote the story long hand, sitting behind the grandstand, and then typed it up when I got back to England. Having a spent another night on the deck, I wasn't exactly in pristine condition when I arrived back at St Kaths for lectures on Monday morning but the job was done. By Wednesday the photographs had been printed and the package was on its way, by airmail, to New York.

My new American boss was delighted. He had a freelancer who could be trusted to deliver and for any editor this is the key criterion in hiring a writer. Being 99% sure that the journalist you have hired will do the job is no good.

Eddie was equally pleased. I didn't crash his bike and just got on with the article without bothering him very much at all.

When he saw the feature, he was delighted. For the cost of loaning me a bike for a couple of hours, he got international coverage for Crooks-Suzuki and this was as good as money in the bank for someone who never took his eye off the PR ball.

There is a postscript to this story which might have been life changing. Eddie was a laser accurate judge of riders and so he urged me to ride the T500 in a Production race at the Aintree circuit on the outskirts of Liverpool. I hesitated and came within a gnat's whisker of agreeing but a lack of confidence stopped me. A year later, I would have done it, and maybe become a serious road racer, but I was still discovering myself in so many ways that I refused.

At one time in my mid-30s, I regretted the decision but now I don't because I have always been strongly attracted to this Anglo-Saxon maxim:

Wyrd bið ful aræd

It translates, more or less, into "Fate is inexorable."

The older I get, the more I believe this and Fate was about to deliver a bumper package of surprises in the next 12 months - the greatest of which was that I fell in love – hopelessly, utterly, totally, every second of every minute in love with a very special girl.

10

May I Speak to Mr. Melling?

I often see life as a trek through a thick jungle. I hack away at the trees and bushes whilst sinking thigh deep in the mud, getting eaten by leeches and bitten by flies. Then, quite suddenly and without any real warning, I make one last cut with the machete and pop out on to a beautiful, sunlit, grassy plateau where everything is perfect.

The next section of jungle is always ahead but, just for now, it's time to enjoy the warmth and relaxation.

The next plateau was just a few cuts away.

First, I fell very heavily in love. I had not been a perfectly behaved young man since I joined S.Kaths and even now, I still feel embarrassed thinking about what happened. There were a lot of very lovely girls at College and I was a very fit male – with all that means!

So, I blundered about falling in out of what I thought was love but which was really lust. I said the wrong things at the wrong time and let my hormones rule my brain.

Then I met a girl who was in some of my History and English classes. She was pretty, had a truly enormous brain and tremendous self-confidence.

We fell in love simultaneously - at precisely the same moment and with an identical passion. It was a beautiful, idyllic, young person's love affair. We walked and talked and loved together, and I made a little creature out of my hand and let it walk up her arm and whisper stories into her ear.

Of course, we felt that no other couple were ever so much in love or had such a perfect relationship. Such is the power of young love.

Eventually, we were married and then there was a divorce which was so sad that it came within a few minutes of killing me. But all this was a long time in the future and, as I walked through Sefton Park with her hand gently squeezing mine and her soft finger tips telling me her story of love and tenderness and longing and wanting to be with me, my life was utterly complete. I wanted for nothing, desired nothing and was replete with happiness.

Even though being in love provided everything for me, Fate was about to throw me another bonus card – and a rather super-duper good one too.

***

The TT winning article did really well and there was an immediate invitation to write more – and at $100 for each feature.

My stories very soon developed a real following and another letter arrived. This one really was a surprise. Would I consider writing a monthly column? I could write about anything I wished as long as it was motorcycle related and I would be paid $75 for each one.

I was stunned and it took me a considerable period of time – about 90 seconds – before I was tapping away at the Adler and agreeing. The truth was that I really couldn't believe my luck. I had opinions on everything, and particularly motorcycles, and now I was being paid to share them. Since I was already doing this for free to anyone who would listen, and many who wouldn't, how good was that?

In writing the column, I continued to have enormous advantages over any other young British journalist of my age. Because I had never been trained to write articles, I produced monthly essays and stories. Rather than discussing sensible, mainstream topics such as when a new bike was going to be launched or who had won what race, I wrote about the things which club racers and the ordinary motorcyclist discussed.

Since I was an industry outsider, I did not have to worry about upsetting or offending anyone in the bike trade. Nor was I concerned about the mag's advertising manager complaining that I had lost him a client. So, I wrote in an anarchic and irreverent style which pulled no punches - and I had a lot of fun every month.

I was particularly critical of the mighty BSA Group, not out of any desire to hurt this Birmingham giant but rather from a sense of utter frustration.

BSA had, at one time, been the world's biggest producer of motorcycles and the company was not only immense but incredibly diverse. In terms of motorcycle production, it owned the BSA brand itself plus Triumph, Ariel and Sunbeam.

However, in some ways, this was only the tip of the ice-berg. BSA made guns and also produced the most sophisticated specialist steels as well as exotic alloys and sintered metals. In short, they were world leaders in engineering.

Yet, the result of all this excellence was motorcycles which were falling behind the Japanese quite literally month by month.

Despite BSA's vast distribution network, which covered almost every country in the world from the days of the British Empire, sales of the Birmingham bikes were plummeting compared with the Japanese.

The problems were manifold and, as a motorcyclist with Union Jack blood running through my veins, they drove me crazy. Not only were the bikes technically ten years behind the Japanese, they were philosophically just as a distant. All BSAs had to be kick started whereas electric starting was becoming the norm for the oriental opposition.

BSA's quality control was vastly inferior too. You could buy a Honda and ride it flat out, all day every day, and it would never miss a beat. Ride any BSA hard and bits would be falling off it all over the place.

So, I wrote of my anger and frustration at the situation and did so unequivocally. I wasn't particularly anti-BSA but I just didn't care what the company thought of me.

When I went home towards Easter, my Mum was in her fussing mode. She said: "Someone from somewhere called BSA phoned and asked to speak to Mr. Melling and I said he isn't in and I was trying to work out who wanted to talk to your Dad. And then they said it was about Motorcycle World and so I knew it was you.

"And who have you been upsetting now?"

By now my Mum automatically, and immediately, expected me to have caused some trouble somewhere to someone.

It would be a lie to say I was confident about the call. My first concern was whether BSA had made a formal complaint to Motorcycle World and that this call was to tell me that I had just been fired: "Ha! Ha! Ha !. That'll teach you to be smarty pants and to criticise BSA!"

Regardless, I couldn't wait to ring BSA and discover my fate. I was put through to one of most interesting characters in the motorcycling world – the urbane, witty and highly burnished Reg Dancer. Mr. Dancer was officially the BSA Group's PR Officer but in reality he was much more. He had an ear tuned to every whisper in the motorcycling galaxy and access to anyone and everyone within the huge BSA empire.

He had been sent copies of my columns from the BSA offices in both California and Maryland, asking what the heck was going on and why was I being allowed to write so much hostile material.

The problem for BSA was that my column was attracting something of a cult following and was generating a vast amount of correspondence from readers. Ten, twenty or sometimes even more letters regularly arrived at Motorcycle World's offices in Park Avenue South. In pre-internet days, this was a massive postbag.

Some were critical, and discussed both my lack of parents and absence of intelligence in great detail, but a lot were positive. Good or bad, the column engaged readers and encouraged them to buy the next issue of the magazine – and this made me flavour of the month at Country Wide Publications.

For sure, Motorcycle World had no intention at all of reining me in.

I must have really been ringing some big bells at BSA because Reg invited me down to meet Lionel Jofeh, the Managing Director of BSA Motorcycles, who would personally explain to me how important customers were to the company and what exciting plans were about to hatch.

As usual, there was a problem. In this case, it was my off blue, Standard Ensign van. I wasn't the most worldly nineteen year old in the country but even I could work out that driving up to BSA's headquarters in Armoury Road, in a seriously derelict van worth £35, was not likely to make the best of impressions.

I waffled and bluffed and told Reg that much as I would like to meet Mr. Jofeh, and have a VIP tour of the factory, I was just waiting for my new car to arrive and so was currently without wheels. Fine tuning the truth for efficiency is a key skill for any freelance journalist!

This was no problem at all to BSA. A First Class train ticket would be winging its way to me post haste and a car would collect me from Birmingham's New Street Station. The die was cast.

The first part was easy. I really enjoyed travelling in a First Class compartment and soon got used to the hostile stares of the blue suited executive who looked at the long haired, flower tied, pink shirted young man with undisguised disgust.

The ticket collector scrutinised my ticket meticulously, and no doubt shared the same opinion as the exec, but having concluded the forensic examination, wished me good day and addressed me as "Sir." This VIP business was good fun.

If the train trip down was a new experience, what happened next really re-set the terminals in my brain. I skipped off the train at New Street and almost missed the immaculate, grey suited and peak capped chauffeur, holding up the meticulously printed sign bearing my name.

He sounded just like an English manservant should and addressed me as "Sir."

After asking if he could carry my coat, the chauffeur escorted me to the grey, London taxi cab bearing the registration BSA 1 and opened the door for me. This was serious stuff.

The BSA 1 registration was easy enough to appreciate for a company the size, status and influence of BSA but the bespoke London taxi was slightly more complicated. One small part of BSA's huge and diverse empire was Car Bodies, the makers of the iconic London cabs, so it was natural that visitors should be collected in one of these vehicles.

We purred through Birmingham with the chauffeur being the most impeccable example of a gentleman's carriage driver:

"Did Sir have a good journey?"

"Was Sir familiar with BSA?"

"Was there anything Sir needed on the way to the factory?"

Bear in mind that, just the day before, "Sir" had been queuing up outside a history seminar room and getting ready for his second Teaching Practice…

As I sat in the back of the taxi and listened to the gentle, solicitous enquiries from the front of the cab I really did expect the Angel of Wrath to reach in through the door, drag me out of the sumptuous leather seat and chuck me into a puddle. Sooner or later, I had to be found out.

We arrived at Armoury Road and pulled up outside the entrance to the factory. My gentleman's gentleman was round at the cab door before I had even got hold of my coat. As he swung open the door, there was a quiet, confident smile – oozing service but not servility – followed by a final: "And I look forward to seeing Sir later..."

Thank goodness my Mum had done a lovely job of ironing my pink shirt and had made me brush my suede, Hush Puppy shoes!

Waiting for me was Reg Dancer along with his assistant. The big guns really were being wheeled out for me. I took an immediate liking to Reg because he was exactly what he both appeared, and claimed, to be. He was polished to a mirror finish, and impeccably dressed, but with just the tiniest whiff of a West Midlands' accent. In fact, his local heritage was important to Reg because he prided himself on being part of the industrial DNA which was Birmingham at that time.

The obverse side of the coin was that he was silky smooth and very sophisticated. City of London investors apparently thought the world of him.

The final part of this quite outstanding servant of BSA was a brain as powerful as a Cray Supercomputer - and one which was finely attuned to the most subtle scents carried on the media winds.

I could never call Reg a friend, because he was old enough to be my Dad, but I did come to know him superficially well and on each occasion that we met I admired him more. Sadly, Reg knew exactly what was happening with BSA, and could do nothing to mend the situation, so he played the hand of cards that he was given to the best of his very considerable ability.

In this case, the cards said that the young man who had just disembarked from BSA 1 was attracting a lot of attention from American customers and so needed to be given the full VIP treatment.

First, there was a guided tour of the factory. The BSA works was not in the best geographical location for a manufacturing centre but it is wrong to think of the Armoury Road site as being some 19th Century hovel with peasants grubbing around in the filth.

In fact, the opposite was true. The factory was, within its physical constraints, modern and well organised. When I first visited, it was also a happy, busy and vibrant place with a lot of skilled workers who had a real pride in what they were doing.

Equally it was old fashioned, not only in terms of the actual building and city centre location but, just as importantly, in its thinking.

Much later, I came across an example of the difficulties which faced all of the

British manufacturing industries at the time but I will slot the anecdote in here to illustrate what was happening.

A new, state of the art, Fiat lathe had been delivered to BSA and sat, pristine in its delivery wrappings, outside the office of the BSA Works Manager, Al Cave. I went back to the factory three months later and the lathe was still there.

I asked one of Mr. Cave's staff why the lathe had not been put to use and he shrugged his shoulders: "We're still arguing with the Unions over the change in the rate for piece work (the amount a worker was paid per item produced).

"They know that the new machine will be much faster, so the turner will get paid more, and we're not letting the bastards have us over otherwise everyone will be at it and we'll have a strike on our hands."

So, at one end of the food chain were militant, difficult and utterly selfish unions and at the other...

The other was a Senior Management of breath taking incompetence, aided and abetted by shareholders who could not look further than their next luxury lunch and oak aged glass of port wine.

In between the two slices of stale and rotten bread was the meat of the sandwich, in the form some of the cleverest production workers and most skilled tradesmen in the world who, if they had been well led, would have taken on the Japanese and won.

If you think that this is simply jingoistic pride in the English workers just look at current Japanese car manufacturing in Britain with the Nissan, Toyota, and Honda factories better than anything else in the world in terms of quality and efficiency.

As the German First World War General, Erich Ludendorff, said of the British Infantry: "They are lions led by donkeys."

And nowhere was this aphorism more appropriate than the way BSA's workforce was led at the time.

Our first stop was to meet Alastair Cave, BSA's redoubtable works manager. Mr. Cave was probably reading an engineering drawing within five seconds of being born and represented all that was good, and bad, about hard core, no-nonsense engineers. He regarded me with the same sort of steely stare – clearly a high tensile, chrome molybdenum one – as my tutors at Warrington Tech had done and which said: "Throw this oik out of my office now and let me get on with the job of manufacturing."

Reg, by contrast – and it was an interesting window on his status – insisted that I have my five minutes of fame and so Al Cave, Master of the BSA Manufacturing Universe, had to be polite to me – at least for a short time.

We then went to the production line for the BSA B.50, single cylinder machines. The motorcycles rolled down the track and the production workers assembled them quickly with a lovely banter going on. However, even to my untrained eye, I could not help but notice the poor fit of the parts for the bikes.

The wiring looms in particular had to be squashed around the handlebars as if they hadn't been designed for the bike. The workers were up to the task but what they were making was very second rate.

Reg took us up to the office section of the factory, through the BSA Quality Control area and this was, in some ways, the most interesting part of the whole visit. In a small office sat Cyril Halliburn, another grey haired, blue suited and archetypal Midlands engineer.

As I have said, Reg was as cute a PR man as I have ever seen and he coaxed Cyril and me on to what he knew was going to be common ground. In front of Cyril, Reg asked me about my racing – as usual I had been somewhat economical regarding the truth in terms of my success – and when we got on to this subject, Cyril's eyes lit up.

Later, I discovered that he had been responsible for the BSA Gold Stars which had raced so successfully on the beaches at Daytona and now, like many engineers in the bike world, all that he wanted to do was play with race bikes again.

We got on well instantly and after ten minutes Cyril was smiling and I felt that I had made a new friend at BSA. How important this was later to be, I had no idea at the time.

Next to Cyril's department was the huge "Tubes In" bay and this gave an indication of what a vast enterprise BSA was. Stacked up in enormous piles were miles of steel tubing, ready to be sent to the frame production area of the factory to make the whole range of BSA bikes.

We walked through the area and across the car park to the temporary buildings which had been tacked on to the old office area at Armoury Road. Again, the atmosphere was happy and positive. I am sure that no-one had the slightest inclination of who I was, and wouldn't have cared for that matter if they had known, so what I saw was very much the reality of BSA.

We went through to temporary, permanent in reality, buildings and finally ended up in the private office of Lionel Jofeh, the then Managing Director of BSA Motorcycles. Again, with the benefit of hindsight, Reg's status was clear. On one side of the table was the head of one of the world's great motorcycling companies. Sat on the other, was a long haired teenager wearing a pair of not too pristine trousers, a fluorescent pink shirt and a velvet tie adorned with pretty little flowers. They were nice flowers though.

In between us was Reg - who introduced me as minor royalty. No doubt Mr. Jofeh thought that it was a case of a chimpanzee with a machine gun, as far as me having access to the media when I really should have been cleaning toilets or brushing up swarf on the BSA factory floor. By contrast, Reg simply made the best of the situation as it existed. My writing was popular and I had influence, so I was going to be courted to the best of his ability – and that was that.

For my part, I wasn't worried or overawed at the thought of meeting Mr. Jofeh. As I have already said - I was, and I remain, my readers so I simply asked the questions they would have asked had they been sitting where I was.

Meanwhile, Mr. Jofeh's PA floated silently in and offered us tiny glasses of sherry in engraved silver goblets which had been made by some unknown department at BSA. What wouldn't I give for that set now?

So, we sat and talked about bikes and I told Mr. Jofeh, politely but firmly, that he did not understand the realities of choosing to buy a BSA when you could get a much better Honda for less money.

I then went on to explain to him that every month we received dozens of letters from upset BSA owners whose bikes had blown up or burst into flames or self-destructed in some other way and that things had to be fixed – and soon too.

Finally, I told him that BSA must make all their bikes electric start and with modern overhead cam engines. If they did this, then the immense amount of residual goodwill still left for the marque would carry them through.

Mr. Jofeh didn't quite pat me on the head and give me a lollipop – but it was a near run thing. After ten minutes, his PA floated soundlessly into the room and reminded the great man of his next appointment and I was ushered out of the office and taken for lunch.

Reg knew that things hadn't gone at all well and, although I didn't understand it at the time, was about to fall back on the golden key which is carried in the pocket of every great PR Officer: bribery.

I went back home, First Class again, and got out the Adler. The next column was not complimentary to either BSA or Lionel Jofeh – all the more so because even I, who knew very little about anything, could see the potential at BSA and I was spitting tacks that the Japanese were being allowed to beat the best of Britain without even a token resistance.

Just how badly things were going wrong was revealed by a huge loss in 1970. From making £3.5 million surplus in 1960, trading had been declining at such a rate that the books showed a loss of £8.5 million in 1970. This was a truly immense sum of money – equating to around £100 million in today's terms.

★★★

If things were looking very dodgy for BSA, the sun was really shining on me at S.Kaths. At the end of my first year, I had submitted an essay on Chaucer. I had been careful to make use of the work I had been doing on my history course and tie it in with the Canterbury Tales option I had chosen in English. The result of welding the content of the two courses together was an A minus grade.

This was a good – an almost impossibly good – result and it altered my whole attitude. Gone were those terrible days of self-doubt where I thought that every morning I was going to be called in and sacked. Now, I was standing on the podium as far as English grades were concerned.

However, like all determined competitors, the A minus grade also caused me a lot of concern. If I could get an A minus why not a straight A? From now on, every piece of work would be submitted with the aim of standing on the top step of the podium.

I was helped in this ambition by Dr. Barnes, a kind, gentle, warm, smiling academic who was Head of the English Department at S.Kaths and one of the country's leading experts on Dickens. I deliberately chose the Dickens' options and Dr. Barnes worked through my essays in the same way as Geoff Leyland had done in my first days at College, unpicking them word by word and line by line – challenging, questioning and praising in equal proportions. The quality of the education I was receiving was incredibly good and, slowly, my thinking, writing and analysis improved and A grades became the norm.

***

Things were improving financially too. With cheques arriving regularly from America, I was able to upgrade my car to what actually proved to be two cars for the price of one. These days, life is constrained and controlled to a very sad degree but there is no argument that there were some very interesting characters about in the early 1970s – and ones who only had the very loosest idea of the truth.

My Dad had been offered one of the last Ford Anglias to be made - a midnight blue, Deluxe model with very low mileage. The price was eye-watering, for me, at £250 but the American cheques kept converting to £30 and £40 pay outs and so it wasn't impossible.

For once, my Dad had done really well so I had a brief look at the car, paid £250 in cash, and drove home as if I had just bought James Bond's Aston Martin DB5.

It was later that night that I noticed something odd as the car stood under the fluorescent street light outside our house. Although the paint work was immaculate, the midnight blue of the rear of the car looked quite different from the midnight blue of the front of the Anglia. How odd was that?

The following day, I started to poke around just behind the back edge of the door. There, running right round the car, was a lovely line of extremely neat weld where the rear of one Anglia had been stitched on to the front of a different car.

There was no use in complaining because I had signed the much loved, "Bought as seen, tried and approved…" receipt but even so, I was disappointed.

Then I stood back and had a long think. The car was very low mileage with less than 15,000 miles showing on the odometer. The paint was better than anything Ford ever produced and whoever had welded the two parts of the car together was no amateur.

I got in and set off to pick up my girlfriend from Chester. Motorcyclists are much more surface conscious than car drivers since the consequences of not feeling a bit of slippery road is potentially lethal on a bike – particularly before the advent of modern, high grip tyres.

I drove the Anglia using just my finger tips on the steering wheel and tried to feel for problems. The car pulled just a tiny bit to the right – and it really was miniscule – but, other than that, it was as sweet as a brand new vehicle. The motor was tight and lively – at least for a 997cc push-rod engine – and the gearshift was precise and light.

Inside, the car was like new and it even had a radio! If it was stitched together, so what? I knew plenty of welders who could join two sections of car so that the finished product would be as strong as anything which rolled off the Ford production line. So I wound the windows down, stuck my elbow out in the breeze and was a happy boy. Things were going splendidly well.

My new found fortune sometimes had unintended consequences. First, Geoff Leyland saw the Anglia and wanted to know how a student had a more modern, and better, car than a lecturer so that weekend we scoured the Liverpool Echo and hunted down a new set of wheels for him.

It was a slightly strained experience. As I said, we were never close but I felt that I owed him a huge amount and so we were, out of need, forced to be together socially. I found a nice Rover for him, haggled the vendor into the ground so the price was really good, and we both went away happy.

There was another interesting experience which came from having plenty of money. At the time, Liverpool had a number of fine theatres. There was the Everyman, located next to the Catholic Cathedral. I liked this theatre a lot. It was a joke, but a true one, that you could sometimes see the stars through the roof, and the seating was rather ethnic, but it produced good plays with real heart. I didn't much care for their "Agitprop" productions but when they put on any performance it was always done with passion and energy. We had a good time at the Everyman.

Down in Liverpool City Centre was the very upmarket Playhouse – a real, national class theatre with a serious reputation and admission prices to match.

When students did venture down to the Playhouse, they sat in the very cheapest seats in the "Gods", right in the top of the theatre, and looked down at their betters far below.

The best seats in the house were located in the Dress Circle. This is the slightly raised area which looks directly at the stage and offers superb viewing in every theatre – but particularly so in the Playhouse.

From our posh seats, we watched Shakespeare's Twelfth Night. The play is one of my favourite comedies and on this occasion was absolutely superb because comedian Ken Dodd, who is a fine comic actor, played Malvolio to perfection. I sat holding the love of my life's hand and we were having a great time.

We noticed that one of our lecturers was in the stalls below us. During the interval when I went to get us both a drink, there in the Dress Circle bar was our tutor. He rounded on me in no uncertain terms. "What are you doing here? You're upstairs and this bar is reserved for the Dress Circle."

I gently, and with commendable courtesy, pointed out that whilst I was entitled to use the VIP bar he, sitting as he was in the stalls, wasn't. It was a wonderful moment.

It was a lovely experience and we both cherished it for many months – but there was more to come because I was about to be introduced to the noble art of bribery.

Mirror, Mirror on the Wall, Can I Really Ride – Or, Actually, Not At All?

THINGS had settled into a real pattern as we began our third year at College. There were some students who had lost their way because of pregnancies, moving to different areas or forgetting that they were there to do a job of work – not play about being children in adults' clothes – but not many.

This latter category, or soft sods as I usually referred to them, ended up re-sitting their final year and this is what they deserved. For the rest of us, it was no more complicated than hard work all day, every day. This is how it should have been: we weren't at S.Kaths on holiday.

I took History and Education seriously and didn't submit a piece of work that I hadn't given my best shot. However English was different and, ironically, my attitude then has helped me understand, and empathise with, the Grand Prix riders' view of racing ever since.

I was such a bad loser when it came to my English assignments that an A minus grade was a disaster and I walked the corridors in a cloud of utter despair. In fact, it was worse than this. Even if the work was marked at a straight A, I scrutinised every comment and pencil mark on the paper and cursed myself into the ground if I should have seen the mistake before my tutor.

This is why you will see a rider stand on the second step of the podium looking as if he has just finished last. Truly, second is first place in the losers' race and once you have tasted the champagne, metaphorical or actual, there is no going back.

***

Things were changing fast on the writing front too. Countrywide Publications had another magazine in their stable called Cycle Illustrated. This was more sport orientated than Motorcycle World so the bulk of my work was moved there. However, the Motorcycle World column was kept on and I was given a second slot in Cycle Illustrated. Now the chimpanzee had two machine guns!

The idea of spending my evenings in the Students Union bar, or partying, never crossed my mind. I was working hard at my College "day job" whilst writing as much as a full time, professional journalist and I also had a side line in selling Honda 50s to impecunious students! Sleeping and eating were non-productive activities so they could be skipped without any problem.

Clearly, the money was rolling in and there was sufficient to buy a really nice Bultaco Pursang motocross machine. The Bultaco was a Spanish made bike and I came to know it through one of the most brilliant riders never to win a World Championship – the Gloucester based Malcolm Davis, who was three times British Motocross Champion.

Malcolm was a complicated character. His father was a successful business-man as well as being a key figure in motorcycle sport's governing body, the ACU. He also had a slightly older brother, Tony, who was almost as good a rider as Malcolm. If he wasn't exactly born with a silver motorcycling spoon in his mouth there was definitely a very high quality stainless one there!

I mention Malcolm's background because, although it opened many doors for him, I also think that it was his biggest weakness as a racer. World Champions, and with his speed this is what Malcolm should have been on multiple occasions, have one common trait: they are appallingly bad losers. It is difficult to overstress just how much they want to win. They will put everything on the line for success – clearly their bodies, and even their life, but also their personal relationships, family and sponsors. Nothing is allowed to come between them and being the best.

Some of the great World Champions cover their rampant ambition with a veneer of courtesy and professionalism – in Malcolm's era, Belgian Roger de Coster was outstanding in this respect.

Others don't even bother to pretend that they are anything but psychopath-ically competitive. I have stood next to a World Champion in the gent's toilet and watched him checking how fast I could empty my bladder so that he could beat me. The idea of being second at anything never crosses these riders' minds.

Malcolm's problem was that he was prepared to ride hard and take all the risks to do his best - but not to put his life on the line, or go the 110% into those areas where lie the greatest dangers, as well as the highest rewards. He once actually told me this, after we had finished testing one of his bikes.

Sadly, for me personally and for motorcycle sport, Malcolm was an innocent victim in a road accident aged just 36 – after a racing career from which he escaped virtually uninjured.

Where Jeff Smith had been curt and dismissive, when I phoned Malcolm he could not have been more helpful – not to say kind. Without asking Señor Bulto's permission, or that of the British Bultaco importer, he agreed to let me ride his works bike one miserably wet and cold day on a track high up in the Cotswold Hills.

Malcolm was utterly sublime. He was one of the most skilful, almost balletic, riders I have ever seen and he floated around the flooded, slippery course as if it was a bone dry track in the middle of summer.

By contrast I slid and struggled all over the place but eventually managed to look something like competent and the photographer got his pics. I ended up in quite a bad way because of the cold, and getting soaked to the skin too, but the job was done and another exclusive was on its way to my employers in America.

I knew that I would warm up sooner or later but the key thing was that the story was in the bag. As each job went by, I was becoming more and more of a freelancer and this state of mind was to cause me some real trouble in the years to come – as well as keeping me employed!

Malcolm and I got on very well and a few weeks after the test, a works Bultaco cylinder barrel arrived at my Mum's house. The factory Bultacos were really close to the production machines which were sold to the ordinary rider. The main difference between the works machines and those you could buy was the cylinder barrel and exhaust.

Señor Bulto thought the world of Malcolm, so much so that he was almost a son to the Spaniard. Their closeness meant that there was always a surplus of factory bits in Malcolm's workshop. I never asked for the details, but my best bet is that one of those works barrels was "re-homed" in my direction and the next time I saw Malcolm I expressed my thanks with three, neatly folded, £10 notes. Nothing more was said - and I now had a really quick 250.

★★★

Little by little, I was coming to believe that I would never make a decent motocross rider, quite simply because I lacked the athleticism for this super tough, physical sport. However, my starting technique was getting better with every race and the Bultaco, with Malcolm's trick works barrel, really was a quick machine. I was winning the odd few pounds here and there and even an occasional 250 class victory where the conditions were stacked against pure grass track machines.

From being in a state of shock at the thought of winning ten shillings I was now getting used to collecting little brown envelopes for thirds and fourths and, once in a rare while, a win.

At this point, I need to digress and illustrate how the minds of the clubman racer and the GP star not only differ vastly - but come from completely different branches of the human race.

Carol and I once had lunch with six times World Champion Jim Redman – as modest, kind and lovely a Superstar as exists anywhere in the world. We were discussing - very loosely - great, compared with merely brilliant, riders and Jim gave us a rundown on the star riders present. "He's rubbish – he hardly won any GPs and he was lucky to even win one World Championship..." and so on.

To Jim, the idea of anyone riding regularly and not winning at least half a dozen GPs was about as likely as stumbling across a vegetarian tiger: inconceivable!

We pointed out that most riders never win anything, at any level, and as for victory in a GP – I had never even fantasised about this happening!

However my ambitions did stretch as far as actually taking home some prize money locally. So, when the word got around about a local rugby club who were running what was euphemistically called a "charity grass track", I smelled the potential to actually be paid to race.

The idea was that the club wanted a new pitch and so they were promoting a grass track to raise funds. It wasn't a million miles away from College so one evening I did a recce and was mightily impressed. The track was going to be laid out on a narrow, rough strip of ground next to the pitch and had two extremely tight corners at each end which the grass track bikes hated.

Above the track was a long, raised embankment for spectators.

When I got the entry form, instead of listing the prize money it just said: TBA – to be advised. I phoned the bloke running the event and he explained that if there was a good crowd then "Everyone will get a drink…" In fact, the bigger the spectator attendance, the better would be the prize money fund.

We arrived on Saturday morning and the sun was out which suited me perfectly. Whilst a good rider does well in any conditions, I need everything in my favour before I can turn in a decent performance. That's another key difference between a quality rider and an amateur.

Even before practice had started, the crowds rolled in and the burger vans were flat out. It was a lovely atmosphere with Mums and Dads and kids and dogs all sat along the banking, in addition to the normal crowd of motorcycle racing fans.

After the lunch-break, it was standing room only. There must have been 5,000 paying customers watching the show – when a typical grass track was doing very well if it attracted 500 spectators.

TBA – was looking like £15 for a win.

In fact, I did much better than expected. The Bultaco was flying and I was starting very well. I won my heat, the semi-final and final and by the time I had got changed and loaded the bike on to the trailer I could barely stop my face from splitting in half, I was smiling so much. As I noted, this is the difference between how easily an amateur clubman rider is pleased and what it takes to make a decent rider happy!

I almost skipped across to the organiser's car and I was all smiles - until he handed me an envelope containing two of the new, decimal pounds and a single 50p piece. £2.50 for winning the heat, semi and final: it was outrageous!

I complained and he simply smiled, explained that the Rugby club had faced a lot of unexpected expenses - but thanks for coming. It was another life lesson: read the small print.

I was about to learn a whole host of new lessons in terms of getting on in life – or not, in my case.

***

Teaching Practices dominated the whole academic year for all trainee teachers and they were hard work. These were the six week blocks where you went into school and taught under supervision.

Even writing and racing was put to the back of my mind for Teaching Practice because, if you wanted to do well, TP required total dedication - and a vast amount of effort. Every lesson we taught had to be written up before we got anywhere near the kids and then we had to evaluate and report on our efforts at the end of each day.

The work load was horrendous, especially in the third year where you were expected to be able to teach properly and up to professional standards. Students who were, "not quite doing as well as they might…" were called in for tutorials before they got on the coaches which delivered the baby teachers to their schools. These guidance sessions took place before dawn!

At the end of the day, the same students reported for a de-briefing. In between the evening and morning sessions, they did their lesson prep, analysis, marking and made visual aids. Sleeping and eating were considered to be unnecessary luxuries and distractions from duty.

Lads receiving "guidance" staggered around ashen faced, with black lined eyes. Girls missed their periods and lost weight by the ton. Yes, TP needed to be taken seriously!

I loved S.Kaths but TP was the one part of the Teacher Training course which I thought could have been done better. In my second year, I met a tearful girl in the corridor after she had just come out of a "guidance" tutorial. I didn't know her particularly well, or like her for that matter, but I did know that she was a good, solid, middle of the road student who had the misfortune to be in a very tough school and so was having a bad time.

She was really struggling with a difficult, bottom set English class, so I wrote four lessons for her which I was certain would work. They weren't great pieces of education but I knew that if she read a certain bit of prose to the kids, and followed that with a particular task for them to do, then the lessons would chuff along okay.

My lessons just gave her a break sufficient to catch her breath, and then she was fine.

What I did was absolutely against S.Kath's policy. The college would have nothing to do with what the tutors sneeringly called, "Tips for Teachers."

The mantra was that no-one was going to help when you were a professional teacher so you had better learn how to cope before you qualified. In theory, this was fine but I still think that the odd spoonful of kindness to get a well-intentioned student through a difficult time wouldn't have gone amiss.

In my case, I had a decent first year TP, a better one in the second year and had set my heart and mind on achieving a Distinction – the highest grade - for my final Practice. This ambition was to cause me considerable problems.

Things went wrong right from the start. When I was introduced to the teacher who was supervising my Teaching Practice, he was all smiles until I quite calmly informed him that there could only be one acceptable result for me from this TP – and that was a Distinction. Anything else was a failure in my eyes. Oh yes, the beloved mantra of: "Second is first in the losers' race…" reared its smiling head again!

He was horrified and explained that students came to his school, which had nationally renowned standards, and were grateful just to pass. I replied that "just passing" was for losers and it was a Distinction or nothing for me. As icicles formed on the window panes, and the snow started falling steadily in the staff room, I could tell that this wasn't the best of starts for my TP.

To be honest, I didn't much care. I worked like I had never worked before, taught well and the job was progressing very nicely.

After three weeks, I was summoned to see the Head Teacher and asked why I wasn't socialising with the school's staff. I explained that I was here to teach, and get a Distinction, not to make friends. Oh dear, oh dear, oh dear. That was the naughty freelancer rather than the team player speaking yet again.

The top few per cent of students, who were in the running for a Distinction, and the bottom few, who were heading for a fail, were always judged by an External Assessor.

I expected to be assessed but didn't get a good hand of cards when I was informed of the timing for the visit. The worst age group to teach in any Secondary School are the thirteen and fourteen year olds. The hormones are raging and, in a mixed sex class, there is usually only one thing dominating all the students' thinking – and for sixty seconds in every minute too!

I was called in to meet the External Assessor and the rest of assessment team – and I almost walked out there and then. There was the school's Head Teacher, whom I had already crossed over my unwillingness to socialise; the supervising teacher – the one I had sorted out on my first visit; the school's Head of Department; my TP Tutor, who was a scientist and who I had barely seen for six weeks, and, with a roll of drums which bounced around my head, the Head of the Education Department at S.Kaths – the very man whose tutor group I had left at the end of my first year in College.

They went through my proposed lesson, molecule by molecule. It was a 35 minute, single period and I was teaching about diet in the 14th Century. A single period means that you really do have to get on with the job because there is no time to correct mistakes. Everything has to go right from the moment the starter drops the flag!

The lesson wasn't a brilliant, world beating piece of education but it was sound, well thought out and thoroughly prepared. I should have been in with a decent chance.

The first problem was that because the assessment team had kept me talking I was late into the class. For all lessons, but particularly so when you are on show, it is essential to be in the classroom long before the first student is even in sight on the horizon. Everything needs to be prepared, relaxed and calm if you are to stand any chance of success.

By contrast when I ran, panting, into the classroom the kids were already climbing up the walls, having been left totally unsupervised for five minutes, and I was chasing the game right from the outset.

The whole of the assessment team filed in with grim faces, sat right across the back of the classroom in a line - and got out their notebooks.

Somehow, I dragged the lesson back on course until the last ten minutes. One of the lads was flirting with the girl in the desk in front of him. They passed notes to and fro and she turned round and smiled encouragingly: lucky boy!

The smart thing to do in these situations is to pretend that you haven't seen what is happening and hope that it just peters out. However, the note passing increased as the lesson went on, as did the giggles, so it was a lose/lose situation. I was either dead for allowing the kids to flirt instead of working, or I had to intervene and risk what was going to happen next.

I walked up to the desk of the lad who was playing the male part in the mating ritual, stopped, and in a voice heavy with a barely concealed death threat said: "Get on with your work – now!" The kid looked up at me, saw the Angel of Wrath in my eyes, and started writing with a real sense of commitment! Sensitive child that he was, he read my mind with complete accuracy!

Afterwards, I was told to dismiss the class and report back to the assessment team for a de-briefing. I was given about ten seconds to sit down and then the Head Honcho from S.Kaths said: "We won't need to detain you long Mr. Melling. Any student who proffers verbal violence to a child will never make an outstanding teacher."

I never even tried to defend myself. I had threatened the kid with the tone of my voice and it didn't matter why. There was no excuse and that was three years of hard work down the drain because a thirteen year old with raging hormones had done what puberty told him to do. Racing was much easier and vastly purer.

With TP over, and I knew that I had blown my Distinction, I settled down to academic work and writing. It was one of the happiest times in my life. I wrote, for College and for Countrywide Publications in roughly equal amounts, made love with the girl I worshipped and sat with her under a soft, summer sun in Princes Park and fed the ducks as "Hey Jude" banged out from someone's cassette tape recorder. Life was perfect in every way.

However, Fate was not happy with this period of contentment because I was about to find out, once and for all, whether I was ever going to be any good as a motocross racer.

★★★

I liked Reg Dancer tremendously and admired his skill as a Public Relations Officer. In fact, he was one of the best PR men I have ever worked with. I think it is fair to say that Reg also had a soft spot for me. Following the Jofeh visit, Reg kept in contact with me informally – and my attitude towards BSA in my columns softened.

The one thing I wanted from BSA was the only thing Reg couldn't deliver. My dream was to have a B.50MX motocross bike on test. The B.50 was the racing version of three 500cc, single cylinder bikes which BSA made and it was, by far and away, the best of the trio. In fact, the two road bikes were dreadful whereas the works versions of the B.50 had won Grands Prix just two years earlier.

At the time, very few bike journalists raced and so Reg didn't have a B.50MX on his test fleet – not that this put me off pestering him for a bike.

I had virtually given up any hope of getting a B.50 when my Mum took a phone call from BSA, asking me to collect a parcel which would be delivered to Warrington's Bank Quay Station in a couple of days.

After TP third year students were expected to work independently, and prepare for our Finals, so disappearing from College for the day was no problem.

Whatever the faults with British Rail, and there were many, the staff at the stations really did try to be helpful – and had the time to be so. I had briefed everyone about this exciting parcel coming from BSA and when the Birmingham train came to a halt, three of us leapt into the guard's van and there was a huge, heavy duty, brown cardboard box. It was a heck of a weight but we huffed and puffed and eventually off-loaded it onto the platform.

The guard was fully supportive of our efforts, as was the driver who smiled encouragement to us and held the train until we were finished.

One of the British Rail staff got out a Stanley Knife and we began carefully cutting the sides of the box away until, like some wonderful mythical creature breaking free from its egg, the most incredible motorcycle in the world appeared.

Even today I can remember my amazement that anyone could make a motorcycle this beautiful, for what Reg had delivered was not a standard B.50MX but the last works bike the factory ever produced.

The reasons for the B.50 being what it was were complicated. First and foremost, Reg liked me. Without this warmth of relationship, the whole job would have been still born.

Reg had persuaded, and/or leaned on, the BSA works manager, Al Cave, to approve the project.

Finally, I had made the right impression on Cyril Halliburn who had a tiny workshop at BSA where the bike could be built. Cyril also had two clever,

116

race inclined, fitters in John Kay and Martin Russell who were able to do the job.

The sum of all these parts meant that it was possible to build a very special bike - if everyone involved was inclined to let this happen, which they were.

Martin later described my B.50 as an "Official Foreigner" – a legally built bike but using all the techniques normally applied to a private project.

At the heart of the bike was a hand-built B.50 engine which gave an honest 32hp. This was good power for a B.50 and about right for the second tier works engines. Cyril had the engine powder coated in a deep, glistening black and also had the engine fins cut back just like the works machines. It was gorgeous!

The frame of the bike had been lightened and chrome plated, again just like the works machines, and the hubs had been machined to save weight. Topping off the package was a tiny, works fuel tank.

Without a word of exaggeration, I wanted to get undressed and make love to the bike there and then on the platform – it was so beautiful.

I was grateful to Reg for getting the bike built and I wrote personal letters of thanks to him, Al Cave and Cyril Halliburn. In some ways, I felt a real cheat because a factory with such enormous status as BSA had built a bike for me - a clubman racer of no great merit – and even then, not because of any riding ability I had but only through the power of my writing. This was a company which had won everything in the motocross world and then they ended up with me. I found the poignancy of the situation very touching.

I later mentioned this to Cyril and he smiled and said: "We really like helping you. You love racing, ride as well as you can and do a good job for BSA. What more can we ask?

"You're also the only thing we have left - so get racing!"

So I did.

The bike's performance matched it looks – it was an absolute rocket ship and had faultless handling. All this was to lead directly to a very important moment in my life. All clubmen racers, and particularly so if they have a little bit of success, harbour the dream that if only they had the same quality of bikes as the top riders they would be just as good.

I was far less inclined to believe that a trophy in a local race meant anything because I knew that I wasn't physically good enough for motocross but even so, there was still that little, nagging doubt. If only I had a GP winning bike then just maybe...

The B.50 showed me that there wasn't a maybe, not then - not ever. Yes, I had the bike but I still couldn't do anything with it of any value. I did win a few, low status amateur races but it was truly a case of so what?

The beautiful B.50 gave me the chance to show the world that I could ride – and proved to me that I couldn't! It was a tough lesson for a wannabee clubman racer.

However, the B.50 did give me one lovely present and again, it has been an immense help in understanding how GP riders think and react to life. It is one of the reasons why I get on so well with Superstar riders. I never, ever, pretend to be within a light year of their skill level – to do so is professional suicide – but I can, just about, empathise with them and how they feel.

My favourite grass track of the year was the one organised by the Fleetwood and District MCC at Fluke Hall, which is on the outskirts of a little village called Pilling, near to Fleetwood.

Pilling has been inhabited since Neolithic times when it was a useful bit of slightly higher ground between the sea of Morecambe Bay and the surrounding marshes. This local history and geography is important to the story.

The grass track was held at Fluke Hall and consisted of two long straights joined by a pair of very tight, hairpin bends. All the way down the right-hand side of the track was a huge sea wall which was essential, to keep the high tides of Morecambe Bay from inundating the village.

Along this sea wall sat thousands and thousands of spectators, in what must have been the biggest natural grandstand in grass track racing.

Finally the track was made up of a heavy, sandy loam which provided superb grip for a knobbly motocross rear tyre and was perfect for lightning starts.

The sun was shining, my lovely girlfriend was all smiles and practice went well. I qualified for the final and made sure that I got into the collecting box, where the riders are gathered before the next race, well before anyone else. This meant that when we were allowed on to the track, I would be first to the start line and therefore have the choice of which position to take. For me, there was only one place to be and that was on the far left hand side, on the inside of the track, right next to the marker pegs.

As always, I had studied the starts before the 500cc final and so I knew that the starter was confident and quick. We would roll up to the line, come to a halt and then the starting elastic would fly back and we would be away. There would be no hesitation or messing about.

On the start line I leaned forward, right over the front wheel of the BSA to stop the bike doing a wheelie, revved the engine hard and almost climbed inside the release pin in the centre of the elastic I was concentrating so hard. The pin moved by half a hair's breadth and I dropped the clutch and kept my weight well forward. The lovely BSA engine snarled and then, it was like being launched from the barrel of a gun because nothing in the world leaves the start line like a good B.50.

I had a good bike's length lead into the first corner and kept the throttle pinned wide open until it was absolutely impossible to stop the bike - then braked as hard as I could and threw the BSA sideways. The super grippy loam let the tyres bite and I got away with what would have been a certain crash on any other surface.

Behind me eleven roaring, snarling grass bikes struggled to slow down and then accelerate out of the tight bend.

Going into the second corner, a rider on a Jawa came tearing past in a massive plume of grass and dirt but, again, I didn't touch the brakes until way past the point where a crash was guaranteed. Then I laid the BSA down, until the engine case dragged on the ground and accelerated away.

By lap two, the other eleven grass bikes were riding all over each other as they battled for track position on the tight corners like killer whales chasing a sea lion. We used to have a lovely picture of me on the BSA coming out of the final corner with a solid wall of grass track bikes filling the whole track behind me it was that close.

The sprint from the last corner to the finishing line was desperate. It was not skilled or sophisticated riding on my part. I simply stretched the throttle cable to breaking point and hung on. If the bike blew up, then this was going to be a disaster - but I had to win.

The B.50 leapt away and the front wheel came up as the acceleration kicked in. I didn't even try to correct the wheelie but just held on and from the corner of my eye I could see the Jawa, which had been chasing me, gaining ground all the time.

Another bike's length and I would have been second but that few feet wasn't there, so I won. The feeling was fantastic.

What was almost more remarkable was the track invasion which followed. Spectators swarmed on to the course and there were hand-shakes and pats on the back – man hugs hadn't been invented at the time! I was forced to stop the bike for fear of running over one of my newly created fans. It was an intoxicating few minutes.

Later, a handful of people came to ask for my autograph which was also a new experience.

My visit to the world of stardom was a brief one, but very enjoyable, and most instructive: so this is what it must feel like to be famous!

It was a wonderful day but just around the next bend, this time in life not a grass track, there was a major set of cross roads – and the routes split in many different directions.

1 2

Cross Roads

I once read a book about the Mafia and, apparently, one of their favourite adages is, or was: "Never complain – never explain."

I like the idea and I have a lot of sympathy with it.

Currently, with the active support of the media, it seems that everyone has some reason why they should receive special attention/care/support/a grant/privileged job access or whatever. If you are not part of some oppressed minority then you really aren't in the game.

For my part, I believe in self-determination. Get stuck in, work hard and take responsibility for what happens without trying to off-load the results on to someone else if things go wrong.

This is why I am not bitter, or even regretful, over what happened next. I played the hands of cards Fate gave me – and did the best that I could with the knowledge and emotions I had at the time. Truly: Wyrd bið ful aræd.

Dr. Barnes called me into his study and said that he wasn't allowed to reveal my results but he could say that I had done well. That meant only one thing because we both wanted a Distinction.

I had toiled night and day, for two years, on my English work and the lowest grade I achieved was an A minus, so anything less than a distinction would have been a disaster – and an A grade one too!

Dr. Barnes also asked me to meet a colleague of his who was the Head Teacher in an outstanding Primary School. The Head was looking for a newly qualified teacher to develop an exciting new programme of language and literature, and he would like to meet me.

Although it was a Primary School, I had done one year of Primary Education in my three year course at S.Kaths so I felt sure that I could manage the work comfortably and with great pleasure.

Today there are formal, monitored procedures which have to be followed before anyone is appointed to a job but things were very different in the 1970s. A smiling school secretary took me through to meet the Head in an unusually, for a Primary school, large office. However, this was no ordinary Head Teacher.

He radiated confidence and enthusiasm and was very passionate about children's literature.

We soon got on to "Frank" terms and it was about this time that I realised I had just been appointed as his new teacher!

We walked down a corridor buzzing with happy kids, chatting, actively working together, sharing and learning. It was the text book perfect Primary school.

At the end of the corridor was a large classroom full of ten year olds – Third Year Juniors in old currency, now re-named Year 5. We walked in and the class all stood immediately and dutifully chanted: "Good Morning Mr. Smith."

Mr. Smith said: "Good Morning Children. This is Mr. Melling who is coming to teach you in September."

The kids squealed with delight and beamed at their new teacher. I smiled in return - but only with my face and not my heart. These lovely, lovely kids wanting to be taught by me: I felt humbled and embarrassed.

It was approaching break-time and "Mr. Smith" took me to the staffroom to meet the other teachers. It was a large Primary school and so there were a lot of them in the staffroom. A big, fat, jolly lady said: "There's always room for one more on the Skylark…" and playfully shoved a younger lady teacher out of the way so I could sit on one of the big couches.

"Here you are Frank, here's a space for you and I'll bet you'll want to bring in your own mug and there's Mr. Pig where we put our tea money," pointing to a large, and inevitably happy looking, pottery pig, "And do you like football? Because we really want a First Year football team next year and it would be so good if you could take them after school."

Everyone was kind, smiling, encouraging, enthusiastic and this was such a good, mutually supportive team - that I wanted to shrivel up and die on the spot.

I was polite, and I smiled too, but I knew that I couldn't come into this wonderful school, with its all-embracing staff and smiling children, without a lifetime commitment - and in truth I wasn't certain. For sure, this was not a place where the freelancer would thrive or even be welcome. It was going to be all or nothing.

For better or for worse, the call of the recidivist freelancer – the same one who slept on the deck of the King Orry to see the TT; rode through Europe navigating with a page torn from an Atlas and really did write to fourteen magazines asking for a job - was too strong.

Like the hard core junkie that I was I promised myself, and every God in the Multiverse, that after just one more column, one more bike test, one last exclusive I would turn my back on writing. Just one more and then I would grow up and settle down.

So I walked out past the lovely secretary and across the sunny car park, marked out so neatly for PE, and drove away from what would have been the start of a wonderful, fulfilling and, I feel certain, successful career in Primary Education.

Back at College, another door opened momentarily – and then closed. One of my lecturers stopped me in the corridor and congratulated me on how well I had done with my English work. He had never taught me, so I was grateful for the compliment. He said that I should really think about a career in university and that he would help me.

He would speak to his old university and get them to accept my teaching qualification in lieu of the first two years of an English Honours degree and then I could do one more year and move on to a Masters and then, who knows what?

The truth is that I was too frightened to accept the challenge. I had already successfully travelled a vast distance from a Council House, scrap metal burning and the Post Office but this next step was just too much. I didn't know anyone socially who had been to a good university and studied, and so I doubted myself and my ability.

As for a Masters' degree, it might as well have been a TV licence on the planet Zog. I had never even thought about teaching in a university so completely incredible was the idea.

With a different social background, or friends who knew about Oxbridge and who had careers in the top flight professions, then perhaps things would have been different and maybe better. But I didn't have any of those so I ran away, for fear of failure. As I did, I felt a real sense of shame at my cowardice.

In fact, what I did was almost nothing – but an awful lot of nothing. I didn't have a conventional job but I was working like a demented thing, writing – and the money was pouring in.

***

In those lovely, pre-internet days the world was a much bigger place than it is now so I sent a few of my old articles to Motorcyclist Illustrated – a British magazine which I much admired.

MCI was a very thoughtful, and even somewhat literary, magazine aimed at the top drawer of motorcyclists. The editor was a highly intelligent, witty and laid back gentleman – and I use the latter word advisedly in this case – called John McDermott.

We immediately struck up a rapport and John took my work to the next level. Much as I worshipped the Americans for all they had done for me, it was essential that the stories I submitted were absolutely ready to roll straight on to the page because they invariably appeared just as I wrote them. This wasn't a problem because I took as much care with them as I did with my English essays but with John, things were better. With infinite subtlety, he honed the pieces so that they were just that tiny bit tighter and crisper- but still retained the Frank Melling style.

Except that they weren't Frank Melling at all now, but were Paul Vilar. For fear of an American version of Frank Melling asking his Auntie Edie to bring back some British motorcycling magazines for him – only to find near identical pieces in both Cycle Illustrated and Motorcyclist Illustrated under the same name – I wrote under the Paul Vilar brand.

What happened was almost identical to America. The articles attracted a lot of fan mail and John soon asked me to write a monthly column and this was popular too. There was a wonderful irony to this situation because Jeff Smith had previously "written" the off-road column for MCI. Now he was in Canada and I had taken his position. You may imagine how I felt.

Things were really busy. I was writing two columns for America, one for Britain and submitting two bike tests a month as well – plus the re-writes for MCI. Smoke was coming off the little Adler some days, I was writing so much!

I had chosen the path of the freelance writer and things were going very well – so far.

***

It was happy days at BSA too. I had become a real insider and remained so until the day that the factory closed.

BSA was a huge works and there were a lot of nooks and crannies and secret cupboards hidden away. Every couple of months, I would take the B.50 back to the BSA to be refreshed and some previously hidden bits would find their way on to the bike. First, it was a magnesium brake plate, then a few titanium nuts and bolts, followed by some magnesium fork sliders and eventually a lightweight frame.

I always thanked Cyril and the fitters for their support and never took their help for granted because I was truly grateful.

Towards the end of BSA, Cyril allowed the fitters to put a special cam into my engine. It was from the speedway engine he was developing. It was a great privilege to be given a part which Cyril had personally developed and I felt very honoured.

However, it was the speedway bike which got me into Cyril's bad books and, except for not being able to walk to the "Naughty Step" at Armoury Road, because I had no bottoms in my shoes, I would have probably been sent there for a week.

By 1972, BSA was in deep, deep trouble and things were happening at the factory that would have been unthinkable only two years before.

It had always been BSA policy not to sell engines to anyone outside the company but now, every potential source of income was being hunted down.

One of the ideas was to manufacture both a complete BSA speedway bike, ready to race, and also sell engines to riders.

The competition shop had closed the year before but Cyril still had my B.50, and this was well known in the factory because it was the only race bike still at

BSA. As I have mentioned, he also had two very capable fitters, a tiny workshop plus the ability to get things done within the factory as "Official Foreigners." It wasn't the best way to do experimental engineering but it was better than nothing – and BSA had almost zero at the time.

Cyril hatched the idea of taking the B.50 motocross motor and turning it into a speedway engine. From the BSA management's point of view, the idea had the dual benefits of being an extremely cheap project and one that might well have shown some income very quickly.

Theoretically at least, the concept looked to be quite practical. The very best B.50 motocross engines were giving around 39bhp whilst the B.50 road racer, ridden by Bob Heath, was up to nearly 45bhp - both running on 5 star (101 octane) pump petrol.

The Czechoslovakian Jawa engines, which were the standard equipment at the time for professional speedway racers, produced around 50bhp on methanol. Since methanol offered around 25% increase in power over petrol it looked, on paper at least, as if the BSA motor would be a sound proposition.

The idea was that standard B.50 castings would be used for the cylinder barrel, head and rocker box and B.50 internals would also be employed. Only the crankcases would be new since speedway engines had no need of a gearbox and a conventional clutch.

The bikes were made in the tiny bay which comprised Cyril's workshop, right next to his office. Martin Russell and John Kay, who built my B.50, were more than capable of putting together what was a very simple race engine.

One day, I was summoned to meet Reg Dancer and Alistair Cave. Reg was, as always, all smiles where Mr. Cave looked as stern and tough as he usually did – and was.

I had seen the BSA speedway bike on a number of occasions and was now asked for my opinion of its sales prospects. The bottom line was that Reg and Mr. Cave wanted a cast iron assurance that they would sell a thousand engines before the project was started. The sting in the tail was that they intended to stop development dead once the engine was made and not to support any riders racing the BSA engines after they had purchased them.

Respectfully, but forcefully, I tried to explain two things. First, that 1,000 speedway engines was a huge number for the market to absorb, bearing in mind that none of the then Iron Curtain countries would purchase them because they were only allowed to buy the Czech made Jawas. Second, BSA couldn't just sell a racing engine and walk away from it: there had to be constant development and support.

Reg and Mr. Cave listened intently, asked lots of questions and took copious notes. Then I was released to go and play again.

Back in Quality Control I began badgering Cyril to let me ride the speedway bike, only to be met with a firm refusal. However, like all loving parents, Cyril eventually cracked and the bike was taken outside the factory. Now the black and white truth was that there was absolutely nowhere to ride a speedway bike in what was a densely packed industrial site but I didn't see this as a problem.

Added to this, I didn't have any leathers, helmet or boots - just a sports jacket and the much loved Hush Puppy suede shoes. But hey, this was the swinging '70s and these were minor details. So, Martin Russell cracked up the bike and, soon, the girls in the new office block were hanging out of the windows cheering and waving. And wasn't I a star works rider? And didn't my public demand a show? Well there was only one answer...

I thought the first run was pretty good. Wind the motor up to 4,000rpm, drop the clutch and the B.50 fairly tore alongside the factory wall with the noise from the straight through pipe ricocheting off the walls like anti-aircraft fire. Even on the brakeless speedway bike, there was plenty of room to slow down and return to Cyril.

Mr. Halliburn wanted me off the bike there and then but the girls wanted more. This time was going to be the big one. 6,000rpm and bang in the clutch. The back wheel spun for 10 yards and then hooked up and we tore down the factory wall in the best possible style. 60mph was there in three seconds and then...

Well, the "then" was a pallet truck full of castings. The driver took one look at the speedway bike bearing down on him and abandoned ship. I shut off, leaned forward and applied both Hush Puppies. My legs buckled, bits of shoe flew everywhere but I just, and only just, stopped.

Cyril was a lovely man - gentle, patient and kind. He looked at the flapping shoes for at least three seconds, said nothing and Martin returned the bike to Quality Control whilst I padded behind dejectedly. He didn't have to say anything. I could read his thoughts perfectly without a word being spoken. So ended my career as a BSA speedway test rider.

As for the B.50, Arthur Browning rode it at a test at Coventry Speedway and declared it a no-hoper. "It just wasn't fast enough. A two valve Jawa would p... all over it and using the same gearing as a Jawa, it wouldn't pull off the line. Professional riders would never have bought it even if it was half the price of a Jawa."

***

Back in my bedroom office I was becoming sadder by the day. I had a deep, soul scorching love for my girlfriend and, since she had started work as a teacher in the September, I missed her dreadfully. Instead of seeing her every day, and feeling her hand in mine, we saw little of each other during the week – and I ached.

College left a big hole in my life too and I was about to learn another important, but painful, lesson. I went back to S.Kaths and suddenly felt like a stranger. There were different notices on the boards, the floor polish had been changed, producing a strange new smell, and the students were unrecognisable.

I climbed the slatted wooden stairs to Dr. Barnes' study, saw he was in and knocked. He invited me in but explained that he was very busy with the new first year students and he hoped that I would understand if he didn't have much time to spend with me. The conversation was stiff and awkward. I was an ex-student and, rightly and properly, he was committed to his current intake.

After five minutes, I left and as I closed the door to his study behind me I had a last, brief glance in and saw the tutor who had done so much for me engrossed in his work, without as much as a glance to see me gone.

There was even more learning to come. As I went down the stairs, Geoff Leyland came bounding up. He nodded the briefest of acknowledgements and that was it: not even a pause to say hello or ask how I was doing.

In the 1950s, chip shops used to wrap their food in old copies of newspapers and there is a lovely expression from the newspaper business that you can sometimes hear even today. It's this: "Today's front page news is tomorrow's chip paper."

It's very true – and I had just discovered what being an out of date product felt like.

***

Where I wasn't out of date was at BSA and I was also becoming known at Triumph. This next story is absolutely true, and you may make of it what you will – but it is accurate and honestly reported.

Reg wanted me to write something nice about Triumph and so arranged for me to have a VIP tour of the factory. It wasn't quite the BSA1 taxi and silver goblets level but I did get to park outside the main entrance to the factory and there was a secretary waiting to greet me.

Opposite me, in the area reserved for Senior Management, was a small NSU Spyder car. It was either black or dark blue and I can remember clearly thinking what an ugly little thing it was. However, the Spyder did have one unique point: it was powered by a Wankel rotary engine and, at the time, BSA/Triumph were betting the family silver that a rotary engined motorcycle would be a world beater.

Out of the car climbed Doug Hele, the legendary Triumph development engineer. He didn't know who I was but, with the secretary smiling and hovering, recognised that I must have some status.

He limped across to see me, made some nominal greeting, and in the back of my car he noticed there was the lightweight B.50 frame I was taking to Cyril.

Although he was a very kind, warm and generous person Doug had a hard face – as if someone had machined his head from a block of high tensile steel.

He was curt and direct: "What's that? What's that frame you've got? Get it out!"

I explained about the B.50 and that I was taking it across to Cyril at Small

Heath. Doug was openly dismissive. BSA? Why should you be going to see that lot – and much more!

Incredible as it might seem, although BSA and Triumph were part of the same group, with the same shareholders, there was barely disguised animosity between the two factories and I often got the impression that BSA staff would rather co-operate with Honda than Triumph – and vice versa.

Doug was blunt: "I want that frame. Give it to me now."

This was a very, very bad place to be. Technically, it was my frame because I had bought it from a bloke who had acquired a job lot of works BSA parts when the Competition Department closed.

However, Cyril thought that he owned it after I had promised that I was taking the frame to him for my B.50.

Unfortunately, now it seemed that Doug had claimed it too.

In the end, I lied and played the Mr. Dancer card and said that Reg was responsible for the frame. Doug grunted and told me that I could have the frame back when I left - but he wanted it for the afternoon because he had an idea.

I felt quite a lot like Icarus flying awfully near to not one, but an awful lot of suns, any one of which could burn me badly. Being a favourite puppy at BSA was a wonderful thing – but it wasn't without its danger!

Many years later, Doug told me that he had taken my/Cyril's frame into the Triumph race shop and slotted a Tiger 100 engine into it. This hybrid then became the Triumph TR5T Adventurer – a very fine bike which, except for a shortage of funds, could have been a world beater.

Was my frame the egg which grew into the Adventurer? No-one will ever know for 101% certain but the following year, I came to know the Adventurer very well.

The Triumph factory was a wonderful place and had a tremendous sense of excitement about it. The workers were the highest paid in the whole area and carried themselves with great pride.

The original Triumph factory in the centre of Coventry had been bombed into extinction during the war and so the new Meriden works was very modern, compared with BSA at Armoury Road.

Maybe the pride was excessive, and mis-placed, because Honda were running rings round Triumph in terms of both the range and quality of the bikes they were selling and the other Japanese manufacturers weren't far behind. Worryingly, BMW's flat twins were first class too – and growing in number every year.

Even so, the Triumph workers were still ready to take on the world and there was a tremendous sense of self-confidence as I was introduced to the various sections of the factory.

Quality control was impressive – even if the bikes were woefully old fashioned compared with Honda. Every crankshaft was checked for accuracy of manufacture on a mercury gauge and the skilled craftsman monitoring the components was adamant that nothing that wasn't perfect would pass through his hands.

Ironically, any parts which were sub-standard went to Doug Hele for use on the works race bikes!

I was to see the very same gauge again a year later – but in hugely different circumstances.

Clearly, Reg had sent some form of memo down to Triumph because I was introduced to Triumph's chief designer Brian Jones but he was bored out of his mind at having to stop work, even for a few minutes, to meet a young journalist and had nothing of interest to say to me.

What did strike me was the tiny size of the Triumph design department. In the late 1960s, Honda had been employing over 200 staff just developing and building race bikes whereas at Triumph, the whole of the road motorcycle engineering team fitted into not much more than a couple of large rooms.

Doug Hele did truly remarkable things with bikes which should never have been capable of being raced but his department consisted of three staff and, as I have noted, a lot of rejected bits from the production line.

Things were truly dire.

★★★

The late summer drifted gently into Autumn, the racing season stopped and it was difficult to find bikes to test. The columns kept the money coming in but now I was spending more and more time entirely on my own and I was lonely. Remember, this was pre-internet and everyone either wrote or phoned and so some days, I would spend all day and neither see nor speak to anyone.

I never let a magazine down but it wasn't the most fun in the world for an active young man.

Then, after Christmas, I went back to the school of life again for another lesson. One of the lads I knew quite well from the race paddock, but who was much older than me, had a terrible nervous breakdown.

He bought a little dog and was arrested trying to scale the railings at Buckingham Palace in an attempt to present it to the Queen as a gift. There were also a number of other incidents which led to him being committed to a Mental Hospital.

I travelled to see him in the grim, Victorian building where he was incarcerated. The first part of my visit was interesting – not to say highly instructive. I parked the Anglia, went straight into the hospital and, fortunately, almost bumped into an immaculately dressed, silver haired doctor wearing a crisp white lab coat and carrying a clip board.

Taking note of his obvious status, I somewhat diffidently asked for directions to the ward where my friend was being detained. The doctor, clearly a Consultant, sighed, looked at his watch, then his clipboard and somewhat reluctantly proceeded to give me the most detailed instructions.

I followed them to the letter, or at least I thought that I did, but after half an hour of trekking along the corridors and through the gardens I was back to where I started. The Consultant had disappeared but there was a green clothed nurse so I approached him and explained about the directions I had been given.

The Nurse smiled kindly: "Ah yes, Mr. Reed. His daughter brings a fresh white coat for him every day, and he never wanders far, so we're happy for him to potter about and meet visitors.

"You didn't take any notice of him, did you?"

The nurse gave me directions and in a few minutes I was at the ward - but I wasn't prepared for what I was about to see. The walls were painted in an off-green gloss paint and there were smears of blood and mucous spattered everywhere.

Some patients were restrained in chairs whilst others sat in corners, crying and sucking their thumbs. Several were screaming loudly and one was, quite literally, trying to climb up the wall to reach a heavily barred window. It was a frightening scene and one which came as a devastating shock to me.

I have tried to be honest and as objective as I can be, writing from a personal point of view, so I need to go on record as stating that I never saw a nurse strike a patient. Equally, when a patient was told to sit down or shut up, the instructions were given as orders and there was no debate regarding whether they would be obeyed or not.

It would be easy, but wholly wrong, to be condemnatory of the nursing staff. They were faced with a lot extremely disturbed and, it seemed, potentially violent patients and the pressure on nurses must have been immense, continuous and relentless.

Today, there is much more humanity and kindness shown to those who have mental illness but it is wrong to re-write history and apply current standards to what happened in the past.

The lad I had come to visit sat against the wall in a high, plastic covered chair. His eyes were vacant and he stared into an unseen and unknowing distance. His face was puffed and ashen and he constantly rolled one hand into the other.

I pulled up a chair next to him and, after a few minutes, he recognised me. This is not quite accurate. He didn't so much recognise me, as realise that I was someone he should know. I tried to talk about bikes with him, the only thing we had in common, but his mind wandered constantly and he asked me whether the Queen was looking after the dog he had given to her.

I said that she was and that she thanked him for the gift. I don't know whether this was the right thing to do clinically but he smiled and seemed to be a little happier, so perhaps I was right to tell lies.

What I did know as fact was that I was way out of my depth – intellectually and emotionally – and that the experience was very, very stressful.

Even so, I felt a moral duty to visit again and continued to do so until he was discharged into the care of his family, after which I never saw him again. Later, I heard that he had committed suicide and that made me very sad.

The visits were hard work for me and they took all my self-discipline. I always came away under a huge cloud of despair at the sadness of the world. However, the visits made me hold a mirror up to my life and question what I was doing with it.

Damaged leg apart, I was super fit, bouncing with health and I had a works BSA in my garage. I had plenty of money and a top quality teaching qualification. Every night, a beautiful, intelligent girl phoned me to tell me how much she loved me. Yet, I was sat in my room moping round like a loser. It was time to get a grip on myself.

The world was moving fast around me. My girlfriend and I were engaged to be married and she was planning our future together with all the enthusiasm that only a young woman in love can. We were going to have a wonderful house, with cottage style furniture and then there would be two children – a boy and girl naturally – and we would live happily ever after until our grandchildren arrived.

I loved her with every ounce of my heart and soul, mind and body, so I agreed with everything. The whole world, except her Mum and Dad who felt that she was marrying vastly beneath her status, thought it was quite perfectly wonderful.

However, to buy a house we needed a mortgage and to get a mortgage I needed a real job with a real monthly income.

So, like a Jumbo Jet rolling down the runway towards take-off, Fate decreed that I should start looking for teaching jobs, security and the life of an adult.

This wasn't a trip to hell by any means. A huge, important part of me missed teaching and the sheer joy of education which, at its best, teaching really is. Another part looked forward to being with other people and seeing something other than my room.

But what followed was going to be another one of the real good news, bad news times of my life in so many ways. Fate was taking me up to the very top of the big dipper – and the ride down was going to be an enormous thrill.

13

The End of the Beginning – and the Beginning of the Start

IT wasn't hard to get a teaching job. I had a glowing reference from S.Kaths and I was articulate, enthusiastic and well presented. I was appointed to the first job I applied for, which was teaching English with a bit of History, in a rather swish Secondary School.

The Head Teacher was a bully and thought of himself as some medieval Baron. His toady was a servile, obsequious Deputy Head. Clearly, there was going to be what is now called "a clash of personalities" between us – and there was.

I worked hard, and taught well, but that wasn't enough. I was accused of showing a lack of respect. Hmmm… That was a first for me – not!

Things reached crisis point one lunch-hour. Newly qualified teachers were not allowed to leave the premises without a written note from the Deputy Head. Clearly, hell would freeze over before I would go grovelling for a pass out - so I didn't.

I had an article to send to Cycle Illustrated so I zipped down to the village, posted the package, had a really nice pie and returned in plenty of time to amble down to my class and be ready for action straight after lunch.

This was a perfectly sensible plan. What happened was very different. My absence had been "noted" and the Deputy Head was waiting for me as I walked in through the main doors. I was told that another teacher was taking my class and that I was to report to the Head – immediately.

What happened next was ludicrous. The Head, with his pet Goblin hovering next to him, raged and foamed and blasted me for my insolence and blatant disregard of school rules. I was not allowed to sit down but had to stand in front of the pair, like some naughty schoolboy who had just been caught with a bottle of cheap whisky and twenty Woodbines behind the school Gym.

I made a token explanation of my side of the story and then shut up and said nothing. Being savaged by bosses was hardly a new experience so, as always, everything just washed over me whilst I stood as an outside observer, in a lovely bubble of calm and peace.

In fact, things were far better than this. I was a successful journalist, and I had drunk sherry from silver goblets with the Managing Director of BSA, so being berated by a couple of teachers was having far less than no effect.

I was told that my future in the school was now in question. They were correct. It was in jeopardy – their jeopardy!

Without saying anything to anyone I applied for, and got, another teaching job.

What happened next was one of the most beautiful moments of my repeatedly-getting-sacked life.

I only had a temporary contract and this should have been really worrying me. At the end of term I was about to be made redundant and I would be left without any wages during the long, summer holiday. It was a big school and there were a couple of other teachers in the same position as me and none of us knew what was happening. Kind heads, with their teachers' best interests at heart, will give staff on temporary contracts a nod and a wink to let them know which way the wind is blowing. This way, those who are not going to be re-employed in September can get a job elsewhere and so make sure that they don't miss out on pay during the holidays. The Baron and his lackey were not kind.

On the very last hour of the final day of the school term I still didn't know, as far as they were concerned at least, if I had a job in September. The kids had gone home early and I was heading for sherry and cakes in the staffroom before we all disappeared for summer. En route, one of the other teachers said that I had been summoned to the Head's Office and that I should get down there forthwith – if not sooner.

"Who've you upset now, Frank?" was the smiling comment as I headed off to discover my fate.

Clearly, my reputation was growing by the day.

In the office was the Baron himself accompanied, as always, by his pet Goblin who was busy licking the floor whilst purring and stroking the Head's thinning hair. They announced that, despite my attitude, they were prepared to give me another chance and that I had better toe the line and sharpen up my ideas or there was going to be big trouble for me.

The Goblin then slid a large, manila binder across the desk containing my timetable for the next year, the clubs I was going to run, the out of school activities I was designated to support and much more. It was a wonderful, golden, full flavoured moment and, as the folder reached my side of the desk, I sat back in utter contentment, smiling the smile of the winner.

"Not for me guys…" I paused to savour the moment. "I've got another job – but do have a great time next term."

They quite literally screamed abuse and threats at me – very unprofessional, not to say extremely bad mannered – but by this time I was back in my bubble, floating above the room and watching the fun.

Out of a sense of courtesy, I let them rage for a couple of minutes then I picked up my briefcase, smiled and walked out. It was the action of the archetypal freelancer.

The new job I had taken was in a lovely Primary School with wonderful kids and a fantastic Head Teacher but before I could take up my post, there was a lot happening at BSA – and it was far from good.

***

Cyril phoned to say that the B.50 had been re-built again but when I collected it, could I make sure that I saw Reg Dancer because he wanted to speak with me?

I duly arrived at Armoury Road and parked my car and trailer against the fence, opposite the new office block whose cheering staff had nearly got me killed on the speedway bike.

By now, I knew this part of the factory well and so I took myself through the Tubes In bay and along to Cyril's office. He offered me a cup of coffee whilst he found Reg but said very little – not even about racing or what had been done to the bike. It was all rather odd and a bit strained. I had always been treated very much like a Labrador puppy by BSA and now I felt as if I had just made a mess on the carpet. Something was not right – and badly so.

Reg arrived, immaculate as ever, and he was all smiles. He had something really important to show me and he hoped that I would give the story maximum publicity in my columns.

We hurried through Production until we reached the Rocket 3 line. The Rocket 3 was BSA's flagship three cylinder, 750cc machine and it was the only bike the factory had which was even half competitive with Honda. Incredibly, but this is absolute fact, Doug Hele had designed the three cylinder engine in his own time, at home, drawing the engine in his front room.

It was a brilliant piece of engineering in that Doug, with real ingenuity, made a 740cc engine largely out of bits and pieces from the existing Triumph 500cc twins: hence the capacity of 740cc which came from one and a half Triumph Tiger 100 engines. As a cost saving exercise, it was outstanding.

Doug told me that he rolled into work with a finished product and Bert Hopwood, BSA Group's Head of Engineering, immediately took the project over and did his best to claim the credit for it.

Despite what you will read in a lot of books, there was no love lost between Hele and Hopwood so although the triple was definitely Doug's design we'll never know how much Hopwood helped, or even hindered, the project.

The triple was running in 1964 and could have been in production the year after, some four years before the 750cc four cylinder Honda, but internal arguments and turf wars within the BSA group meant that it didn't see the light of day until 1968 – and, by then, the bike was too late. It was also a styling mess which motorcyclists hated.

I have already mentioned the intense rivalry between BSA and Triumph and this led to one of most stupid errors ever – even by BSA Group standards.

Instead of standardising on a single, three cylinder machine for both BSA and Triumph there were two, quite different motorcycles for the two marques – and this pushed up the cost of production tremendously.

Even so, the BSA Rocket 3 was the better looking of the two triples and was selling very well, at a time when BSA needed every penny of revenue they could get.

This is why I was shocked by what Reg showed to me: the Rocket 3 production line was being broken and in its place was what can best be described as a child's tricycle with a 50cc engine.

This abomination was called the Ariel 3 and came about because of Jofeh's total lack of understanding of, and empathy with, motorcyclists. Jofeh's idea was that motorcyclists were out of date and yesterday's story. The way to make the BSA Group profitable was to develop a "product" which would sell high numbers of "units" to "buyers".

It didn't matter in the slightest degree what that product was. It could have been toothpaste, floor cleaner or dustbins – just as long as it was profitable. It also mattered not one iota whether the buyers wanted, or cared for, "the product" just as long as they paid.

If you had tried to design a business model less suited to the motorcycle market than Jofeh's concept, you would have failed.

BSA owned the Ariel name and it had proved to be a popular, and lucrative, marque for the group in the past. In fact, the brilliant Val Page designed the 250cc Ariel Arrow/Leader range of bikes. These had the lowest warranty claims of any BSA Group product and had been highly profitable.

BSA had halted production of the Arrows in 1965 and so the Ariel name was available for use in the biggest mistake ever made in the British motorcycle industry – the Ariel 3.

The idea behind the Ariel 3 was that millions of commuters would buy the tricycle and zip round town centres much more cheaply and easily than in a car. The front end of the trike leaned over in corners but you couldn't fall over as you could with a conventional motorcycle. To someone who didn't like bikes, or motorcyclists, this looked like a good idea.

It would take a book entirely of its own to describe how bad the Ariel 3 was. The little 50cc Dutch Anker engine which powered the trike, and that is using the word power in its loosest form, over heated and the Ariel's handling was scary over 25mph but, most of all, it looked silly – and I really do mean utterly ridiculous.

I can give you a first-hand example of what killed the Ariel 3 – and it wasn't just the engineering problems. It's worth remembering my record of riding any motorcycle of any kind under any conditions. I was a petrol engine junkie – and I remain so to this day.

Cyril's tiny work bay where the speedway bike and my B.50 motocrosser were built. This picture is probably unique because, strictly speaking, the bay was off limits for photography. I snapped the pic just for my own use when Cyril was distracted on the phone. I am glad that I did.

The truly lovely Cyril Halliburn — a brilliant engineer who had the misfortune to finish his career baby-sitting me. He must have wondered what he did wrong to deserve this!

I wanted to include this picture because it shows what a happy time I had at BSA and how kindly I was treated. Can you imagine a cheeky young man, in a sports jacket and suede shoes, being allowed to ride an un-braked speedway bike flat out through a factory now? The girls did cheer though!

Preparing for launch. Ten seconds later, this ended up in disgrace!

Eddie Crooks – naturally in a Crooks-Suzuki branded shirt - was not only a fantastic sponsor but also taught me so much in so many ways.

The TS250 Suzuki was brilliant after the disaster of the Fantic Caballero. I loved this bike and it made a lot of money for Eddie – which was great because it is why Ed sponsored me.

The Crooks - Suzuki PE250. The bike which almost convinced me that I could race a motorcycle. It was telling fibs!

Pressing on with the PE250 in the Welsh Two Day International. The Suz was brilliant in these fast, long distance enduros.

John Banks — riding as hard as ever, this time on his works BSA.
John had only two speeds. Parked in the paddock and absolutely flat out.

I am trying, and failing, to look competent here on the works Cheney.
As Eric said, it needed a real man to master it!

Husqvarna PR guru Norbert Kunze tries to convince me that the Army bike isn't going to get me killed – probably!

The 608cc Clews Stroka which caused the interesting discussion between Alan Clews and me. I still wrote the story as I saw it.

Tense times at L'Enduro des Sables. The little Kwack was doing 10mpg —
and I was deeply grateful to still be alive at the end of the first lap.

This is an unpublished pic and is interesting because it shows the height of the Dakar
bike. A few moments later, a mad BMW mechanic tied a rope to the front forks and
towed me up and down that track behind a G-Wagen.
As the saying goes, you don't have to be mad — but it does help!

*Giving Hubert Auriol's Paris Dakar winning bike some air,
the day before the Dachau visit.*

*Doug Hele said that the Adventurer needed running in because it had new barrels and
pistons. Somehow, I got distracted…
This isn't the works TR5T but one of the test fleet I borrowed later.*

At the end of the Rocket 3 line was an Ariel 3, built up and running. Reg encouraged me to have a ride round inside the factory on the little trike. Had this been a 140mph race bike I would have been tucking my trousers into my socks and tearing down the line – regardless of the danger to me - or anyone else! The same would have applied if I had been offered a go on a motocrosser - but with the Ariel 3 I was just too embarrassed to even try it.

Bill Weatherhead was either the Line Foreman, or perhaps Line Superintendent, I can't remember his precise title, but he knew me well through my B.50. He was falling about laughing at the thought of BSA's last factory rider being seen on an Ariel 3 so, much as I respected and liked Reg, I just refused. If I had been seen on that thing I would never have been able to show my face at Armoury Road ever again.

However, the tour of the House of Horrors was not over yet. Reg showed me the huge bay which used to contain all the BSA spares dating back to the start of the factory. These were now being unceremoniously piled up in heaps, and in their place were tens of thousands of boxes containing the Anker engines.

I don't know if anyone ever knew precisely how many engines had been bought for this stupid project but Reg told me that there were 50,000 in the spares bay alone. There could have been even more than this, so grandiose were Jofeh's fantasies.

As politely as I could, I pleadingly explained that the project was doomed and that it was going to destroy the factory. As I am writing this, I can remember the long sigh which came from Reg and his next words. "Frank, this is what is happening. It's been decided, Can you help?"

I explained that the best thing I could do was nothing – not to mention the Ariel 3, nor even acknowledge its existence. Much as I wanted to assist BSA, I could not, and would not, tell my readers gargantuan lies by saying that the thing was anything other than an utter disaster. So, I didn't – but I knew that this had to be pretty well the last straw in the history of this iconic factory.

Ironically, there would have been a way out of the mess - if only Jofeh had been a motorcyclist. It is difficult to over-state just how clever were the BSA craftsmen. Some years later, I saw an incredibly talented fabricator/frame designer called Rob Homer produce a complete chassis for a bike, called the NVT Rambler, in one working day. That's not an exaggeration. Working with an engineer's eye, and a craftsman's skills, Rob bent the tubes round the Yamaha donor engine, welded them up and the bike was done – and a lovely little thing it was too.

Given the support of BSA management, Cyril could have built a complete mo-ped in less than a week. Using existing BSA parts, and some simple pressings which the factory could have almost done as a foreigner it was so easy, there could have been a viable little mo-ped on sale in a less than a month. This would have used the engines profitably and brought in some much needed revenue. But, with Jofeh at the helm, this was never going to happen – and didn't.

***

BSA was in a bad way but teaching wasn't. I first met my class at the Parish Junior School in Runcorn towards the end of the summer term. Mr. Teare, the Head, introduced me. "Good morning children. This is Mr. Melling. He will be your teacher in September and I am sure that you will have a good time together."

And we did. I was about to start one of those idyllically happy periods of my life.

George Teare was a wonderful man – a real educationist with a tremendous interest in the kids. He was also a motorcycle racing fan so we got on really well.

This next part of the story is slightly out of time context but I think that it needs telling now because it ties in with the Ariel 3 fiasco.

On a lovely October day, Bill Weatherhead phoned my wife with an urgent message: BSA was going to close – and that day. If I didn't collect the B.50, it was certain that I would lose it: absolutely guaranteed!

This was a double tragedy because clearly my career as BSA's last ever works rider was fast coming to an end but, by this time, I had a bought the bike from the factory so I was also going to lose my bike!

My wife rang school, and this was where working for a Head who was a bike racing fan really paid off!

He came down to my room, explained what was happening and said: "Look, you'll be useless teaching today because you'll be worrying so much. I'll take your class and you go and rescue the BSA." Now that was real kindness.

I said a very hurried goodbye to the kids and screamed away from school, heading for home to collect my trailer.

On the grounds that I might still incriminate myself after all these years, I will say only that if there has ever been a faster time to cover 85 miles towing a trailer I would be very surprised.

My wife had also phoned Bill Weatherhead to tell him that I was on my way and so when I arrived, the B.50 was parked against the tubes, just by the entry to the Tubes In bay. We loaded the bike on to the trailer in seconds.

But Bill wasn't finished yet. He grabbed an enormous cardboard box and we ran down the B.50 line. Into it went valves, two cylinder barrels, a couple of cylinder heads, five pistons and much more. It was like one of the "All You Can Grab in a Minute" supermarket competitions.

We were out of breath when we reached the end of the line. "How much you got with you? Quick!" panted Bill.

"I've got a ten quid - but that's all."

"Give it me! Give it me now! Quick!" Bill barked.

I gave him the two five pound notes and he scribbled a receipt for me: "Assorted BSA spares - £10."

"Go on, get out now. Go on, go on, go on. Get out now."

I ran across to my car, which I had reversed up to the Tubes In bay and so was pointing in the right direction to leave the factory. Spinning the wheels, I accelerated towards the security cabin by the gate whilst, behind me, a group of blue suited men were descending the steel stairs from the new offices.

The security guard looked at the B.50 on the trailer and hesitated. "It's mine honestly, it's mine. Cyril Halliburn looks after it for me and Bill Weatherhead has just sold me some spares. I'm Frank Melling and the B.50's mine - honest..."

There were tears welling in my eyes. The guard looked at the box of parts on the back seat and then back at me.

"Look, I've got a receipt. Bill has just sold the bits to me, honest he has, honestly. Look at the receipt."

The suits had reached the bottom of the stairs by now and the factory gates were just a few seconds walk away.

The guard looked at the bike, back at the BSA box, with parts spilling out everywhere, and then at my ashen face. Finally, and with what felt like infinite slowness, he took the receipt and waved me through.

I was shaking like a leaf and pulled up on Golden Hillock Road, just to calm down. I was panting for breath and flopped forward across the steering wheel completely exhausted.

I raised my head and looked out of the driver's side car window and across towards Armoury Road. The suited gentlemen from Cooper Brothers Accountants were locking the gates to the factory and that was the end of BSA as a major manufacturer of motorcycles. The work force was slashed from 4,500 to just 1,500 and all production finally stopped on 14 April when just eleven Rocket 3s and seven B50SS Gold Stars were built.

My days as a BSA works rider were well and truly over!

***

By contrast, things were great at school. The kids were lovely and I was allowed to teach them without petty interference. What more could anyone ask for?

However, once again, Fate was about to slide some interesting cards across to my side of the table.

In the Spring, before the closure of the BSA that Autumn, I had received a phone call from Triumph: Doug Hele wanted to speak to me. I phoned the factory and was put through to Doug, who asked me to come to Meriden urgently because he wanted my opinion of the bike he had just built.

This was a real out of body experience, not unlike Michelangelo asking the Meeter-and-Greeter at B&Q for some advice about what colours to use in the Sistine Chapel.

I duly arrived and Doug took me through the factory to his competition department, which was at the back of the works. The atmosphere was hugely different from my previous visit. There was a sense of greyness and apathy which was palpable. I passed by Quality Control and saw one of the lads who had previously been so meticulously checking every crankshaft.

His mercury gauge was dirty and the knife edge wheels, on which the cranks sat during checking, were dumped on one side of the gauge. As Doug was speaking to one of the other staff, I chatted briefly to one of the Quality Control fitters. He looked a broken and angry man: "They (the management) don't give a flying f**** about quality any more. Everything and anything goes out now. They just want the money in."

These were desperate times.

The bike Doug wanted me to see was a works prepared Triumph Adventurer – a remarkable dual purpose, off-road and road motorcycle.

The Adventurer was, to use that hackneyed football expression, a game of two halves. Of all the bikes I have ridden, this was the one which was so near to being a motorcycling icon that I could weep at the missed opportunities. If only Jofeh had spent a fraction of the money which was wasted on the Ariel 3 fiasco in developing the Adventurer, BSA Group finances would have been vastly healthier. This isn't a rose coloured view either, simply because I am a great fan of the bike, but absolute hard core fact.

You may remember that the heart of the TR5T, which was Triumph code for the Adventurer, was BSA's B.50MX - and that the germ of the idea is supposed to have come from my frame. Truly, a legend in my own lunch-time!

The B.50 had much to commend it as both a motocross bike and a road machine. The main frame of the bike consisted of an extremely strong, large diameter spine which housed the oil. This made the motorcycle very narrow and compact, and easy to ride off road.

The B.50MX forks were okay too. They were not state of the art for the time but perfectly serviceable. The same could be said of the hubs, which were too big and heavy to be ideal but still not a million miles away from being excellent.

Finally, in BSA's parts' bins were all the expensive bits which really add costs to a new motorcycle. On the shelves were fine quality alloy fuel tanks, high level braced handlebars, off road footrests and everything else needed to make a dirt bike.

The final part of the equation was that there was plenty of room inside the chassis, because the B.50 engine was tall.

The problem was that the B.50 had a truly dreadful engine. It could be made to go fast, as Cyril had done with my bike, but in this state it was fragile. The gearbox was weak, the clutch suspect and the cylinder head had to be kept perfectly torqued down or the head gasket would blow.

Worst of all, a quick B.50 was almost impossible to start - and not just by amateurs like me. The situation was so bad that the BSA factory riders never even had a kick-start on their bikes and relied on push starts all the time. Not for nothing did you always see B.50 riders parked on the highest ground at a motocross meeting so that they could bump start their bikes downhill – and this was a motorcycle which was supposed to be sold to the general public!

If a B.50 was detuned so that it would start, the motor did not make sufficient power to pull itself out of bed in a morning. It was a real donkey!

By contrast, Triumph had a very fine 490cc, twin cylinder engine. This made as much power as a good B.50 but without the vicious acceleration which made the BSA such a formidable beast off the line. However, anyone could fire it up no matter how inexperienced or cack handed they were. The Tiger 100, as the single carburettor version of the engine was known, was heavier than a B.50 motor, and wider too, but vastly more user friendly.

In terms of ease of use, the Tiger 100 was a peach. Riding a quick B.50 was hard, unforgiving work and guaranteed to generate plenty of blisters on both hands. By contrast, the Triumph twin was as docile as a pet Labrador - and silky smooth. This was a bike for everyman. In short, it had that most desirable of traits – a truly broad market appeal.

Critically, the Tiger 100 engine slotted into the B.50 chassis perfectly.

The huge issue was with the gearbox. The Tiger 100 had only four speeds when it needed five, or ideally six, to be a true dual purpose bike. This would have enabled the new TR5T to be ridden at low speeds off road and still have relaxed cruising speed on tarmac.

Years later, Doug told me that Triumph had made a one-off five speed, 560cc version of the Adventurer and it was a peerless motorcycle with a genuine 100mph performance and excellent handling both on and off road.

Tragically, the Adventurer was a re-run of Doug's triple project. By the time BSA Group management had removed their fingers from their bottoms it was too late. Again, like the triple, it was going to be many years before the Japanese made a bike anything like as good as the Adventurer so nearly was.

However, history can't be changed and as I was shown the Adventurer which Doug's team had prepared, I was mightily impressed. One of the weak points of all BSA group products was the appalling Joseph Lucas electrics. Not for nothing did riders refer to "Joe Lucas – the Prince of Darkness" because the lights on bikes fitted with Lucas electrics failed so often!

To overcome the unreliability of the electrics, Doug had a complete dual ignition system on the bike which was accessed via a neat panel on the right-hand side of the bike, where the oil tank would have been on a normal Triumph.

As I have said, the handling on an Adventurer was excellent but Doug had given the Tiger 100 engine a serious re-work and it was now effectively a Triumph Daytona race engine with a single carburettor. One of the fitters fired up the bike – and it sounded lovely.

I tucked my flared pants into my socks and took off on Doug's creation. Naturally, with an audience I had to ham it up and so I pulled a few neat wheelies, slid the bike around on the grass and, thankfully, managed not to crash and look a Muppet.

Triumph were supplying three supposedly standard, except that they weren't, Adventurers to the Royal Marines' team which was entered in the International Six Days Trial that year – the World Championship of enduros.

I must have had quite a good reputation at Triumph because Doug was asking me to do a shake-down ride of the bike so that any bugs could be sorted out before they were handed over to the Marines.

Enduros, as these long distance off road events were called, were just starting to become very popular. An enduro in those happy days had extensive off road sections linked by public highways. Riders needed an ability to ride any sort of terrain quickly and the self-discipline to keep going when things were tough. In short, enduros had my name written on the tin and they were to become an important part of my riding life in the next ten years.

I had never ridden in an enduro before but this didn't put me off in the slightest degree. One of the more high profile events was a night and day event called "The Tour of Wales." The idea was that riders set off from Newtown, which is in Mid-Wales, in the middle of the night, navigated by a series of symbols written down on a paper route map, and then ended up in the forests around Dolgellau – where the event would be won or lost in a series of high speed, off-road tests.

The Tour of Wales proved to be one of the more impressive good news/bad news stories in my life. The good news was that Doug's Adventurer was an absolute rocket ship and revved all the way up to 9,000rpm as smooth as an electric motor. I could pull wheelies everywhere and the B.50 chassis handled exceptionally well on the road.

In pre-event practice, I also took an instant delight to riding fast on the shale roads which comprised much of the Forestry Commission land. The Triumph engine was powerful and easy to ride and again, as I knew from my grass tracking days, the B.50 chassis was a pussy cat in a power slide.

But there was bad news – and this time it was gift wrapped with a big shiny bow. To say the least, I am not a gifted navigator so the start of the Tour of Wales was both predictable and hilarious.

Riders were despatched at one minute intervals and, as the three of us rolled up to the line in the pitch dark, I looked at the two trials riders either side of me, and their knackered old bikes, and I was already wondering what the winner's trophy looked like and where it would go on my trophy cabinet. This is always a dangerous mind set.

By the light of a small, portable spotlight the starting official held his five fingers out for the three of us to see. Five, four, three, two, one – go! And I went. After all, I was winning money at grass tracks so there was no way that I wouldn't lead everyone off the start line – especially riding a factory Triumph.

Bang in the clutch. Nice controlled wheelie and we're in the lead. Great. Now where the heck do we go at the end of the street? To my acute embarrassment, I actually managed to get lost within sight of the start. Thank goodness it was dark and no-one could see me!

The next five hours were spent groping around the lanes of Mid-Wales whilst vastly slower riders came pottering past me, knowing precisely where they were.

Eventually, as dawn was breaking - tired, frustrated, cold and hungry - I found the forestry: what a relief. Now the course was marked with big, fluorescent arrows, I was riding off road and I could go quickly.

However, Fate wasn't quite satisfied and was wearing a rather self-satisfied smirk on his face.

The sun had come up but, in the dips, a heavy mist still lay across the road. I was also dog tired not to say fed up. Okay, that's the list of excuses…

The Adventurer was flying along the shale road and in the distance, floating in and out of the mist, was what looked a little bit like a gate. But it couldn't be. The gates were surely open on the shale roads….surely?

The gate disappears into the mist and I wind the Adventurer on. The non-existent gate appears again – and then sinks out of sight into the mist once more.

The Adventurer is really singing now as I put the bike into a lovely power slide and the world is looking a wonderful place. Then the mist clears and there is the gate again, now looking very rural with moss growing beautifully on the brown, five bars - but also, most definitely, firmly closed.

I am doing a genuine 60mph and so this is going to hurt – and good style too. There's only one solution. Lean back, pull hard on the 'bars and the lovely Adventurer stands up on its back wheel and we smash into the gate with the front wheel over the top bar. This is good – very good – because underneath the engine is a big steel bash plate and this cuts through the gate like a knife through butter as I go sliding down the road. As I skid along on my back, I watch the gate slowly fold into two halves - and then collapse.

The damage could have been much worse. I was cut and battered but nothing was broken. The Adventurer had done even better with only the handlebars bent and just a few scratches. Of the three of us, the gate had come off by far the worst.

Being the responsible racer that I was, I left an apologetic note wrapped round the gate hinge along with my phone number but, strangely, I never heard a word from the farmer or anyone else. Perhaps gates regularly got cut in half on forestry roads.

Doug's reaction was equally surprising and showed the difference between the way professional and amateur racers think. My concern was the damage I had done to the bike, and the cost of reparation for my war crimes The big question on my mind was whether Doug was going to have his fitters turn me upside down and shake the money out of my pockets to pay for the repairs.

By contrast, Mr. Hele had less than no interest in the crash or the damage. The only thing he wanted to know was how the bike had performed. He probed and explored and then checked my answers so much that I felt I had been in one of those science fiction films where the victim is put on a machine which sucks out their memory.

At the end, Doug gave me the briefest of thanks and then the interview was over and that was the end of my career as a works Triumph rider. Still, having ridden factory bikes for both BSA and Triumph wasn't a bad thing to have on my CV – even if I was the least talented rider to have ever ridden a works bike for either, or both, of them!

Now, I was about to be told just how bad a motocross rider I was and also how much I loved being a freelance writer. There were exciting times ahead.

14

Two Great Men, One Enormous Row and a Best Selling Book

ALTHOUGH BSA was finished as a factory, the B.50 was still very much alive through the actions of two brilliant, but very different, men. One of these was Eric Cheney - a man who I came to know, like and respect so much that I was privileged in being allowed to call him "Uncle Eric."

The other was the equally talented, but in a quite different way, Alan Clews – the founder of CCM Motorcycles. I respect Alan hugely, but without any affection because it was with him that I had my first major, five star, journalism argument.

First, the gifted, mercurial and eccentric, Eric Cheney.

The BSA competition shop closed in 1972 bringing to an end the Birmingham factory's domination of British motocross whilst simultaneously making some of Britain's best motocross riders redundant. Team leader Jeff Smith moved to Bombardier to develop the Can-Am two strokes; Dave Nicholl continued as a privateer on his old, ex-works BSA whilst John Banks campaigned a two-stroke CZ - with spectacularly poor results.

Banks' results in particular were noted with interest by the pundits since at the time, "Big John" was arguably Britain's best off-road racer, having narrowly missed the 500cc World Championship on two occasions - first in 1968, by just one point, and again in 1969.

The second element in the saga was Eric Cheney, the sensitive genius whose fertile mind and skilled hands had built the bikes which regularly challenged the factory BSAs.

Eric had been a very fine rider in his own right as well as a gifted mechanic. He joined the Navy, aged just 18, and spent the whole war in Motor Torpedo boats working in the claustrophobic confines of the MTB's tiny engine room.

This was considered to be one of the most dangerous jobs in the whole fleet. Eric worked on three huge, V12, supercharged Packard Marine engines surrounded by thousands of gallons of fuel. Safety clothing amounted to a pair of navy blue, cotton overalls!

The engine room was completely unprotected and the MTBs were made of wood. If there was a fire, it was certain death for the crew. I remember once chatting to Eric about how quick he was whilst working on bikes under pressure at races and he came back with one of the best quotes I have ever heard.

"Frank, if you're stuck out in the Channel with a pair of Messerschmitts shooting lumps out of the boat there's a big incentive to work fast and get an engine running!"

Eric's riding career came to an end in 1961 when he contracted a serious blood infection, after competing in Algiers. Following this period of acute illness, he never re-gained his former speed so he decided to retire and concentrate on bike preparation.

Eric was a lot more of an artist than an engineer and he provided a fascinating window into the mind of a creative genius. On one occasion, I visited him in the old tobacco drying house in Hampshire, which was his workshop at the time. You might, reasonably, think that gas welding with an open flame on the wooden floor of an all wooden building was pushing Health and Safety boundaries somewhat but this never occurred to Eric – not even for a second.

He had just concluded the manufacture of a revolutionary, lightweight motocross machine using a Honda engine and I was fascinated by how he had conceived such a radical design.

Eric explained: "It's simple. First, you get the boys to hold the engine up against the wall. (which, conveniently, was made of fairly flat pieces of wood).

"Next, you get a piece of chalk and you draw the frame tubes round the engine.

"This'll take a few goes because you need to see the frame grow and change until it looks right."

In fact, I have poshed this bit up because Eric was utterly dismissive of the creative process and felt that it was no more complex than brushing your teeth or combing your hair.

"Then," Eric explained patiently as if talking to a rather slow witted five year old, "you put the tubing up to the chalk drawing, cut it to size and make the frame. It's as simple as that!"

This artist's approach to design meant that Eric would never slot into a mainstream bike manufacturer's pre-defined box, as a salaried employee.

By their very nature, creative people are dissatisfied with the status quo and want to change it. This is the way that even low grade creatives like me, as well as geniuses such as Eric, are hard wired. We can't help ourselves. Water is wet. The sun is hot. Creative people don't want to follow what is known and predictable.

It would be wonderful if teachers today had the flexibility to say: "I don't quite understand what you are doing, or why you want to do it in that way, but I'll support you regardless. Let's have a go."

Give a creative kid an exercise about being creative and the first thing he will want to do is change all the parameters to suit what he has in mind - or what he might have in mind at some time in the future.

In a society where everything is known, planned, predictable and capable of being monitored and assessed, the creative kid will be left outside in the cold, usually because he isn't comfortable, or happy, with life as it is.

What society needs are gifted, bold people like the Senior Librarian in Warrington Library who took a bet on the little boy who wanted adult library tickets. Now that was allowing individuality to flourish.

A few hundred replicas of Sammy Green's wash house in every town, where sub-micro businesses could set up cheaply and free of regulation, would also be immensely helpful and might even give rise to a new Eric. Sadlly, I doubt whether either will happen in the current climate.

The relationship Cheney had with the BSA factory is worthy of some consideration. You will often read that Eric and BSA were daggers drawn but this was not the case. Rather, BSA - through the medium of Competitions' Manager Brian Martin - tried to help Cheney as and when possible but they were often thwarted by the fact that Eric was totally unemployable in any conventional sense of the word.

Eric was another hard core freelancer, who would never do even what was necessary for his own good if he wasn't inspired by whatever creative muse drove him on. Steering committees, five year business plans and spread sheets did not exist in Eric's world.

So, Cheney received help from BSA in the form of bits and pieces on a semi-official basis and, in return, BSA benefited from having their engines power some very successful, and newsworthy, racing machines.

By the end of the 1972 season, Banks was clearly going no-where at all and was weary of the CZ and ready for a change.

The aptly named "Big John" was arguably England's best motocross rider at the time but was something of a mixed blessing for any team. On the plus side was a heady mix of aggression, courage and riding skill, whilst the debit column would have recorded a violent brutality to the bikes he rode. John's determined temperament also sometimes led to a tactical weakness, particularly in GPs.

However, with Banks on one of your bikes there was always a chance you might win and this has a tremendously positive effect on any team - witness the Rossi phenomenon today.

The other factor to bear in mind is that John raced for personal satisfaction. Certainly, he was as cash conscious as any other rider of the day but he did not need to race to live, enjoying the support of extensive business interests in Suffolk as he did. Having begun his sporting career as a horse rider, it was not for nothing that he was known as the Baron of Bury St. Edmonds. Thus, to a certain extent, he could afford to indulge his preference for riding four-strokes.

***

Signing a rider is always a strange business and rather reminiscent of a 19th.

century courtship. In this case, it was Dave Nicoll - sometime teammate of Banks at BSA and a near neighbour of his - who introduced the blushing couple. Following the end of season Fox and Hounds meeting at Newbury, Banks, Nicoll and Cheney retired to a local pub and a deal was struck.

Cheney would provide Banks with six bikes and all the spares he needed, as well as £1,000 to seal the contract. In return, Banks would compete in all the Grands Prix and the British 500cc motocross championship. In less than an hour, the deal was done. There was to be a further £1,000 for Banks at the end of the season when bike sales had paid for the year's racing. Banks negotiated his own personal sponsors.

In 1973, £1,000 clearly had more buying power than today but even so it wasn't a lot of money. Remember at the time, Banks was earning between £300 and £500 in start and prize money from a French International race. Nevertheless, both parties were ready to go out and win the world championship: this was to be no token, half-hearted attempt.

Cheney already had the basis of the bike built, in his Victor Mk. IV. This was a neat, light, slim bike which handled very well. Eric now planned a development of the Victor using a BSA B.50 engine which was lightened and tuned to produce the aggressive power which Banks liked so much.

The care and attention lavished on the bikes was incredible. For example, Eric insisted on using his own front forks which were manufactured from billets of solid Dural – a very light and tough alloy. These were machined by the old London gun firm of Mollants, using an Eldorado gun drill which Eric had imported from America.

Manufactured like this, it meant that the forks could be finished to an extremely tight tolerance - there are no bushes in the design - in one pass and the finished product was a front fork about as good as one could get at the time. Eric never even considered the costs, or practicalities, of making suspension in this way.

The end result of the 200-300 hours spent on each machine was a bike which weighed some 235lbs (106kgs) wet and produced around 40bhp. This package was equal to the last works BSAs and the team was competitive.

The new JBR (John Banks Replica) first appeared at the Cadwell Park TV scramble, in February 1973, and immediately attracted attention with its nickel plated frame, blue anodised petrol tank and side-panels and, rather eccentrically, the latest Preston Petty plastic mudguards which were bright orange. Banks too proved to be on the pace and BSA fans all over the world looked forward to the new season.

It was at Cadwell that I was formally introduced to Banks and what followed was one of the most interesting experiences of my riding career.

I took an instant liking to both Cheney and John Banks. Eric was highly eccentric but he was, very clearly, a completely bovine excrement free zone.

He told things exactly how he saw them and whether you agreed with him or didn't made no difference, because he was right and you were wrong!

I got on well with John too. He was a big man, built like a rugby player, but with a ready smile and a quite touching modesty. At the time, Banks was one of the best motocross riders in the world but he never made any mention of this. In summary, Banks was a complete gentleman and behaved as such.

Both were happy to acknowledge that, whilst I wasn't anything other than a club rider, I did have a lot of influence in the press and so everyone was happy.

It's worth explaining how the relationship between the media and manufacturers works at its best. The riders and manufacturers have one set of skills and abilities. Decent journalists have another set. If both parties are honest, then the relationship can work to everyone's benefit.

I have never claimed to be anything more than a Muppet when it comes to riding ability – but I can write. If the manufacturer I am working with acknowledges both of these facts then everyone will get on fine. If they don't, there will be conflict. Later in the year, I was to meet this problem head on.

***

At the time, I had the very great pleasure, not to say honour, of working with one of the best motorcycling photographers of all time – a young man called David Dewhurst. David had only just finished a photography course at Blackpool College but was already better than other snappers who had been doing the job all their lives. At the risk of using the word genius again, David was simply incredible. Later, he emigrated to America – something which should have been declared illegal on the grounds that he was a major national asset and therefore an export licence for him ought to have been refused!

We duly arrived at John's large house and were treated like royalty. John and his wife Mary could not have been more welcoming or effusive. Despite the hospitality, I wanted to get on with the job because, for once in winter, the weather was kind and the light useable for a photo shoot.

We arrived at the test track and immediately got the first shock. John reached into the back of the van and did not roll the Cheney down a ramp but simply lifted it out and onto the ground. This could have been a round in "The World's Strongest Man" competition.

David and I looked at each other but didn't say a word. Fit as I was, John made my muscles look like knots in wet cotton!

John bump started the Cheney and the noise from the straight, unsilenced exhaust pipe sounded like gunfire. Even today, the memory of the B.50's staccato crackle sounds just as fresh as when Banks first fired up the bike on that cold winter's day.

John warmed up the bike with a few runs round the test track – and I became ever more depressed. Banks was clearly playing about - but at speeds which I couldn't even imagine. Goodness only knows what he was going to think of my performance.

One bit of the track in particular was a nightmare. It was a steep, cambered bank which was partially frozen. I was all over the place trying to ride it and so John kindly helped by showing me the correct technique.

John was patient and thorough. All that was required was a more aggressive approach, he explained. Get the engine revving really hard in second gear and then, as the bike slides downhill, ride it up the camber and just control the slide with extra revs. It was easy.

David and I looked at each other again and then I tried to explain, gently and kindly, that I just couldn't do it – I simply did not have the ability or physical strength. John was puzzled. He went through everything again and, once more, I failed miserably. After another five minutes I took the route used by so many losers – I feigned injury, we packed up and went home.

That's the difference, not only in riding ability but in the mind set too, between those who really can ride a motorcycle – and the rest of us.

There are three postscripts to this story. As might be expected from a team operating from little more than a four car garage, there were ups and downs in the season. John led the French Grand Prix by a handsome margin and then had the nylon heel of the contact breaker seize on the ignition cam.

However, he did finish a joint second in the American GP at Carlsbad, beaten only by Gerrit Wolsink on the factory Suzuki.

By the end of the year, Banks had also dominated the British 500cc Championship and was the last rider to win this Blue Riband event on a British bike.

I loved the Banks bike and so Eric built me a cheaper replica of the machine. It gave me a lot of pleasure and, at the microbial level at which I raced, a fair amount of success too. Incredibly, Eric also delivered the bike on time – and there are not many of his customers anywhere in the world who can say this!

At the end of the 1990s, I heard rumours of a Cheney for sale in the Oxford area and, on the way back from a Vintage grass track meeting, Carol and I decided to track the story down.

There, buried deep within a storeroom inside a palatial farm complex, we were shown a very special JBR. After two hours of intense negotiation, we headed home much, much poorer - and with a JBR on the trailer.

I was beside myself with excitement and the same night, I 'phoned Eric who confirmed that it was indeed one of the batch of bikes which had been built for Banks but in this case, it was the spare machine which had never been delivered and, when finances got tight at the end of the season, had been sold to raise money.

The bike had clearly been little used from new but it had not benefited from being stood idly for so many years. Carol and I worked every spare minute to get the bike ready for what was going to be its debut event – the Farleigh Castle "Pre-65 Grand Prix" for classic motocross machines.

Now, at this point, the story should finish with boy-racer-journalist-makes-good-riding-the-bike-of-his-dreams. Except, well, there always has to be an exception doesn't there? In this case it is the simple fact that putting a good clubman rider on a GP bike does not make the amateur into a world champion superstar. I know this to be fact!

Despite the quality of the handling, the superb brakes and the Warp Factor Five motor, I hated riding the thing. The Banks' Cheney was not a user friendly motorcycle in any sense of the word and needed the skill, and fitness, of a GP star to be useable.

When I complained to Eric, he summed up the situation easily and as accurately as ever: "Your balls aren't big enough! It needs a real man to ride it."

★★★

Eric wasn't the only one trying to make use of the demise of BSA to his own advantage. I know this because I was about to test another B.50 engined machine, produced by a very different character to Eric. The bike's creator was Alan Clews and the machine was the Clews Stroka – later to become known as the CCM.

I was introduced to Alan Clews through Doug Hacking, the genial, wheeler-dealer entrepreneur who was the mastermind and driving force behind Doug Hacking Motorcycles in Bolton.

In some ways, Doug was another Eddie Crooks. He would do a deal on anything and in any way. In his farmhouse were juke boxes, suits of armour and antique guns which he had taken in part exchange against motocross machines. I can't think of anything which would not have been accepted in a "swop" – providing Douggie turned a copper or three, as the Bolton expression went.

Douggie knew of my journalism, and that I could ride a motocross machine, so he proposed a marriage which would benefit everyone.

Doug explained that he had just become the sole agent for a new bike: the 608cc Clews Stroka.

Alan Clews was a hugely different character from Eric Cheney and both his courage and vision need recognising. When the BSA competition department closed in 1971 Clews managed to buy a lot of the contents. 99.999% of the motorcycle trade, including me had I not been concentrating on my College work, would have kept a few choice parts for themselves, sold the rest on and had a good time with the profits. Clews wanted more – much more. His aim was to be a motorcycle manufacturer and, to his immense credit, that's what he became.

I first met Alan in a newsagent's shop. He wasn't buying a motorcycling magazine but was serving behind the counter - at the same time as lacing a wheel for one of the bikes he was building.

Alan had a hard face and it struck me as haunted too. There was a lot going

149

on behind his eyes and the nervous energy crackled so fiercely that it was surprising the newspapers didn't burst into flames! However, one thing was clear: Douggie had clearly co-coerced him into doing the story and Alan wanted me in, and out, as quickly as possible so that he could get on with his master plan.

For my part, I was only there because of Douggie. The Clews Stroka had never been in the media before. Now, it was now going to get a lot of international publicity thanks to Doug's PR acumen. I didn't expect gratitude but a modicum of recognition from Alan, at how clever Douggie had been in getting me over to Bolton, would have been nice.

I rode the Clews Stroka and didn't much like it. Alan asked for my opinion and I said that, compared with my works BSA, it was a crude thing with an engine which vibrated fiercely and very stiff, uncompliant suspension. Mr. Clews was not best pleased and I was told that I was in no position to judge whether the bike was good or not because I couldn't ride to save my life and that I had better write the truth – or not write anything at all.

This was not a good thing to say to any journalist - and it was a particularly sensitive subject with me.

Alan was correct. By GP standards I was a rubbish racer. That much was true and there was no argument between us on this point.

However, he completely mis-understood just how seriously I took the responsibility of having a duty of care to my readers.

I carried an immense sense of gratitude for standing in my readers' place and representing them through whatever article I was writing. Just how fortunate I was came flooding back to me every time I remembered painting shelves, or being trapped at the Post Office watching the minutes tick by.

This belief is almost a religious tenet for me. I am clearly not even a half decent rider and I would never win any awards for literature either. However I am, and always will be, a clubman racer who often finds himself in places of real privilege. Hell would have to freeze over and produce large glaciers before I would ever abuse that position.

This determination to tell the story as I see it has got me into a lot of trouble over the years, and on innumerable occasions too, but it still won't shift me from my core belief that I must be my readers – and if this means getting into a war as a result then so be it.

The fact that someone was raging at me in an attempt to change my view of a bike meant less than nothing. After all, getting shouted at by people who thought that they had power over me was hardly a new experience.

I also think that Alan made a fundamental mistake. Yes, he was correct in stressing my incompetence compared with top quality riders but he mis-understood my position in the racing galaxy too. Those little brown envelopes containing a few pounds in prize money were a common occurrence by this time - as were the cheap little trophies I was taking home.

If I won at Fluke Hall - then there were eleven riders behind me who didn't. Sponsored riders didn't buy CCMs – decent, ambitious clubmen like me did. Even down to buying bikes, I was my readers – and they were CCM's potential customers.

The other key fact that Alan overlooked was that I would have the last word in this argument – and I did.

I was going to write the story exactly as I saw it and my editor was going to run the piece untouched. These things I knew to be fact – and they were.

Douggie, as always, was charming, kind and the eternal diplomat. He ushered me out of the room before things got really out of hand – and this wasn't far from happening. Afterwards, he phoned me in an attempt to calm things down but it was too late. I wrote what I believed to be the truth and Cycle Illustrated published the story.

None of this prevented me from developing an immense admiration for Alan and the truly amazing things he did. Equally, I was never added to CCM's Christmas card list!

***

Back in the classroom, things were moving on too. George Teare was sent on a Post-Graduate training course and the school had a new, peripatetic Head who didn't like me and who I could not respect. The job was going only one way.

Except for one factor, I would have been over the hills and far away sooner but this was my final year of teaching in Primary School and I had been entrusted with the 11+ class.

Of all the tasks I have ever undertaken, nothing was as important as coaching the kids for their 11+ examination. We went through day after day of drills, revision and exercises until we were – both my pupils and me – at the point of tears.

For those kids who were good at formal tests – and that is all that the 11+ examination was – the prize was a place in Grammar School and, maybe, a way out of a poor background into university and the professions. For the rest, there were Secondary Modern Schools - and very little chance of tertiary education.

There was a lot hanging on the 11+.

The brightest children handled the pressure well but at the bottom end of the class it was tough. The kids in my class were used to hard work but not of the kind which was based around rote responses to rigid questions. Yes, I demanded high standards but the work I set was flexible and, I hope, fun too.

One lovely little girl found everything too much and, during the 11+ Maths paper, started sobbing uncontrollably. This was very bad, not only because she was so upset but also in the way the more able children were being disturbed by her distress.

She had answered all the questions she could – which wasn't very many – so I gave her a box of felt tip pens and asked her to draw a picture of her dog for me, and then write a sentence underneath.

She immediately settled down, I wiped her eyes dry with a tissue from the box we kept in my desk drawer, and she smiled. What the 11+ examiners thought of a large, brightly coloured dog sat on their test paper I don't know but I did wish that it could have been incontinent too because that's how I felt about the distress this lovely child had suffered.

If wanting to represent my readers was a religious calling, then trying to help children at the bottom end of the ability spectrum was another. A love of books had got me out of the prison in which I had been trapped, and I wanted every kid I came into contact with to be able to read and write. I believed then, and still believe now, that literacy is the golden key which opens up an escape from poverty and deprivation.

With this in mind, I took a job in a High School which wanted a teacher to develop a literacy programme for the least able students. It was a dream job for me – and there was a pay rise attached to it. Happy days all round.

However, it was another good news/bad news story. The good news for a freelancer was that when I arrived at the school, there was quite literally no, as in zero, resources with which to do anything. I thought that this was great and worked night after night, until the caretaker threw me out, building a literacy programme.

My writing, and health, suffered but I loved the idea of having a blank sheet of paper and creating something which was really going to benefit kids who needed all the help I could give them.

It was such an exciting time that I couldn't sleep at night.

The bad news was that I was given two much older teachers to help me. These gentlemen were maybe forty years older than me and had served our country nobly in the war. Now, I was being asked to direct their teaching and manage them.

I didn't have a clue about how to approach what was an almost impossibly difficult task and so I ricocheted about, making mistakes which could have been avoided if only I'd been given some training – or at least a bit of advice. But neither was forthcoming so I blundered around in turn hyper enthusiastic, impatient, respectful, insensitive, tolerant and crass.

With as much effort as I have ever made in my life, I got the programme started, the kids began learning but I arrived at the end of the Christmas term in a bad way - both physically and mentally exhausted: I was truly burnt out.

★★★

I remember sitting at home with a huge cup of milky coffee and a thick round of toast when I heard the letter box click open and closed. I had a long debate with myself as to whether I should leave the Christmas cards there and just fall asleep but, after five minutes, the enthusiast in my mind kicked the rest of my body reluctantly into life.

I staggered to the door mat and there, surrounded by Christmas post, was a letter with my name typed on the envelope. As well as my name and address, it should have had Fate's logo emblazoned on it because this was another fork in my life's pathway – but in this case it was an easy one to take.

I now had the writing of feature articles fully sorted out and, after producing something in the region of 150 columns, spread over three magazines, I had this branch of journalism cracked too.

In terms of writing, the one thing which kept me awake at night was the idea of producing a book. It wasn't the money, because journalism was paying very well, but something which was infinitely more important. I wanted to be on the shelves of Warrington Library along with all the other authors.

I ached, lusted even, to cross the literary Rubicon and become the read, rather than the reader.

You can put on it whatever metaphor you wish – the Holy Grail, the crock of gold at the end of the rainbow or Santa arriving with a sleigh full of presents. Nothing is sufficiently powerful to explain just how much I wanted the ten year old who had battled for his adult library ticket to be able to look at the shelves and find a book written by Frank Melling.

The letter had arrived on the 23 December and this was a cruel blow of fate. It came from JH Haynes who were, and still are, known for their workshop manuals. They had a book publishing arm operating under the imprint of GT Foulis and the letter was signed by Tim Parker.

For the next ten days, I was driven to point of insanity. Here was an offer to talk about writing a book and … fill in the expletives here … Haynes were closed for Christmas!

It was like going up to someone who was walking across the Sahara, and who had run out of water, and then saying to them: "Here is lovely big bottle of chilled, sparkling water – but unfortunately I don't have a bottle opener for a couple of weeks."

Tim Parker was also the driving force behind the project. He was full of excitement and energy and goodness me, he really did he know how to stroke authors' heads and make them purr! Many years in the future, Tim and I fell out over another book, which was very sad because I really did like him.

Tim told me how much he enjoyed my writing, and respected my work, and how I was the only person in the world who could produce the book he had in mind. It was going to be called "The Complete Book of Motocross." This was to be the companion to another book which Foulis had already published, entitled "The Complete Book of Trials" and had been written by Don Smith.

I just lay on my back and let Tim tickle my literary tummy. Truly, I thought that I had died and gone to heaven.

The key thing was that Tim promised no interference. I would have complete control of the content, style, photographs and everything else. It was great. This was the freelancer's dream.

Interest in off road sport was about to explode – and on a world-wide basis too – so my book was soon selling like crazy and re-print after re-print followed.

Don's trials' book was just doing as well and, sadly, this led to a real tragedy. I have tried to be totally honest in this book but in this case I can't remember the precise details of what happened to us both. In essence, John Haynes thought that we were both earning too much money from royalties. From his point of view, dealing with authors of dull as ditch water technical books who wrote page after page of lifeless prose, this might be understandable.

But Don and I were not technical writers churning out information about which oil to use in which gearbox and how to remove a rusty stud from a crankcase. We were named, known personalities and our books were selling because of this.

John did some nimble work with our contracts so that we got vastly less money than we should have done. I was upset – but Don was out of his mind with frustration and a sense of injustice.

I took my contract to a commercial lawyer in Manchester and he shrugged his shoulders and said that what had happened might not be sporting but it was legal, so basically shut up and get on with my life. Five minutes after I walked in, he had pocketed my £75 - and his secretary was showing me the way out.

Don taught himself law, battled on and died at the tragically early age of 66. I think that the strain of fighting an unwinnable battle took its toll.

My view was different. It was not that I didn't care about what had happened but I am always looking to the next day – not worrying about the past, which can't be fixed no matter how hard you try.

It was the right attitude because Fate had packaged a very nice present to cheer me up – two in fact. How good was this going to be?

15

Enduro Days

IF you wanted to read a book about motorcycling success then you've picked up the wrong volume because, as I have said on a number of occasions, I have never been much of a rider in terms of real quality. However, I have had some very lucky breaks and at this time two arrived simultaneously.

The first was that enduros took off as a sport. In fact, it was hugely the biggest participant activity in motorcycling, with thousands of riders taking part almost every weekend. With enduros, I found a niche where I was actually not too bad. I won lots of club enduros and occasionally had a good ride at national level. This was never going to happen with either motocross or grass track.

The reason that I did so well was that, in those days, enduros were much faster, and less physically demanding, than they are today. So a rider who could deal with the off-road going competently, which I could as a motocrosser, ride the shale roads in the forestry which was grass tracking territory, and who was also handy on road sections had a decent chance.

The other piece of good fortune was that I had stayed in contact with Eddie Crooks after writing the article on the TT winning T500. I want to talk about my time with Eddie in some detail because it was the best period of my serious riding "career" - in every respect. It's also a window on to how blurred, and overlapped, the line became between a very heavily sponsored club rider and someone who rode for a living in the mid-1970s.

Eddie would be the last person to argue that he was perfect in every respect but, from my point of view, I have never been happier with any sponsor and he treated me extremely well – almost embarrassingly so.

I was with Eddie for five years and we never once had a single cross word – not one, ever. He was kind, supportive, enthusiastic and provided me with the very best bikes he had available.

For my part, I was scrupulously honest with him and worked very hard to sell his products because I was very conscious of how fortunate I was to have a sponsor of this calibre.

I had heard that the Fantic importer, a chap called Roy Carey, was looking for a major dealer to push the new Caballero enduro machine. Although Eddie was heavily into road racing, he was a very fine enduro rider in his own right and Crooks-Suzuki was the biggest off-road Suzuki dealer in Britain.

The Fantics were made in Italy and really looked the part, with a beautiful red and silver finish and a six speed Minarelli engine which, although only of 125cc capacity, had immense fins. Enduros were big in Italy and Fantic was one of a number of small Italian manufacturers who made serious, focussed, pure enduro machines with every part of the bike being designed for these events. In every way, the Caballeros looked like serious racing machines.

As I have said, but it's worth repeating, Ed was laser sharp when it came to seeing business opportunities before anyone else. At the time, Suzuki did not have an enduro bike so the Fantic looked like a good bet for a machine to sell into this new, and fast expanding, market.

Eddie never played about at being a motorcycle dealer and I seem to remember that six, or maybe even eight, of the lovely little 125s ended up at the Crooks-Suzuki shop and I headed north to collect one of them.

Although I was tall and heavy for a 125, the Caballero felt really good as I ran it in and got to know its handling characteristics. In fact, it was a little flying machine which braked and handled a treat. Eddie valued my opinion and he was as pleased as I was when I phoned in to report on the good progress.

The problem is that testing is never quite the same as racing. Even in a hard test session, the bike is never under precisely the same stress as it is during actual competition – as Ed and I were to find out.

At most events in the 1970s, there was no specific class for 125s. To get the results which Eddie wanted in order to sell the bikes, I had to ride the Fantic very hard so that I would do well in the 250cc class against bikes of clearly twice the capacity.

This meant that I was simply flat out everywhere. I was, and still am, a very smooth rider, and easy on bikes, but with the Caballero I just had to ride it into the ground from the moment I left the start line.

The first event was the White Horse Enduro in Wiltshire. I was doing really well up to about half way through the event and, as I came screaming into a 90 degree right hand bend, the gearbox locked solid. This is the most frightening of all mechanical failures on a race bike because the rear wheel simply skids and there is nothing the rider can do about it.

I came off heavily but didn't break any bones. Ed and I shrugged our shoulders and said that it was simply one of those freak mechanical problems which happen in racing.

Roy Carey sent a brand new engine to me and I fitted it – which just shows how simple the job was!

The same thing happened during the next race in Mid-Wales and this time there was a sharp inhalation of breath from both of us because I had another big crash – but again with no serious injuries. The problem with gearbox failures is that they soon start eating away at the rider's mind. It doesn't matter if it is a World Champion or a Muppet like me – there is nothing you can do except hang on, and pray, when a gearbox gives up the ghost.

In the case of the Minarelli engines which powered the Fantics, the failures were very serious with the gearbox breakages being so severe that the whole crankcase was torn apart. It was not encouraging.

Another new motor arrived and this time I fitted it with far less enthusiasm. Eddie's reaction to all the problems is worth mentioning in some detail and it explains why I thought so much of him. He never once criticised me, or my riding, for the engine failures but was overwhelmingly supportive.

I entered the bike again, this time in a forestry enduro in Mid-Wales and, as usual, the bike flew as I started to regain my confidence. The Fantic really did handle well and I was pressing on down a fast, smooth fire-road and catching a quick KTM 250 in front of me. I came down from sixth – fifth, fourth and into third gear – then there was the all too familiar clonk. Unfortunately, I was slightly banked over at the time. The rear wheel snapped out and I was spat over the handlebars and into a rocky stream.

I took a real bang on the head and I was also very wet and cold. When I staggered back to the bike I was not in a good way.

On Monday morning, during the kids' break time, I phoned Ed. The conversation was short and, by his standards, very brusque. "Just leave the bike exactly as it is. Don't touch it. Bring it back to the shop this weekend.

"You're not going to ride it ever again. We'll find something better than that bloody thing."

And that is how a real sponsor looks after his rider. I learned an awful lot from Eddie which I carried over to my own teams when, later, I owned them.

Nothing much happened for five months and I didn't pester Ed because I had complete faith in him to find a bike for me. In any case, things were hectic at school.

***

I was really enjoying my work and I felt that I was doing what, morally, my teaching qualification allowed me to do in terms of educating kids who really needed help. The problem was that the pace was relentless. All day, every day, there were major social problems, as well as educational ones, and I ended up taking on God's role far too often for my liking.

There was a non-stop stream of Court Reports to write up and Case Conferences to attend. There were pregnancies for really young girls, which I found very upsetting, really bad marriage break ups, abusive parents and a myriad of other things - all of which impacted on the children's learning.

If a youngster was falling asleep at his desk on Monday morning because his parents had been at each other's throats – quite literally – all weekend, what was I supposed to do? Keep him in detention for lack of effort?

So I worked the kids hard, marked their work meticulously and demanded the highest standards from them and, through literacy, hoped that they would find the same way out of their environments as I had. In my eyes, literacy was the Holy Grail and so my classes read and wrote at a frenetic, non-stop pace and even the least able kids improved. The one phrase we never used was: "Can't do that..."

The greatest difficulty I faced was being required to make subtle, complex, choices about when to press a kid and when to turn a blind eye in kindness. It wasn't straightforward teaching and making these decisions really took its toll on me. Sometimes, at the end of a day, I used to sit at my desk unable to move I was so exhausted. It was only bikes which kept me sane.

***

One Friday evening in late Spring, the phone rang and it was Eddie. Could I get up to the shop the following day because he had something to show me? I had been through all of Autumn and Winter without a race bike, so you may imagine that I took very little persuasion.

When I arrived, Ed was all smiles. He took me through the shop to his tiny workshop and his young mechanic, John Wren, was pushing a lovely red and black Suzuki trail bike up the ramp and into Allison Street. Eddie beamed like a proud Dad with a new baby, and introduced me to the Suzuki TS250A trail bike.

The bike was not registered but Eddie was such a deity in Barrow that trivia like legalities tended not to get in the way of racing. The Suz was much bigger than the Fantic, and very much a trail bike rather than a thoroughbred competition machine, but it looked solid and friendly and, after being spat off the Fantic so often, these were big plus points. The bike started first kick and sounded lovely with a deep, confident, chuckling sound which said: "Come on, let's go riding."

I rode the new baby up and down the alley behind Ed's shop a couple of times and was immediately impressed. Where the Fantic was very much a 125, and small for me, the Suz was a big 250 with loads of room.

The Fantic needed buzzing flat out to make any progress but by contrast the Suzuki pulled like a train and was more like a 500 than a 250. I fell instantly in love. That's how complicated a racer's mind is!

I brought the bike back after a couple of minutes and Ed said: "Right, if you're happy we'll race it. But leave it here with us for a week because we've got some ideas."

Eddie had some clever mechanics in John Maddison and, although both were very young at the time, John Wren and Nigel Birkett. Plus, he had access to every part Suzuki had ever made.

When I went to collect the TS250 the following week, the bike had been put on a severe diet and all the road bits and pieces were back on the shelf ready for sale. In their place were lightweight racing plastics, a race carburettor, exhaust and air filter. In one week, Eddie's team had done a very neat job of converting what was very much a road biased bike into a proper off-roader. I was chuffed to bits.

I loved the TS250 – I really did. Just writing these words brings back memories of the friendliest bike I have ever raced. I rode it all that season, during which time that wonderful motorcycle never once let me down, and on the rare occasions I did crash the Suz it was always pilot error.

I won plenty of club enduros on the bike, and had some good rides in bigger events too, but this book is not a catalogue of the modest, the very modest, achievements of a club racer. I could ride enduros competently but no more. However, what I did do well was to promote the new sport and, of course, Eddie saw a business opportunity in my skills.

Whenever possible, I would loan the TS250 to other riders of my status – upwardly mobile clubmen. Often, they wanted a TS250 like my bike and Eddie was quick to sell them one. Just as importantly, all the parts to convert a standard TS250 were available for next day delivery from Crooks-Suzuki so Eddie sold loads of conversion kits. For a very modest investment in a bike and in me, Eddie got a really sound return.

For my part, I started a club aimed at trail bike sport. This was called the North Cheshire Trail Bike Club and we ran enduros, motocross and grass tracks just for trail bikes. We attracted huge entries because there were an awful lot of race converted trail bikes about at the time. In every way, it was a golden time for enduros and every form of trail bike sport.

***

My writing was pretty well flat out too - despite the fact that Motorcycle World and Cycle Illustrated simply disappeared. There was no explanation – and, by the way, they still owe me $800 – and this is the other side of the American way of doing business. If you are useful and productive then you will get paid without any recourse to your qualifications, background or even experience. If you can do the job, and make a profit for your company, you will be flavour – or flavor – of the month. Once your skill set is no longer needed, the Americans won't even waste a bullet on shooting you.

Motorcycle World and Cycle Illustrated were no longer profitable so they were closed down and I didn't exist anymore. There was no letter of thanks for my efforts, a leaving present or anything else. Instead, my letters didn't get answered and when I phoned, the receptionist told me that she knew nothing of the magazines. Click. Bang. You're gone!

To a lot of Brits, this seems harsh but I have no problems with the American way of doing things: it is the perfect way to live for the freelancer. When I couldn't get a word of my work published in England, the Americans took me purely on merit. For this, I will be eternally grateful. If I'm still owed $800, I'll take that as collateral damage – and a fair exchange for being collected at New Street Station, by a chauffeur holding a board carrying my name. That experience alone has got to be worth $800!

Not that the demise of the American magazines mattered much because I could barely keep up with the amount of work I was being asked to write in Britain – and the rest of the world. I produced articles for Motorcycle Weekly, Motorcyclist Illustrated and a new off-road newspaper/magazine called Trials and Motocross News.

Mainly I had great editors who left me alone to write what I was good at - which was irreverent feature stories. When they didn't like the content or style, as happened fairly quickly with Trials and Motocross News, I took my work elsewhere.

This is both the strength and weakness of the good freelance writer – and I do claim to be extremely good at my job. If you can find the right niche for a quality freelancer then we are an editor's dream. There is no need for any support, monitoring or supervision. We can handle all this ourselves. The ability to a complete a job without any help is in the DNA of the good freelancer and, in this respect, we are a magazine's lucky lottery ticket.

Equally, a magazine can never own a freelancer. An editor can only ask a freelancer to write for him and that relationship has to be mutually beneficial. Yes, the money is important – vitally so – but if you are going to have a, fairly, tame wolf cuddle up to you then it will need the occasional bone and its ears tickling every now and again.

The clever editor understands this and, during this period, I worked with one of the smartest editors ever to walk the planet: Colin Mayo of Motorcycle Mechanics.

At the time, "Mechanics" was hugely the biggest monthly magazine in Britain with a mammoth circulation of 112,000. Colin had both a good, and very tricky, hand of cards to play. At the core of the magazine were three very good writers in John Robinson, Brian Crichton and me. John and I were very strong willed and highly opinionated – "Badger" was more amenable.

Colin played the three of us like a Ringmaster in a circus – alternately tugging gently on the reins and feeding us sugar lumps when needed - with the occasional flick of the whip too. In so doing, he produced a really interesting magazine which melded three very different writing styles into a cohesive whole whilst still allowing each of us to retain our individual style.

It was a masterclass in management and I learned an awful lot from Colin.

***

It might seem odd to constantly swing between writing, racing and teaching but, in practice, all three fertilised each other – constantly and consistently. On an obvious level, I took racing into writing but I also transferred the freelancer's skills into teaching – and this was beginning to show because I was soon promoted to Head of Department. In this respect, I was one of the youngest teachers in Cheshire to achieve this position of responsibility.

Being HoD carried with it a lot of pressure but it also opened a whole host of new doors.

Some were really interesting. For the first time, I was being asked to lecture other teachers and give them advice on the education of less able pupils. In a spirit of modesty, I suppose I should say that I found the experience terrifying; that I was full of self-doubt and all the other blushing virgin things. However, none of that would be true. I prepared the course well; arrived at the venue early and worked everyone hard all day.

At the end, the Advisor who had booked me asked me to do another course later in the year. It was a freelance job done well – the only galling thing was that I didn't get paid a fee!

At the other end of the scale, being a hard core freelancer sometimes didn't quite fit the job specification. I was sent on a Senior Management training course to, of all places, Llandudno where Cheshire Education Authority had rented a big hotel as a training base. During one of the sessions, we were split up into groups and given a hypothetical educational problem to solve.

I was the by far the youngest teacher in the group but no-one objected when I offered to lead it. The experience was interesting. I found that almost everyone will follow a confident leader. They don't have to like you, or even agree with your ideas, but they do have to trust that you know what you are doing. These much more experienced teachers were willing to do what I asked them because they felt that we would be successful.

As things turned out, we were a bit too successful. I divided up the tasks equitably, everyone worked well and by 2pm the group was in the hotel bar, relaxing. The course leader was not best pleased and I was summoned into a private room for some personal re-education regarding the behaviour of a true leader. Why wasn't my group still hard at work until 5pm like all the other teams on the course? The answer came straight from the freelancer's bible. We had been given a job, done it well and finished. What was the problem?

On my appraisal sheet, which was sent back to my Head Teacher, the lead comment was: "Excessively goal orientated". I think that was meant to be a black mark against my name but I thought it was the highest praise. There had been a task which needed completing, we had done it successfully and moved on: that's what freelancers do.

***

Back on the racing front, Fate was about to give me a golden card and it carried the name PE250B. Eddie was the biggest Suzuki off-road dealer in Britain – and by a considerable margin. He moved dirt bikes in truly industrial quantities! Therefore, it was to be expected that he was one of the first people to hear about the all new PE250B. PE stood for Pure Enduro and B was the Suzuki model year designation for 1977. I stared at the brochure he sent to me and thought that I was looking at the Angel guarding the Gates of Heaven.

Where the TS, brilliant as it was, could only ever be a converted trail bike, the PE was a genuine competition motorcycle in every molecule of its being. At its heart was a proper race engine, with a wide ratio gearbox which meant that it could deal with everything from rocky climbs to fast forestry tracks.

The PE had a serious race chassis, with good suspension and brakes, and there was nothing to remove from the bike because it only carried the bare necessities to make it road legal. I was in love again!

PEs were criticised by the top flight riders for not being fast enough but I never had this problem. John Wren tuned the barrel on my bike so that it was a rocket ship which would catch anything my riding ability would allow.

The bike's only real fault was that it was made for durability and was therefore a bit on the heavy side. Against this, if you seriously bent a PE then, for certain, you would be looking down at the accident from a grandstand seat next to St. Peter because the bike was unbreakable.

Even more than my works BSA and the Cheney which Eric built for me, I loved that bike and, for a couple of years, it caused me to have dreams above my status. The PE arrived at the right time in my riding career. I was young enough to be super fit and had sufficient race experience to know the ropes inside out and back to front. If I was ever going to do anything in terms of competitive success it was at this time and on this bike, with Eddie as my sponsor.

The truth was that I did not do too badly on the PE. I won lots of minor enduros and even had the occasional good ride in a national event. However, the PE proved that most accurate of racing adages: class is forever – form is for a day.

If everything had gone well at school during the week; if the weather was perfect; if the course was fast and I got up with a beaming smile, then I could turn in a good performance which actually looked as though I could ride a motorcycle well. If everything wasn't absolutely perfect then it was back to being a racing Muppet.

However as well as being a wonderful motorcycle, the PE was very naughty in persuading me that I was a better rider than I actually was – and this delusion nearly got me killed.

★★★

To be fair to the Suz, the fault was as much mine as the bike's. I had reported on lots of GPs and travelled extensively throughout Europe and America. As a result, I really had a hot and heavy lust to walk out on to the start line carrying a Union Jack flag and waving to the crowd. Intellectually, I knew that I could never, ever - not even if the Archangel Gabriel was sat on the handlebars giving me advice - ride in a GP but that didn't stop me from dreaming.

It was following these fantasies which made me the first British entrant in what was, at the time, the most dangerous motorcycle race in the world. L'Enduro des Sables, or as it is known in English the Le Touquet Beach Race, was truly an event to die for - and in. The year I rode, it was still in all its pristine glory with 1300 or so entrants in a mass start, a five mile long straight and five fatalities. A Sunday afternoon club race it was not!

Le Touquet is in Northern France, just a few beaches away from the D-Day invasion sites, and is comprised of an ultra-swish and sophisticated town, some utterly enormous sand dunes and, when the tide is out, a wet, concrete hard beach stretching for something in the region of seven miles.

The reason that I ended up at Le Touquet in February was that I should have paid more attention to Miss Pillar's French lessons instead of spending my time surreptitiously reading motorcycling magazines under my desk.

The story begins in August 1977. The weather at the Belgian round of the 500cc World Motocross championship was blistering and, inside the Citadel of Namur, the dust hovered like dense clouds of light brown talcum powder for the whole of practice.

Whatever you think of the GP motocross riders in the 1970s no-one can doubt their courage. Truly, they had cojones like fit Hereford bulls but on that August Sunday they just refused to ride, so dangerous were the conditions. The track at Namur threaded its way one bike wide through the trees and around the houses, and visibility was zero – as in you couldn't see the bike three feet in front of you. Someone was going to get killed - so there was a strike.

I was writing a feature on the GP, and also taking pics, so to fill the time until the GP was on again I gossiped to a French journalist. Ahhh, Miss Pillar was sitting at her desk in Heaven smiting me for my inattention.

The Gallic journo explained that every February there was a light-hearted mess about at Le Touquet, where a few of the off-road boys got together for a sort of track day on the beach, glugged a lot of wine and ate some rather fine food.

After a good season with the PE, I was very full of myself and ready for a European adventure. If it wasn't exactly a GP, it was riding in a foreign country and I could pretend.

The plan was to show off to the French with a few power slides on the beach and then get stuck into le menu Gastronomique. At least, this is what I thought I had translated.

The first problem was that at the end of the season my 1977 Suz had been sold and the 1978 model had yet to arrive. Still, with Ed's permission I was allowed to ask Arthur Arnold, the owner of Knott Mill Kawasaki in Manchester, if I could borrow his Kawasaki KE 175 trail bike demonstrator.

It is important to put the little Kwack into perspective. The bike was an utterly non-competition spec. road biased trailie aimed at commuting and light recreational use. In fact, it was a gentler, more road orientated version of my much loved TS250. However, there was a smattering of these inoffensive little bikes being used by total beginners in club enduros and they had gained a reputation for being bomb proof reliable – not to say surprisingly competent off-road.

I explained to Arthur that Le Touquet was a bit of light-hearted fun but he was concerned. What if it wasn't such a play event as I thought? What if it was actually a race? I dismissed his worries but Arthur still insisted on putting a crash resistant enduro light kit on the bike and a set of race knobblies.

So now we had a cute little street trail bike which looked as if it might manage some light trail riding. How cool would that be when I was doing my demo do-nuts on the beach?

The first hint of suspicion came when I received what looked awfully like race entry forms. The man behind L'Enduro des Sables was Thierry Sabine – master mind of the Paris-Dakar races – and the man who invented extreme off road events. Thierry's reputation was based on never, ever doing easy.

Still what could go wrong? If it was a bit of a demo race so what? I was winning plenty of trophies and was confident that a few inebriated Frenchmen wouldn't embarrass me.

Sometimes racers just can't take a hint. As we drove down to the docks at Dover to catch the ferry across the English Channel to Boulogne, the rain attacked the van like 20mm cannon fire whilst the wind tried to roll us off the approach road and into the sea. In all the many times I had made the Channel crossing I had never, ever seen a ferry rocking so violently – and that was whilst it was still tied up in Dover Harbour!

Still, we had a brilliantly cheap deal on the trip to Boulogne and at least I didn't have to sleep on the deck of the King Orry like the early TT days.

The English Channel isn't considered to be a proper sea but the masses of green water breaking over the upper deck's lounge window gave a good imitation of the perfect storm in the mid-Atlantic. I was sick, my unpaid pit-crew-cum-general-dog's-body was utterly sick, the ship's crew were sick and I guess that down below the little Kawasaki threw up too.

We staggered off at Boulogne and I had to stop the van almost immediately – to be sick again. Thank goodness it wasn't a serious race the following day.

Ten miles out from Le Touquet it finally dawned on me that this was a major event. The roads were absolutely jammed with bikes large and small. Full-on enduro bikes screamed past on the grass verges, mo-peds pushed through on either side whenever we stopped and passengers in Wehrmacht replica BMW sidecar outfits swung their machine guns round on the cheering crowds. I had dreamed of riding in a GP – now my wishes had come true, certainly in terms of the number of spectators.

Scrutineering confirmed my worst nightmares. This was a race – and a proper one too. We unloaded the little Kwack and joined the end of the queue. An hour later, a snowdrop appeared. It blossomed and died. In front, a bored French couple made love. She became pregnant and gave birth. The lined moved again. Continents were formed quicker than our progress to the scrutineering team…

What made things worse was that everything which obsessed British technical control held no interest for the French. Brakes: don't care. Self-closing throttle: it's up to you. Race numbers: oui, parfait. But the lights – goodness me the lights! Did they work? Being a road bike they actually functioned quite well. Now main beam, now dip, now main beam again. I was beginning to think that this was a night race.

Cold, tired and feeling as if I had just spent three hours throwing up on a Channel ferry, I slunk off to the hotel. The mussels in white wine, garlic and parsley looked delicious. And indeed, they proved to be so – until the first one hit my stomach and it was off to les toilettes again.

It was a long night and an interesting one. I lay on the bed, doubled up in agony whilst outside the hotel the final of the all France, unsilenced mo-ped race was in full swing. As the last mo-peders exited at 5am I crashed into a tortured sleep – until the alarm went off 20 minutes later.

One look at the croissants convinced me that food was not a good option so we set off to retrieve the little Kwack and discover what the day held.

The first problem was that the bike, in the Parc Fermé, and the work area on the beach lay a couple of miles apart – and of the three of us, only I would drive in France. Still, with much arm waving, horn honking and "Allez! Allez! Je suis un pilote!" I forced the borrowed van down to the sea front – and got a real shock!

Next to us was the factory SWM team who had travelled all the way from Italy - complete with spare wheels, quick filler fuel cans, three factory mechanics and a Team Manager. I looked at our single jerry can of pump fuel, one tin of chain lube and the Kwack's tool roll and realised that Monsieur Cock Up really had come for afternoon tea.

Now the van was in the right place, in the work area, but the bike was still in the Parc Fermé, outside the Town Hall, where all of the bikes had been stored over night after scrutineering.

Getting to the Kwack was not as difficult as it seems. I had paid a little bit of attention to Miss Pillar so it was merely a case of standing in the middle of a stream of traffic doing 60mph, flagging down the first bike to make eye contact and demanding a lift to the Town Hall. Simple, if you have no sense of danger and you're desperate!

When I arrived there it was like the Challenge Cup Final at Wembley, half an hour before kick-off. Bikes were everywhere and a dense fog of two-stroke fumes hung over the Parc Fermé as riders battled with their bikes, arm waving officials, increasingly tense police dogs and each other, for a slot through the one bike wide exit gate.

Once out into Le Touquet's elegant town centre things became even worse. You've never seen true danger until an amateur tries to pull his first ever wheelie, surrounded by 1000 over hyped racers – and then crashes into a lamp post bringing down five of his fellow competitors.

Girlfriends rushed out to plant kisses on the cheeks of their heroes, Grandad was wheeled out into the centre of the road to shake his grandson's hand. Mum stuffed a baguette sandwich down the riding jacket of her little boy. The amateur racer's life was revealed in living colour!

By this time, I was feeling fine. The threat of real, serious danger and a lot of racing experience had combined to kick in the adrenaline and focus my mind. This job had the potential to get me killed if I didn't start to take it seriously.

The chaos was even worse at the start. I never did find out the exact number of starters but the figure lay between 1200 and 1500. The idea was that there would be three rows of 500 or so – and that's a lot of bikes – arranged on the beach with the quickest riders seeded to row one.

I was directed to the third row back and I could immediately see the problem of hurtling down the beach with 1000 bikes in front of me. So, with a bit of polite elbowing and convenient mis-understanding of instructions I soon manoeuvred the Kwack to the first row.

Directly facing us was a water-filled ditch which stretched the whole width of the beach and into the sea. In fact, at the far right, 50 or 60 riders were actually in the water. In front, stretching away out of sight, was flat empty sand.

I hadn't a clue where the course lay so I asked the KTM rider next to me how far it was to the first corner. He smiled and said, "Huit kilomètres sur la gauche."

8 kilometres – that was five miles and flat out all the way. Suddenly, the cross channel sea-sickness returned.

We were told to watch a Landrover parked in the water and when someone waved something, the race would start. It didn't happen like that. The waves started breaking over the bikes in the sea and, with the wholly reasonable excuse that they were drowning, off they went and L'Enduro des Sables had started.

For the first 25 yards, the Kwack was competitive and I was in the leading group. Then we weren't!

I simply pinned the throttle, lay flat on the tank road racing style - and prayed. Why the sudden affection for God? All around me were high speed crashes, as riders with more bike than ability discovered that riding at 90mph on wet sand demands a considerable degree of skill.

In front of me, a tricked out Yamaha XT500 started to weave. The golden rule in these situations is to sit back and nail the throttle. The Yam's pilot shut off and leaned forward.

It's a fascinating sight to see a rider cartwheel through the air in front of you but not nearly so interesting as observing a white fuel tank, gushing fuel, bounce down the track directly at your bike.

The tank is travelling at 60 mph up the beach and I am travelling at 60 mph down the beach. This is going to hurt. I tuck my left shoulder tight into the Kwack and petrol sprays from the Yam's tank as it neatly pirouettes over my shoulder. It really was that close.

The first corner is a motorcycling version of a medieval cavalry charge. Bikes are everywhere – on their sides, upside down, on fire, bent, broken and no longer of this world.

I came down two gears and blasted through, round and yes, I have to admit it, over bikes and riders. Even so, it was surprising how long you can hear the scream of someone who has just had a knobbly tyre spin over his manly parts!

The rest of the 15 mile course was very natural and simply ran up one giant sand dune and down the other. Chaos ruled but the baby Kwack ran to perfection – all the way up to within half a mile from the service area. Then it started to cut out. I flicked the fuel tap on to reserve, in case sand had got into the tank, and pressed on. Clearly, the bike wouldn't do another lap like this with sand in the tank so I pulled in for a check. The answer was obvious. There was no fuel.

Normally, the KE175 would do a comfortable 40mpg even off-road. At Le Touquet, I was caning the bike so hard that this had fallen to 10mpg.

Lap 2 showed that sometimes the God of Racing loves amateurs. The blast down the beach was as bad as ever but the first corner was ten times worse and the hills were blocked solid with the dead bikes and nearly dead riders. Then, the sun came out.

Factory Yamaha rider Serge Bacou came blasting past me and as he reached the base of the first killer hill, an army of hitmen from Sonauto – the French Yamaha importer – appeared. Two of them grabbed the fork legs on Serge's bike and another four ran in front and hurled bikes and bodies out of the way. I stayed glued to rear wheel of the Yam and suddenly I was rising up the race order - and rapidly too. It must have been the slowest ever slipstreaming but it was effective.

In between hills I rode with reckless determination to keep Bacou in sight and it worked. Another hill and a further 100 up the order.

On the final lap, I actually waited to be lapped by another factory Yamaha rider and off we went again.

I did three laps without getting killed which I count as one of my best ever rides but I wasn't looking forward to the second leg, to be held after lunch. I need not have worried. The gale force winds drove the tide up the beach and even the bonkers French had to abandon the job.

So, I can claim – I think – to be the first Englishman ever to compete in L'Enduro des Sables and with 135th place, from an entry of over 1300, probably the happiest – thanks of course to being an unofficial member of the works Yamaha team and whilst riding a Kawasaki too!

Le Touquet was a real experience but freelancing was going to take me on some more very interesting foreign ventures.

Now, I was about to find out how cold Sweden is in winter - and I came across some very strange weather at a Concentration Camp.

16

Concentration Camps and Skis
– the Freelancer's World

I want to avoid turning this book into a replica of one of those racing memoires where the story is that I raced at this event and got that result on a 250cc works whatever.

So here's a summary. I rode a lot of factory bikes, which no-one else got to test, and I worked with a lot of world champions. My favourite of them all was Roger De Coster, who I came to know quite well. He was gracious, modest, patient, courteous and helpful – and still managed to win five World Motocross Championships. If you ever wanted the perfect role model for a professional motorcycle racer, it would be Roger.

As a by-product of my close connections with the top echelons of motocross, I was able to pursue an idea which had been gnawing away at me for a number of years. By 1978, motocross was an intensely professional sport. Yet, just ten years earlier Paul Friedrichs had become World Champion whilst riding part time and also working as an East German policeman.

In 1978, the paddock was full of race transporters and motorhomes whereas Friedrichs arrived at events with his CZ bikes on a trailer. The rate of change was amazing!

I wanted to chart this meteoric development whilst it was still fresh in everyone's mind. Moreover, I wanted to do well what Miss Boardsley at S.Kaths had said I was good at: be a Chronicler rather than a Historian. So my new book, which was called "The Big Leap", was far more an epic tale than it was a list of dates, riders and results.

Roger De Coster was particularly helpful and it was from him that I got the story of Yamaha, Suzuki and Honda all vying for the first practical Monoshock suspension system to be used in motocross. In the end a French speaking Yamaha engineer, with a gut feeling for what would work, bought the Monoshock from Belgian Lucien Tilkiens and took it back to Japan. The Big Leap is full of stories like this which tell the human side of racing.

The book was published by Hamlyn and they were great to work for. The editor rang me every couple of months for a chat and I delivered the manuscript ahead of schedule. At the start of the project, I had been offered two options by Hamlyn. The first was a standard royalty contract and the second a serious lump of money as an advance, followed by double that amount on completion. To a simple freelancer, having this much money on the table looked too good to be true so I took the cash offer. As it happened, I was wrong because I was later told that The Big Leap sold tens of thousands of copies and I would have done well with a royalty contract.

What Hamlyn did was very smart – and new to me. Instead of selling the book through motorcycling channels, as GT Foulis had done with The Complete Book of Motocross, Hamlyn whacked it out along with cookery books and footballers' autobiographies. It was a really odd experience to walk into WH Smiths and see stacks of the book piled high, with non-motorcycling customers browsing the pages to see if it was birthday present material.

I used to get really embarrassed as I stood there, because there are a few pics of me in the book and I would have been mortified if someone had recognised me. So I would play the voyeur, pick up a copy and pretend to browse through it - all the time listening to what my potential customers were saying. Fortunately, with sales of many thousands it was clear that quite a lot of people liked it!

The 1970s was a wonderful period, with a freedom which is unimaginable today. In the rest of this chapter, I want to try to give you a flavour of the freelancer's life at this time.

First, the summer of 1976 – and before you read the next section I know what we did was wrong, irresponsible, reckless and every other adjective which today's society would apply to our behaviour!

It was an August of astonishing heat and I had a contract to write features about European GPs. The race reports were to be written by real journalists, who were good at facts, whilst I was to convey the look, feel and taste of Grand Prix racing.

I borrowed a 750cc BMW from the British importer and my wife and I loaded it with two saddle bags, plus all my photography gear. We rode across Europe in the baking heat – she wearing a t-shirt, jeans, tennis shoes and a helmet and me, only slightly better protected, in identical gear, plus a pair of thin race gloves.

Cruising at 90mph, we felt we were riding inside the wind as we ate the baking air, swallowed it and let the torrent wash over and through us. We were one with the bike, and the heat, and the immortality of youth.

Deep in Eastern France, we stopped at a restaurant and the Patron told us tales of the French Resistance and blowing up German trains. Afterwards, we lay in the shade by a sun dappled stream and slept off the wine before riding again.

Coming back from Italy over the Gran san Bernardino Pass, I looked down at the BMW's twin exhausts glowing cherry red in the dark as my wife slept soundly, her head resting on my shoulders.

It was a wonderful time to be immortal.

★★★

Being a well-known freelance author conferred many benefits and a warm relationship with BMW was one of them. This next story is rather strange but, as with the rest of this book, it is as true as I can tell it and you may judge what happened, or perhaps didn't, for yourself.

I have stressed that I was never a good rider against top quality opposition but in terms of journalists I was at, or very near, to the best around. This is why I got an invitation from BMW to write an article about their 1981 Paris Dakar winning bike, which Hubert Auriol had ridden to victory.

I liked the BMW competition department staff a lot. They were a million miles distant from the suits and slick presentations of the road bike PR staff. They knew I could ride so, basically, we went to BMW's off road test centre, played about on the bike for a day and pretended that it was work when it wasn't really.

Not that everything went exactly to plan. The Dakar bike was just as Auriol had finished the rally and there was about half a ton of sand in the petrol tank and it wouldn't start. To get it going, the bike had to be towed behind a Mercedes G-Wagon along an unmade road. Now, hands up all those riders who want to be towed, at high speed, down a dirt track, by a mad BMW race mechanic, when the bike is so tall that it's impossible to touch the ground.

Nevertheless, we eventually got the big Beemer fired up and BMW's photographer was a dream to work with so we got some nice pics.

However, by the end of session the bike was really coughing and spluttering and, rather than come back the following day for another go, as had been in the original schedule, we jointly agreed that the job was over.

The race staff wanted to get on with their jobs so they dug out an R75 road bike, which was being used as a test mule, and told me to go for a ride. They would see me in the evening for dinner. The weather was stunning – a wonderful late Autumn, Bavarian day – and I had just got a world exclusive in the bag, so professionally and personally every box was ticked. Just as good, I knew that tonight would be great fun with the race shop lads. If this wasn't a perfect day then it was "or very near offer".

I always liked the R75. The 750cc motor was the smoothest of the BMW large capacity flat twins and so I set off with a happy heart and a big smile. As I have said, the weather was truly beautiful and I cruised through the back lanes riding in just in a thin race jacket, jeans and my helmet.

I was in no rush to go anywhere - and had nowhere in particular to go. It was recreational motorcycling at its most relaxing. That's why what happened

171

next was really odd. I was riding along a pretty little lane and suddenly felt very cold. There was no apparent reason for the change in temperature - no trees or water filled valley, nothing which could account for the penetrating cold which immediately ate right through my gloves, jacket and jeans. What was even more puzzling was that the sun was as bright as ever.

At the end of the lane was a sign to the Dachau Concentration Camp. This was the first of the Nazi death camps and opened in 1933. It even managed to get into German popular culture of the time with this chilling rhyme:

"Lieber Herr Gott, mach mich stumm,

Das ich nicht nach Dachau komm"

"Dear God, make me dumb,

"That I may not to Dachau come"

No-one knows accurately how many people were murdered at Dachau but the Nazi records admit to over 31,000 deaths. There were, no doubt, many more.

I parked the bike outside and walked in, still inside the bubble of inexplicable cold. The camp is a mere shadow of its original self but I could still get an idea of the industrial scale of the organised, thorough, every day massacres which took place at Dachau.

I was shocked at how different Dachau was compared with the Prisoner of War camps I had seen in war films. There were no wooden posts or barbed wire fences for the brave RAF prisoners to dig under and escape. No plucky heroes, armed only with home-made identity papers, bluffed their way to freedom here. Dachau was a large factory for killing people with the minimum of cost and maximum efficiency.

I must have spent three hours silently walking the site and looking at the photographs of the emaciated prisoners jammed into their four tier high bunks. Their gaunt, grey, hopeless faces still haunt me today. Rarely can the word hopeless be more accurately applied to humanity.

Afterwards, I walked back to the R75, fired it up and rode off. Two or three miles from the death camp, I suddenly rode out of the bubble of cold and into the warmth. There were no marker posts to indicate the boundary I had just crossed or any other conceivable reason why I should go from cold to warm in just a few yards. Regardless, this is what happened and the memory remains as clear to me today as it was at the time.

That night, I was quiet at dinner.

I'm not superstitious, or given to believing in magic or the paranormal, but I do wonder whether Dachau was so evil that something beyond logic and current understanding was apparent that day.

That story needed telling, lest we ever forget what happened in those death camps, but the next tale was a more accurate reflection on what a great time I had writing about bikes.

Being a freelancer took me to places and situations which I would have never seen if I had been a successful teacher and nothing else. One of these avenues led me to the wonderful town of Husqvarna, home of the iconic Husqvarna motorcycle factory, located in the centre of Southern Sweden.

Husqvarna had originally been gun manufacturers and the factory was the site of the Swedish Royal Armaments factory. When I got to know these lovely people the factory was the world leader in two-stroke motocross machines and had won 12 World Motocross Championships, in the 250cc and 500cc categories.

I had been introduced to the factory through the British Husqvarna importer, Brian Leask. Brian belonged to the Eddie Crooks/Doug Hacking mould in terms of PR awareness. He was keen to harvest the publicity which he knew would result from my visit and so fixed it up with one of the most amazing men in motorcycling PR – the one and only Norbert Kunze. Norbert was so special that I'll come back to him in some detail later.

Husqvarna is on the northern edge of Jönköping, in southern central Sweden, and in winter it is cold! Reaching Jönköping wasn't easy and I flew first to Schipol, the huge air terminus outside Amsterdam for international flights. Then it was a short hop up the coast to Copenhagen and, finally, a local flight to Jönköping in an ancient DC4 propeller engined plane.

This aircraft was almost a commuter bus for Swedish and Danish business-men and their families, and they treated it as such. We took off in the driving rain, at what felt like10mph, and I wasn't best pleased. In fact, as the plane was weaving its way down the runway I was beginning to have serious doubts about the whole exercise.

We bumped and snaked across the sky - whilst I sat rigid in my seat, muttering prayers to every sky God I could contact. Meanwhile, across the aisle, a Mum and child were colouring in Mickey Mouse. Clearly, I didn't have the right mental set for this journey!

It was an absolute blizzard as we approached Jönköping and, from my window seat, I couldn't even see the nearest engine. All around me, Swedes folded up their papers ready for exit and Mums chatted to their kids and tickled babies' cheeks. As this domestic bliss went about its happy way, my finger nails dug holes in the seat arms!

The DC4 slewed drunkenly all over the sky and the snow got ever heavier then, without any warning, came the black blur of a forest. I adopted the brace position – whilst the jolly Swede next to me kindly offered to help me find whatever I had dropped on the floor. After all, why else would I be in a ball, with my head between my knees?

Truthfully, the plane touched down not so much with the thump which all airline passengers know so well but with far more of a large plop. It was all that I could do not to fall on the floor and start babbling prayers of thanks.

Meanwhile, the Scandinavians bustled about and hummed to themselves because, clearly, this was a completely normal way to arrive.

Norbert was waiting for me in a Russian fur hat with his coat collar turned up to his ears. Welcome to Sweden!

Mr. Kunze had a rather thin, somewhat pinched, face which was split into an almost permanent smile. Before we had left the airport terminal, a real bond had formed between us.

Of all the characters I have met in the bike industry, Norbert was one of the most interesting. He was an Austrian who, in 1939, really had found the lucky ticket in life's lottery because at the outbreak of World War II he was studying Scandinavian languages at Stockholm University. With a commendable soundness of judgement he had ignored the call to join both the Nazi Party and the German Army, and had stayed in neutral Sweden for the duration of the war: what a smart decision that was!

Even though officially neutral, Norbert's political views were what might charitably be called somewhat right of centre – especially after a few drinks. With wholly commendable wisdom and foresight, he never fired a bullet during the conflict and so, unlike many millions of his countrymen, stayed alive.

However, his defining trait was a burning loyalty to, and enthusiasm for, Husqvarna. If you had told Norbert that he could have good press coverage if he walked naked across Lake Vättern in the middle of winter carrying a reindeer on his back, he would have been on the ice in an instant: he loved Husqvarna.

There were a number of reasons Norbert and I got on so well – and some of them were quite unusual. First, it was recognised at Husqvarna that I could ride a motorcycle competently and this was respected. The second group of reasons was rather odd. Husqvarna was owned by the Electrolux group at the time and many journalists pressed Norbert for gifts – whether this was in the form of fridges, chainsaws or anything else which took their fancy. Even blonde haired, Swedish prostitutes had been on the wish list.

By contrast, I wanted only exclusive access to bikes which would make a good story. My puritan attitude got me a world exclusive test on the 360 Husqvarna which won the 1974 World Championship – and only three days after Heikki Mikkola took the crown. This was when every magazine in the world was beating on Norbert's door to write about the bike.

Yes, I did get some nice presents from the factory but I never demanded or even asked for them. In a way, this made things like the hand-made Husqvarna cuff links which I was given all the more important to me. I was really grateful for the factory's kindness.

Finally, I could take alcohol or leave it – I really wasn't bothered one way or the other. At the time, alcohol was incredibly expensive in Sweden but factories were given an allowance to entertain foreign customers and guests. I fell into this category and so had an alcohol allowance attached to me. Since I was more than happy to have a Coke or mineral water my allowance could go straight to my Swedish hosts – and goodness me, they did enjoy a drink!

I visited the factory on a number of occasions, and every single one produced a good story and warm memories but the one trip which stands out was the not the Mikkola bike but the time when Norbert phoned and asked me for a favour.

Just after the Christmas of 1978, Norbert contacted me and asked whether I would like to try an all new bike which would change the face of motorcycling forever. I was keen on anything which would make a good story and we agreed that I would fly into Jönköping - which I hoped would be blizzard free this time because I was still terrified of snow landings.

The new motorcycle had been developed to fulfil a Swedish Army contract and there were potentially large sales hanging on the success of the deal. If the Army took the new Husky, it would be hugely helpful to the factory and so Norbert was a lot more tense than normal. Not only were the numbers important but military contracts were highly lucrative because armies order precisely the same item for the whole of the production run - and then buy loads of spares. No wonder Norbert wasn't in a jovial mood when he met me - there was so much to play for.

The Swedish Army had demanded a motorcycle which would transform a raw beginner into a competent rider in five working days. The bike had to be a true, multi-purpose machine which would have decent highway performance, be good on the tens of thousands of miles of forestry trails which cover much of Sweden and, critically, would work in snow and ice. It was a demanding specification to meet.

Husqvarna's solution was a most elegant piece of engineering. Using most of the bits from their existing 250cc enduro bike, the factory designed a truly remarkable gearbox which would make the bike instantly easy to ride.

The initial drive from a static position was taken up by a centrifugal clutch just like a Honda 50 Cub. This was well proven practice and nothing radical. As the rpm increased, a series of dog clutches engaged ever higher gears until top in the three speed 'box was reached.

When the throttle was closed, the engine free-wheeled. As power was applied again, the rear wheel speed told the gearbox what gear it needed - and off you went. It really was that simple.

In fact, it was easier for non-motorcyclists to ride the bike because they knew nothing about engine braking or using a clutch.

Remember also, that all this happened a long time before sophisticated electronics had been developed and so, being a completely mechanical system, it was both very rugged and easily repaired in a war zone.

When the bike was used in the snow, two enormous skis - one on either side of the bike - pivoted down to touch the snow. This gave the Husky a true, all terrain performance.

The overall concept was, in theory at least, very simple. On highways or trails clear of snow, the rider put his feet on the normal footrests. To give drive on ice, the rear tyre was studded with what looked like pop rivets - but with sharp heads. These dug into the ice and gave, I was assured, enormous grip. Once in snow, the rider half sat on the saddle and half stood on the skis whilst the rear of the bike provided the motive power.

The following day we met the design team. Rubin Helmin was Husky's Chief Designer. He explained how important the Army contract was to the factory, patiently talked me through the engineering and was at pains to stress that the joy of the concept was that it required virtually nothing new in the way of fresh tooling or R&D. Clever though the new 'box was, it was a real "garden shed" effort which would have horrified the Japanese.

The army bike was built in Husky's race shop. This was a tiny affair for a company which lived and died by its racing success and again reflected the fact that the Swedish factory really had its back against the wall and just had to make the Army contract succeed.

That night, Norbert took me out to dinner. The Husky team drank my alcohol allowance and I sipped water and listened to stories which, even today, are wholly unprintable.

If nothing else, the Swedes could hold their drink and in the cold, dawn light I was heading out in a Husqvarna van to try the new bike with the Husky R&D staff as fresh as daisies. We arrived somewhere deep in the countryside with an arctic wind blowing and the thermometer showing a brisk, minus 15 centigrade.

I went to get changed in the back of the van. By now, I was becoming distinctly edgy over the whole exercise. I just wanted to finish the job and get back to some nice English drizzle and mud. My first mistake was to put a damp finger on the unlined van wall. It stuck instantly and one of the Husky staff had to melt the area above my frozen fingers with a cigarette lighter. They sighed at my stupidity and were even less impressed with my motocross gloves. Ride in those, I was told, and you are certain to get frostbite. This was even less encouraging.

They dug around in one of their toolboxes and found some reindeer skin mittens which were their most essential piece of winter riding kit.

Everyone was really tense and this worried me because Husky staff were normally very laid back and relaxed. They kept on re-assuring me that the concept, and the bike, were both totally idiot proof and that nothing could go wrong. As the snow whipped through the flat grey light, I was given my instructions.

Take the Army bike on to the damp, Tarmac surfaced road. Open the throttle flat out and the bike would accelerate effortlessly. Continue – still flat out – on to the sheet ice of the access road. And no, don't worry because each knobble on the motocross tyres carries a little metal stud which means that perfect grip is assured.

I looked at the tiny studs - and the sheet of polished ice on which we were standing - and I felt horribly sick.

When I hit the packed snow, I was told to treat it the same as firm loam in an enduro and just keep the throttle pinned. When I finally arrived at the big right-hand corner, I was to lean forward just as if I were broad sliding an enduro bike, put my foot on the ski and the bike would float round effortlessly. My freelancer's danger warning system was screaming one question to the rest of my brain. If everything was so simple and fool proof, how come everyone was looking so very nervous?

I was under a lot of pressure and the fact that virtually the whole of Husqvarna's Senior Management, all wrapped in their heavy coats and fur hats, were lining the outside of the big right-hander only heightened the tension. This was strange – and very disconcerting!

Norbert forced a smile and waved encouragement - and I set off down the Tarmac with all the enthusiasm of a condemned prisoner on the way to the gallows. However, I was immediately impressed by the Auto. I nervously opened the throttle, just as a raw novice would do, and it pottered away like a 50cc scooter. The studded tyres made a droning noise on the Tarmac but not to worry - I wasn't going road racing.

Half a mile away, I turned the bike round and the Husky staff waved - more desperately than enthusiastically. I whacked the throttle full open and the little two-stroke ambled off briskly down the tarmac. So far, so good.

We hit the sheet ice and I tensed, ready for the inevitable crash, but the Husky just wriggled a little and we carried on effortlessly. It was bizarre.

Now we were doing around 50mph. On to the snow and another wriggle but nothing worse than riding in loose earth. This was fun. Those studs - tiny though they may have been - really worked.

Then into the 90 degree right-hander. I dropped the bike in, leaned forward and put my right foot firmly on the ski. The springs allowed the ski to touch the snow, the back-end floated out and a really satisfying rooster tail sprayed snow over the great and good from the factory. This was easy - and fun.

In really deep snow, I simply put both skis down and the bike's rear wheel acted rather in the fashion of a Mississippi paddle steamer and we powered along leaving huge grooves in the snow. A change of career beckoned. Did the Swedish Army want an English recruit?

The Husky staff eventually dragged me off the bike, ignoring my pleas for just another ten minutes. I got changed, without touching the van wall, and was driving back to the factory hot, happy and feeling good about life in general. Norbert was happy too - and visibly relaxed from the morning. I pressed him to know what had caused the tension.

He explained. There were a lot of jobs hanging on the success of the Army project. I was only the second person outside of the Husqvarna test staff to ride the bike - and the first one was still in hospital recovering from injuries sustained on the fast right-hander where I had playfully been showering the Husky staff with snow.

That night, I did drink my beer allowance.

17

All Change - the Train Finishes at This Station

THIS is going to be a difficult chapter to write because so many major changes happened in such a short time. I have already mentioned that, in my eyes, there were very blurred boundaries between teaching, writing professionally and riding and all three experiences always fed each other. However, during this period of my life the demarcation lines really did become fuzzy!

Writing was as successful as ever but it wasn't so satisfying. I could write bike tests all day long but because I could do them they were in danger of being formulaic. My saviour came through teaching. My department was developing a national reputation for excellence and so we were visited by two educationists, who were collecting examples of best practice from all over the country.

They made lots of positive comments about the department but expressed their concern at the lack of books written for the least able pupils in Secondary Education. The same thought had already crossed my mind and so I eased off writing about bikes and produced the "Project" series for Heinemann Educational.

Writing for this very mainstream publisher really was an odd experience for a hard core motorcycle freelancer. I caught a train to London and hopped across to the posh Heinemann offices on the edge of Soho. The Commissioning Editor was a very sophisticated gentleman who personified English courtesy. He was so incredibly well-mannered that I became quite confused!

I was used to working with editors like Colin Mayo who made decisions on the hoof and in seconds! "Okay Frank, what's the idea? Yes, great! Send in 1500 words by the 23 March."

Or: "No, that won't fit with what we're doing at the moment. Remind me in a couple of months. Gotta go now. Cheers."

Editors like this I could understand.

I made my pitch to Heinemann and was greeted with a lovely, warm, all enveloping cloud of ambivalence. Yes the idea looked good and yes, it fitted in with what Heinemann were trying to achieve but, on the other hand, no-one had done anything like this before and therefore it might not be a commercial success but, then again, it met Heinemann's philosophical aims - but looked at from a different perspective..."

Arrrghhh! I was being driven crazy. Look. I'm a freelancer and I can do a good job for you. Do you want the thing or not?

Eventually, Heinemann did take the book and the first one grew into a series which did very well commercially. Heinemann and I both made plenty of money from these books.

If the commissioning of the work was different from working with a bike magazine then the way I was treated was a very new experience too. Every month or so, my editor would phone me for a chat. We talked about education, literature, art and politics and then, almost in the last breath, there was a passing comment about the progress of the latest book.

This was a real out of body experience for me. Editors of bike magazines almost never phoned and when they did, the #1 topic was the work they had commissioned. It wouldn't have mattered if I had just broken both legs or got Ebola virus, the conversation would have been the same.

"Don't be a selfish b*****d and die - until you've finished the job!"

That was their mantra – and I loved it.

★★★

I continued to do well at school and my success opened not so much one potential fork in my life's path but a myriad of them. Where to start?

Things are no doubt much better now but, at the time, the management training of teachers was dire. All of my promotion had been based on my skill as a classroom teacher and this led to huge gaps in my management skills – immense ones.

In fact, schools throughout the country lacked professional managers. The Heads of Department were often skilled teachers, and had the best interests of the kids at heart, but everything was short term. Get through the lesson, the day, the week, the term and the year will sort itself out.

I became increasingly dissatisfied with what was happening around me and one thing in particular caused me genuine distress. There was a national initiative called "Language Across the Curriculum." It was one of the best concepts ever to be devised. The idea was that, instead of the English Department taking the sole responsibility for literacy in a school, every Faculty would teach language skills to a common, agreed standard. So, if a pupil made a spelling error in a Science subject it would be corrected in the same way as it would in English, Humanities or Mathematics. The kids would be immersed in literature, of every form, and so written and spoken English standards would be raised. That lovely lady from Warrington Library was calling to me again!

My fellow Heads of Department listened politely, murmured approval – and in just one term the whole project had died. The problem was that although my Head Teacher backed me in theory, he lacked the long term vision to force the changes through.

In three months, I knew that I had failed – and it hurt.

The first step towards solving this problem was for me to teach myself management skills. That way, maybe the next time I could carry my ideas forward and take my colleagues with me too. Inevitably, I turned to books and spent a small fortune on management tomes so that I could learn the theory behind the practice of leading people.

Not a minute of the hundreds of hours was wasted because if I couldn't be the manager I wanted to be at school, then my aspirations were to be fulfilled later, when I owned a race team.

I need to jump back to racing now because a lot was happening there too. First, and to my everlasting sadness, Eddie Crooks stopped sponsoring me. It was for the silliest of reasons and, ironically, had nothing to do with me.

Suzuki had an off-road department, as well as a road division, and the dirt bike section was run by an ex-motocross rider called Graham Beamish. Eddie got a small extra discount from Suzuki for my bike. In the wider picture, it was buttons – maybe £200.

I rode all over the country and so not only sold bikes for Eddie but for every other Suzuki dealer in Britain too. Eddie was relaxed about this and considered the extra discount from Beamish as fair recompense.

Then, for some incredibly trivial reason which I never discovered, Beamish would not give Ed the discount so my sponsorship was stopped on a point of principle by both parties. It was silly beyond words for everyone but that is the nature of sponsorship – and particularly where racing egos are involved.

Still, I rarely even remember this part of my time with Ed because there were vastly more good times.

***

I learned an awful lot from Eddie – a vast amount – and added my own layer of honesty to the way I thought sponsored riders should behave. All the time, I was learning the skills necessary to manage my own team.

It would be a lie to say that I was as white as the driven snow. For example, I have sometimes sold a tyre, when it had gone past its best performance, to some less fussy rider further down the racing food chain. Strictly speaking, the £5 I got for the tyre should have gone back to the tyre supplier but I admit that I have pocketed it. All sponsored riders have done things like this and I was no different. However, what I have never done, and never would do, is to exploit the situation. Sometimes this view of sponsorship had hilarious results.

My agreement with Eddie, I never had a written contract, was that I could find my own personal sponsors and because I was good at this it meant that racing cost me nothing. I never showed a net profit on a season but to race all year cost me hardly anything.

I had a reputation for being an expert at publicity and got far more press coverage than riders who were vastly more successful than I was in terms of race results. This meant I wasn't too surprised when I took a phone call from a well-known "fixer" in bike racing. He wanted an enduro rider for a multi-disciplinary team which he had "sold" to the oil company Duckhams. The international riders further up the ladder got the actual cash for signing, plus win bonuses but I would receive all the lubricants I needed for the season, some overalls and a couple of nice anoraks. Down at clubman level where I lived, this looked like a good deal.

I wrote to the fixer with my requirements, which were very modest. Having free lubricant was a very good thing because it meant things like the bike's chain could be lubed very regularly during an event and the gearbox oil changed after every meeting – all those little luxuries which were beyond a clubman's budget.

It was late afternoon when a huge Duckhams truck pulled up outside our house. The driver checked that I was Frank Melling and then pulled back the curtains on the truck to reveal four wooden pallets of oil – there was what looked like a ton of it! Next to the pallet was a huge box containing clothing.

I was embarrassed and explained to the driver that there had been a mistake. This wasn't my oil but all the lubricants and clothing for the whole team. He looked at his sheet and, somewhat irritably, confirmed that this was just for me and the rest of the load was for everyone else.

It took some time to unload the products and my two car garage was absolutely full of oil and clothing with hardly any room for me or the bike.

I phoned the fixer and asked him to sort out the mistake. I was told to mind my own f******g business and shut up if I ever wanted to be sponsored by anyone ever again - this was the deal which Duckhams had agreed and I needed to zip my mouth and keep everyone happy. So I did - and I've still got some odd bits of Duckhams products three decades later!

I never sold any of the Duckhams oils but I did do something else which strictly speaking wasn't legal - but I think was morally right. I had so much product that I had to reduce the sheer quantity of it because I could barely get to my bike. I wouldn't sell it out of the back of the car but when I saw a promising clubman, who was on the point of doing well, I would give him a tin of chain lube or whatever along with my personal recommendation that Duckhams was the best lubricant manufacturer in the world.

In this way I became Duckhams' unofficial sponsorship representative at enduros and another piece of the management jigsaw fell into place.

I had a lot of fun with all of my other sponsors too and through one of them I made a lot of money in just a few months – and completely legitimately.

I was sponsored with free helmets by a firm called Griffin who were based in Halesowen, in the West Midlands. The company was owned by Terry Oglivie Hardy who had been a good car racer before he started making helmets.

Griffins were excellent quality, although they were made in rather Third World conditions which would have got Terry hung, drawn and quartered today.

This led to a rather interesting situation. The production line was more than rather basic. Particularly during the final finishing, there would sometimes be hairs dropped into the wet paint or bits of dust blown across the shop floor which would stick to the helmet shells.

These helmets were structurally perfect but the cosmetic flaws meant that they were called "seconds". At first I bought a few of these seconds to sell at races and, gradually, the business grew until I was shifting a lot of cosmetically sub-standard helmets.

In fact, the situation became truly farcical. I visited Griffin unexpectedly on one occasion and one of the lads was going down a line of helmets which had just been sprayed, sticking his thumb into the still soft paint. When I questioned what was happening he said: "Oh, we're making some seconds for Frank. He's coming to collect them later…" Enterprise really was valued then!

On another occasion, I called at the factory and Dave Woolgar, the lovely Works Manager, looked really fed up. He explained that Terry had bet the company fortune on an Italian made helmet called the "Superstar." The helmet was a "tribute" to the market leading Bell Star lid. The Italian helmets were beautifully made and so should have sold well. The problem was that the Superstars were vastly too expensive, and lacked Bell's strong brand reputation, and so Griffin had 5,400 of them piled up in a huge, damp barn.

Now I have to say that 5,400 helmets is a lot of product – it really is an immense quantity -and, stacked up, forms the size of a small house.

Even to this day, I don't know what possessed me to think that I could go from selling twenty or thirty seconds to shifting this huge quantity of helmets but a light came on somewhere and, five minutes later, I was sitting in Terry's office concluding a deal. Instead of the £45 he had been trying to sell them at, I would put them on to the market with a retail price of £20. The dealers would pay me £15 and I would buy them all from Terry for £13 each – and regardless of the condition.

The offer was more generous than it seems because the bottom of the pile had suffered badly from damp, and the helmets were also very popular as family homes for upwardly mobile rats. After all, what better place could Mummy and Daddy rat find than a dry, well insulated, nicely curved helmet with the benefit of a convenient front door?

We agreed that I would make an immediate payment of £3,000, and that the helmets wouldn't all arrive simultaneously because this was going to take a lot more than Sammy Green's wash house to store them!

The £3,000 needs seeing in context. At the time, our bungalow was worth around £15,000 – around £200,000 in today's prices – so I had just bet £60,000 plus of the bank's money that I could move an awful lot of helmets very quickly.

The next week, the deliveries started, and when the first lot arrived I felt like hiding. Griffin had a big Fiat panel van and it was full, floor to roof, with helmets.

They were everywhere! Clearly, both the garage and my workshop were rammed solid but they also filled every corner of the house. Just to really crank up my blood pressure Benjy, the driver, said he would be back next week with the second lot. Things were looking hard core bad!

I often smile when I hear the latest lot of whingers on TV, saying that they can't do this or that because they haven't got a grant, or a support group or a mentor. Just try to use the toilet when you're sharing the bathroom with fifty helmets and you will soon find out how to be motivated!

Every night after school, I got on the phone and sold to every dealer in the North-West of England. At first, the reactions ranged from polite apathy to outright hostility. The Superstars were well known in the bike trade as being far too expensive and a disastrously bad seller.

Still, with a mixture of evangelical selling, pleading and even the occasional offer to take the helmets back if they did not move, I got rid of the first 200 – and there was just about space for Benjy's second delivery.

By the Friday of the first week, a very strange thing was starting to happen. The dealers were still far from enthusiastic but the answering machine had plenty of messages on it asking if I had two more helmets in this or that size, or some blue helmets instead of red or gold. The Superstars were on the move.

In a month, there was Superstar fever. Now, the minimum order was twenty helmets – unless you were a favoured customer who had previously purchased a lot from me.

I had a Honda Accord hatchback and, incredibly, I could get 35 helmets crammed into it. Thank goodness that driving conditions were easier at the time because I could see very little out of anywhere except the bit of windscreen in front of me.

The Superstar fever absolutely destroyed every other helmet vendor in the North-West of England and led to some really bizarre situations. One of my best dealers was "Skidlids" in Manchester. They had placed an urgent order for 35 helmets on Friday evening. I arrived at their shop, bright and early, at half past eight on Saturday morning and I was surprised to see a crowd of about fifteen bikers milling around outside the door.

As we were unloading the helmets, customers were pouring in through the door like the January sales – it was that manic.

By the time I returned home there was a message waiting for me, asking for another 35 helmets – and be quick about it – because there wasn't a Superstar left in Skidlids.

It was an exhausting six months and I enjoyed every minute of the rocket ship ride. At the end, I had made enough money to look at a posh new house and so I was very grateful to Terry and his Superstars.

Although things were going very well on every front in Britain, I came awfully near to emigrating. My wife and I had been to America on a number of occasions and I loved everything about the country. On one trip, we had played in the surf at Newport Beach, driven up the Pacific Coast Highway to Malibu in a Ford Mustang and dined in a beachside restaurant, watching the sun set over the Pacific.

Then I had slept under the stars in Lucerne Valley and, the following day, even won a trophy in a desert race. In short, it was one heck of a package.

The problem was that people emigrate to better themselves and my British lifestyle was already very attractive. So with the help of a sad face from my Mum, and a bit of persuasion from my wife, I found an excuse not to take the plunge, stayed in Britain - and that door closed.

I suppose the real reason for not getting on the plane to a new life in Los Angeles is that I was, for the first time since I left school, unsure of what to do next. In the early days, the decisions were easy. Get a bike which didn't break. Find a nice bed instead of the deck of the King Orry and so on. From such low base lines, progress was easy.

Teacher training was also straightforward, in that my life was controlled by someone else. Then I wanted sponsorship and a few trophies and this path was clear too.

Now I was thirty-five years old and, in some respects, I had reached the end of the line. The biggest change was racing. Anyone who races regularly gets hurt. When you are young, none of this really matters - but one day it does. I wasn't so much bothered about the pain but rather the inevitability of getting injured – weekend after weekend.

Some of the accidents were just irritating – loads of broken bones – but occasionally they were serious. I rode in a charity grass track, to try to help a local Church raise funds for African war victims. The event was hardly more than a mess about in a big field but I came to lap a bloke who had never raced before, he pulled in front of me at 45 degrees to try to move out of my way and his handlebars went through my ribs. The next thing I remember was hearing the sirens as I was rushed to hospital with five broken ribs and a punctured lung.

On the basis of the conversation going on between the two medics in the ambulance, I was certain I was about to die but a clever surgeon in Accident and Emergency threaded a catheter into my lung and saved my life. I just got away with what was a very near miss in terms of fatal accidents but, even so, it wasn't the most fun I had racing.

The end of my serious racing career, if it can be called this, came quite suddenly. I rode in a Hare and Hounds event at Sproston, near to the M6 motorway at Middlewich, in Cheshire. It was a team event and I was paired with a brilliant young rider called Colin Jones. The course was a mile and a half per lap and we had to do sixty laps each, in thirty lap sessions. To win, we had to ride relentlessly and pass slower riders ruthlessly and without hesitation.

Colin was the faster of the two of us and this really put the pressure on me. I got stuck behind a slower rider who had a very quick KTM and so was difficult to pass. Colin was going berserk at the delay, jumping up and down at the side of the track, waving his arms about and shouting at me to get on with it.

I really felt that I was letting Colin down so, as the track ran down alongside the River Dane and into a 180 degree hairpin corner, I slid my machine up the inside of the bloke who had been delaying me and, as we reached the hairpin, I simply flicked the rear wheel out into a slide and punted him into the river.

To say the least, he wasn't best pleased and the following lap, still festooned with river weed, he was waiting to kill me with a four foot (1.1m) long marker stake: that was a real encouragement for quick acceleration out of the hairpin bend!

Fortunately, he had calmed down by the end of the event and took what happened as a "racing incident" – which was just as well, because he was much bigger than me and I didn't fancy having my face re-arranged by a 4" (100mm) wooden post!

I crossed the finishing line in a real mess. I had ridden myself into the ground and I was in a lot of pain from hitting trees and getting smacked by the stones thrown up by other riders. Colin and I won and this should have cured everything. Racing success, in whatever form, had always been an instant fix for any injuries ever since I rode in my first scramble in the fog and rain at Oswestry. For some reason, this time was different. I stopped the bike and just let it fall on to the floor as I sat against my trailer sobbing for breath. I had a brilliant pit crew man called Russell Foulkes who never said a word but just picked up the Kawasaki and passed a bottle of water to me.

This was no fun so I decided that I never wanted to race under such pressure again and this would be the end of racing for me. Of course, like all junkies, I was lying to myself but at least I thought that I was being honest and it was good to finish with a win.

By now, I was giving a lot of thought to the idea of owning my own team. I had been sponsored for fourteen years and knew a lot about the optimum way of supporting a rider. This is where my professional duties at school tied in beautifully with racing because, not only was I teaching myself management but I was also studying a lot of marketing books. When I had a team, it was going to be commercially minded and focussed.

The result was Tsubaki Racing – a source of immense pride to me at the time and now.

Much of what I am going to say will seem obvious and standard practice for today. However, I put these ideas into practice thirty-six years ago and things were very different then. In every way they were innovative and ground breaking.

Tsubaki Racing was the result of forging many different strands of my knowledge and experience into a single concept and I was incredibly proud of it.

At the heart of the team was the Japanese Tsubaki chain company. They wanted to raise their profile in Britain and I pitched the idea of a motocross team to them because they were trying to sell a racing chain into dirt bike sport.

They had a decent budget and on to this base I grafted support from other companies so that my team riders had a really good package. I chose to run the team in AMCA racing because this was where the bulk of Tsubaki chain would be sold.

It was also easier to win in AMCA amateur motocross than it was in the British Championship, so I was more likely to get Tsubaki the publicity I had promised them.

Another key factor was that the weekly, off-road newspaper Trials and Motocross News was very pro-AMCA so every success garnered lots of positive coverage.

Finally, the numbers worked. From the outset, I was determined to run the team at a profit. I intended doing a good job for Tsubaki and I wanted paying for my professional services. Tsubaki Racing was never a case of being on an ego trip or wanting to act out some sort of fantasy as Master of the Universe. The team was first, last and middle, a business – but one which I ran with my heart as well as my brain.

At the core of the team ethos was all that I had learned from Eddie Crooks in terms of caring for my riders. In my team, there would always be humanity. Not that this was to be interpreted as weakness or being a soft touch. On the contrary, Willy Street, one of my favourite riders, told me a long time after the team disbanded that when I walked into the paddock all the riders used to give their bikes a quick clean, to make sure that they represented Tsubaki to the highest possible standards. They knew that my eyes were everywhere and that they would be under the microscope – and would be told unequivocally if they hadn't reached the expected level.

I did not ask that the riders like me but I did want their respect – and their belief that, come good results or bad, I would be on their side.

Running in parallel with what Ed had taught me was what I learned from other sponsors who were clueless. Intimidating a rider was never going to improve results and so I didn't do it. I owned the team, and there was no mistaking who controlled it, but I wanted to manage with compassion – not bullying or abuse.

Then there were the Duckhams type lessons. No rider would be short of support – but that help would be targeted, fair and accurate. We would not be a wasteful team.

We would do what I had done throughout my riding career. We would be loyal and proactive to Tsubaki and sell product for the company, as I had done all the way from BSA days, rather than just take the money without thought or care.

This policy, very occasionally, led to a showdown. The early Tsubaki chain gave problems and the rival DID company made a better product. I saw one of my team using the DID chain and he argued that he needed it, to be sure of finishing in championship races. I told him that we were there to help Tsubaki develop their chain for racing – not just put their stickers on the bikes.

I also informed him, with the utmost clarity, that if he did this again I would remove all sponsorship from him - on the spot. There would be no second-chance. He and his mechanic said nothing but I saw them smirking to each other as my back turned. This was not a smart thing to do.

The next meeting he was using DID chain again and, to add insult to injury, I found out that he had been selling his Tsubaki chain from of the back of his van.

Russell Foulkes, who had been my enduro pitcrew for many years, was a lovely person but at six feet three inches tall he was also a popular and effective nightclub doorman. When Russ spoke, very few people didn't listen intently.

I asked Russell to remove all Tsubaki sponsorship from the rider, and his mechanic, immediately – there and then in the paddock. Russ did and there were never any other mis-understandings after this.

Finally, we re-wrote the book in terms of the way we represented Tsubaki, and the team's other sponsors, in the paddock and on the bike. At one end of the scale, everyone had a sticker chart and they placed the sponsors' logos exactly where they were supposed to be.

This policy had a number of advantages and all were of equal importance. First, sponsors could come to a race and see that they got exactly what their contract said they would receive in terms of exposure. They had a chart showing where their stickers would be and when they saw the team, that's what they got.

It was a form of light discipline too. No rider ever appeared at a race meeting unless their bike was immaculate and was following team protocols. This led to a wonderful esprit de corps. Tsubaki riders looked the best in the paddock and so felt the best too. Whenever a Tsubaki representative saw their team, the quality of representation we gave to them was obvious and so they were keen to support us.

Another wonderful team rider, Alan Handbridge, told me that much later than Tsubaki Racing, he went to work for a top international Honda road racing team and the Principal there showed him a brand new idea which Honda had introduced: sticker placement on the bike precisely by contract: Alan just smiled.

Because I had spent all my working life as a photographer, I knew what colour schemes would work in both colour and black and white. Colour was quite rare in the print media, and clearly there was no internet at the time, so I designed bold, simple, dramatic team clothing and then mocked it up and took photographs.

When I was certain that it was going to work, I put the team clothing into production and ensured that riders always had plenty of product so that they always looked immaculate when they went to the start line.

In every respect this was a professional team, the equal of anything around at the time.

In some ways, Tsubaki Racing was practice for when I ended up owning, and running, the Thundersprint which was one of the world's largest motor-cycling events but at the time I did not have a long term vision. On the contrary, I just loved managing the team. I took tremendous pleasure in working with the riders but I also enjoyed incorporating the marketing theory which I was learning into a motorcycle racing team.

I mastered the concept of brand properties, and how to construct these. Soon, press releases were pouring out telling the world about our successes – and there were plenty of them. I learned about socio economic groups, how to identify and sell to them, and brand loyalty and how this could be inculcated. In short, I was like a child in a sweet shop, I was having so much fun.

***

Things were not nearly so happy at school. I had been promoted again and I was now a Year Tutor as well as a Head of Department - plus doing a lot of work with Court Cases and Social Services' reviews. It was not only hard work but depressing too because now I seemed only to teach in between fire-fighting. It became a really sad way to spend each day.

I would still do my lesson preparation over the weekend but I knew that I would be lucky to get through the first lesson uninterrupted on Monday morning, before the deluge of problems arrived.

If this sounds like a moaning teacher then please forgive me because it really was tough and emotionally draining. Let me give you a flavour of what faced me on a daily basis – although this story is a particularly good one.

I saw one of the lads chewing gum – or at least he looked as if he was chewing. I really wanted to get on with the lesson so I called him to my desk and said, "Look Billy, empty your mouth in the bin now and get back to your desk so we can all get on with our work."

It should have been a 30 second long interruption.

He replied: "Am not chugging er. Am not."

This verbal rally went to and fro across my desk until I started to get really fed up. What happens in these confrontations is that the whole class stops work and gets agitated, so it's a real pain to settle everyone down again and usually the lesson is lost.

Eventually, Billy said: "Orry 'er." Hung his head over the bin - and spat out two 9mm, automatic pistol bullets. They hit the metal bottom, one after the other, with a very positive clonk.

Now there are a number of interesting things about this story. I never did find out why "Billy" was chewing bullets but I was so fed up with my lessons being interrupted that I couldn't even be bothered to ask and make a fuss. I left the 9mms in the bin, carried on trying to salvage the broken shards of my poetry lesson, and told Billy to report to me at lunch-time.

One of the reasons I was so sanguine is that I used to shoot pistols so I knew that modern ammunition is very hard to fire but even so, you can imagine the situation today where a kid spits ammo into the class bin - and then then the teacher bashes on with some epic poetry. Not!

The truth was that I was suffering from battle fatigue. If it hadn't been the ammo, then it would have been a knife, or stealing motorcycles, or – really – putting a cigarette lighter to the fuel filler cap of a car to see if there was enough petrol in it to be worth stealing. Nothing was too bizarre and the stream of incidents was non-stop.

However, this particular story wasn't over yet. After my English lesson, Billy went to woodwork and, half an hour later, the Head of the Technology Department came down the corridor in a state of some distress - frog marching Billy in front of him.

I had been somewhat peremptory in sending the lovely child back to his desk because the two rounds were not all his brother had stolen from the Army: there were more. In fact, there was sufficient for Billy to put a couple of bullets in a vice and start belting them with a mallet.

As you may imagine, his teacher was not best pleased. The story had a happy ending though. Because little Billy was doing a woodwork module at the time, hitting the ammo with a wooden mallet was cool. It would have been interesting to see what would have happened in the second half of the term when he did six weeks of metalwork. Then he could have smacked the rounds with a metal hammer and a centre punch…

My Head knew I was getting tired and he called me in to see one of the county's Senior Advisers. She knew me well and it was understood that I had been marked out for more promotion. She asked me what I wanted to do next and I said I would like my own school. She nodded in agreement and I knew then that I would be put into the unofficial pool of teachers who would be expected to go on to Senior Management.

However, before this could happen, I would need a Post Graduate something or other so I had better take a year off teaching and get myself the required bit of paper.

I chose a Reading and Language Acquisition course because I was interested in the psycholinguistics elements of language but I was unhappy and frustrated at the amateurish way everything was run and had a rotten time.

But if the course was bad, there was much, much, much worse to come.

18

Wyrd bið ful Aræd – Fate is Inexorable But Freelancing is Very Good For the Health

I have debated for many months whether to include this final chapter, but I have decided I will, because it exemplifies all that is good about the professional freelancer and I am very proud of my calling and my profession. Yes, we freelancers have innumerable faults, and can never be true team players, but you can always trust a decent freelancer to deliver – regardless of the circumstances. I was about to show how true this was.

The story has multiple happy endings too because I now have the most wonderful, kind, brave, patient and loving wife who has been with me for twenty-five years. On the way we have had a lovely daughter, who I worship, won loads of races and run the Thundersprint. So, it's all good.

However, the next bit isn't.

I finished my post graduate course and couldn't wait to get back to school. I badly needed a break, so my wife and I planned a fantastic trip through Europe. At least, I thought that we had planned it. She was planning something even more impressive – and memorably so too!

On the final day of term, she gave me a big kiss and said she was looking forward to me coming home in the evening. I left school as soon as I could after the sherry and cakes and counted the seconds until I could be with her.

When I arrived home, her car wasn't there which I thought was rather unusual but she had left a note. It was brief and to the point. It said that she knew I loved her but she no longer loved me and she had left me - forever.

It was a devastating blow.

My first concern was for her safety so I spent the next few days just trying to find her and make sure that she was well. She was, so that was good.

All divorces are sad and, from my point of view, this one was no different.

I am constantly restless and hard work at best, and impossibly fidgety and irritably dissatisfied at worst, so I can understand why she wanted a new life. However I was, and I still am, sad that she felt she had wasted seventeen years with me when I would have preferred her to be happy from the start with someone else.

Her departure hit me very hard, in so many ways, and there is no point in recounting them here.

Eventually I couldn't manage another day of sadness so I decided that I would end my life. It wasn't an irrational, spur of the moment decision but rather a case of arriving at the end of the line emotionally, physically and intellectually.

It wasn't a cry for help either because I didn't want any help from anyone.

I just wanted to stop going to sleep on a tear soaked pillow and waking up the following morning with the feeling of infinite emptiness which was life without my precious wife.

I had nothing left to give, even to myself: I was just an empty shell.

In those days, Valium used to be given out very freely and my Mum had numerous bottles of this powerful sedative. She also had industrial quantities of really powerful sleeping tablets. Over a week, claiming that I couldn't sleep, I acquired a good supply of these narcotics from Mum and I also scrounged some from one of my colleagues at school who was suffering from depression.

I laid all the tablets out on the dining room table along with a bottle and a half of whisky. I didn't write a suicide note or leave anything at school. Nor did I tidy the house or try to leave things in any order because I didn't care what anyone thought.

As I got ready to take the pills and drink the whisky, the phone rang. I still don't know why I answered it. Maybe it was just an automatic reaction, from a lifetime of answering calls.

It was Jeff Clew from Haynes. I had nearly finished a book for them – but not quite. I had been very ill for some months and it wasn't so much that I wouldn't finish the last chapter but that I couldn't. I had nothing to say to anyone, except that I was very, very sad and no-one wants to hear this. My typewriter's dust cover hadn't been moved since the summer and why should it? A writer needs something to give the reader – ideas, passion, information, opinions but something - and I had nothing.

The bulk of the manuscript and photographs had been with Jeff for some months and the book was nearly ready for production. Jeff was sympathetic but he had problems too. Haynes had paid me a generous advance against future sales and now, quite reasonably and fairly, Jeff wanted his book – and immediately too, because he was getting some serious stick from the upper echelons of management.

I was stuck in a corner with no way out. Here was someone who was, quite literally, pleading for my help. He was desperate. What could I do? To put my needs before his was unthinkable and so, in a few seconds of confusion, I agreed to get Jeff out of his corner – and, without knowing it, me out of mine at the same time.

Once I had given my word, I was trapped by the code of the freelancer: never let anyone down, no matter how much effort it takes. It was all the way back to promising a test report on the bike which had won a TT for my third article – and delivering it.

Why did I agree? That's more difficult to answer. First, as I have said, it's in the DNA of every thoroughbred freelancer never to let an employer down. A freelancer only stays employed by being reliable.

Then, perhaps I felt wanted and needed by someone so that was a factor too.

Kindness also had a part to play. I couldn't see someone in a mess I could fix and not help.

Maybe it was a combination of all these and more but I pushed the tablets to one side for later, made a cup of coffee and started work. Just before midnight, I faxed the chapter to Jeff - and then fell fast asleep without even getting undressed.

The following morning, I saw the tablets and whisky - but also the faxed sheets and I knew why I should stay alive. For the freelancer, every day is a new day and the next job is always round the corner.

I'm glad that I did do the job for Jeff because I was about to climb aboard another adrenaline ride which was the second part of my life.

Yes, Fate is inexorable - but freelancing is very good for the health.

The Flying Penguin

More Stories of a Freelance Motorcycling Journalist

AFTER helping Jeff Clew out of his corner, things didn't get any quieter!

First, I avoided getting killed during the Winwick Quay riots, when Eddie Shah's Messenger Press was threatened with fire bombing.

Next, I produced the world's biggest children's magazine and, at the same time, worked with some of Britain's most serious and accomplished young criminals.

I discovered classic motorcycle sport and became a national club champion as well as coming awfully near to winning a race at Daytona – but didn't!

Writing was booming and I became a mainstay of the Daily Telegraph's Motoring section before discovering the internet and finding my happiest of homes at MotoUSA.

I took everything that I had learned from teaching, racing and team ownership and bet our house that I could persuade 150,000 spectators to watch blokes on classic motorcycles race round a car park in Northwich. That bet was called the Thundersprint – and we won.

Finally, I found a lovely wife and we had an equally lovely daughter – both of whom were very unexpected bonuses.

On the way were lots of ups and downs and near misses - so please join me for another roller coaster of a journey. There really are some cracking stories to tell – honestly!

Thanks for reading

**See you for
The Flying Penguin**